*Fundamentalism, Revivalists and
Violence in South Asia*

Fundamentalism, Revivalists and Violence in South Asia

Edited by
JAMES WARNER BJÖRKMAN

The Riverdale Company
Riverdale, Maryland
1988

© J.W. Björkman 1988
First Published 1988

ISBN 0-913215-06-6
LOC # 85-61080

Published in the United States of America
by The Riverdale Company, Publishers,
Suite 102, 5506 Kenilworth Avenue,
Riverdale, Maryland 20737
by arrangement with Manohar Publications,
1 Ansari Road, Daryaganj, New Delhi-110 002, India.
Printed in India.

Preface

In November 1984 a two-day workshop was held at the University of Wisconsin on the changing division of labor in South Asia. Half of its emphasis was on the emerging role of women in social, economic, and political affairs; the other half covered the increasingly violent role of religion. In 1986 Manohar and Riverdale published nine of the much revised papers as *The Changing Division of Labor in South Asia*. This volume completes the task of presenting for public discussion the sometimes painful issue of modern religious violence and communal politics in the major countries of the subcontinent.

Although several years have elapsed since the workshop, the following chapters have been so thoroughly revised and rewritten that they are almost completely current. I must thank the authors for submitting (not always cheerfully) to my requests, requirements, and periodic badgering. The editorial process was compounded with abnormally high postal costs because the editor, the authors, and the publishers are spread over three continents. Nonetheless, I believe the final result to have been worth the wait.

If, then, you have been perplexed about the chronic religious violence in contemporary South Asian states, you need search no further for relief. The following chapters examine, explore, and explain aspects of religious fundamentalism, self-righteous revivalists, and murderous mayhem among the four major faiths of South Asia. With due respect to my colleagues and co-authors, there is good reason for being confused. South Asian politics *are* exceedingly complicated and the religious factor is particularly complex. After reading the case-studies and interpretative chapters, one may justifiably conclude that a "no win" situation characterizes the South Asian mosaic. Contemporary reality is depressing, if not gruesome; the daily documentation of death and destruction, cruelty and carnage, is sufficient evidence thereof.

Knowing that things have gone wrong, however, is not nearly as beneficial as discovering *why* things went wrong. Essential questions include: who are the real participants? who is battling for power? what are the payoffs? why do the few continue to dominate the many? why are combatants so fearful of applying democracy to their disputes? One can come away from this volume wringing one's hands in despair at the utter hopelessness of human foibles. Or one can catch glimpses of truth and possible points of leverage by which the certain slide into anarchy might be arrested and even reversed. Sigmund Freud once wrote:

> The truths contained in religious doctrines are after all so distorted and systematically disguised that the mass of mankind cannot recognize them as truth (Freud 1928:78).

The aim of this book to uncover some of the socio-political truths disguised by the frequent invocation of "fundamentalist" and "revivalist" claims in contemporary South Asian religions. If the reader, after having thoughtfully interacted with the authors following, comes at least to question the almost constant use of those terms in political discourse, then one small step will have been taken in the direction of our purpose.

As editor, I cannot guarantee whatever conclusions you may reach; but I can and do assure you that the chapters which follow have been thoroughly thought through in terms of some of today's most persistent, perplexing and profound problems. While their authors may not have come up with any durable answers, or even guidelines to answers, they have starkly illuminated the realities of fundamentalism, revivalists, and violence in South Asia.

Terrace House	James Warner Björkman
Ootacamund	26 January 1987
The Nilgiris	

Addendum

Through a tragicomedy of errors, accidents, and misunderstandings compounded by transoceanic communications, publication of this volume was delayed by a full year. Its contents remain valid, however, despite marginal changes in current events (e.g., the impositon of President's Rule in the Punjab in May 1987).

Because endemic religious violence in South Asia puzzles pundits both politically and analytically, the contributions herein are even more relevant for understanding fundamentalism and revivalists throughout the subcontinent. Although belated, such understanding would be a modest measure to mark this 40th anniversary of that violence wreaked by a revivalist motivated by fundamentalism: the assassination of Mahatma Gandhi.

River House   J.W.B.
Madras   30 January 1988

The Contributors

JAMES WARNER BJORKMAN, educated in political science at the University of Minnesota (B.A. *summa cum laude*, 1966) and Yale University (M.Phil., 1969; Ph.D., 1976), is Director of the American Studies Research Center in Hyderabad, India, as well as Executive Director of the International Institute of Comparative Government in Lausanne, Switzerland. He has held faculty appointments in Sweden (University of Linköping), England (University of Essex), Pakistan (Institute of Development Economics), India (Institute of Economic Growth), and the United States (Yale and University of Wisconsin). Author of *The Politics of Administrative Alienation in India's Rural Development Programs* (1979) and editor of *The Changing Division of Labor in South Asia: Women and Men in Society, Economy and Politics* (1986), he has also authored books on American health policies; co-edited a book on health professionals in western societies; and published articles on South Asian ethno-political relations, Panchayati Raj, accountability in health care, professionalism, South Asian social policies, and comparative methodology. During 1985–89 he is conducting a major comparative study of national health policies in South Asia

MUMTAZ AHMAD studied political science at the University of Karachi, the American University of Beirut, and the University of Chicago. He has taught at the National Institute of Public Administration, Karachi; Columbia College, Chicago; and the Chicago State University. Currently working as a consultant in Southwest Asian Affairs in Washington, D.C. and a lecturer at the Foreign Service Institute of the Department of State, his publications include: *The Kashmir Dispute: A Study in Diplomacy* (1969); *Bureaucracy and Political Development in Pakistan* (1974); *Studies in Local Government and Rural Development in Pakistan* (1976); and *State, Politics, and Islam*, ed. (1987).

KINGSLEY DE SILVA holds a First degree in history from the University of Ceylon, and a Ph.D. from the University of London. His doctoral dissertation was published by Longmans, Green and Co., London, for the Royal Commonwealth Society in 1965. He holds the Chair of Sri Lankan History at the University of Peradeniya (since 1969) and is presently Vice-Chairman of the University Grants Commission, and Vice-Chairman of the International Association of Historians of Asia. He has held visiting appointments at Cambridge (in 1968–69) as Smuts Visiting Fellow in Commonwealth Studies and Visiting Fellow of Clare Hall, Manchester University (1976–77) as Commonwealth Visiting Professor in the Department of Government and as Fulbright Scholar in Residence and Visiting Professor of South Asian History at Bowdoin College, Brunswick, Maine. He has published books and articles on the history and politics of Sri Lanka. Among his other areas of interest are higher education policy and ethnic problems in Sri Lanka and the third world. He is the Chairman of the Board of Directors of the International Centre for Ethnic Studies, Kandy/Colombo.

ROBERT ERIC FRYKENBERG was born and reared in India. He studied with Richard L. Park in Berkeley and with Percival Spear of Cambridge before going to London (SOAS) where he completed his Ph.D. (1961). After a year at Chicago, he went to Wisconsin where he has remained ever since. Professor of History and South Asian Studies since 1970, he has served as Chairman of the Department and Director of the Center of South Asian Studies (1970–73). His specialty lies in the history of local influence upon central authority since the rise of the East India Company. His *Guntur District, 1788–1848: A History of Local Influence and Central Authority* (1965) was his first major work. This was followed by *Land Control and Social Structure in Indian History* (1969), *Land Tenure and Peasant in South Asia* (1977), *Delhi Through the Ages* (1986), and *Studies of South India* (1986) to each of which he contributed chapters as well as edited. He has published some thirty articles in various scholarly journals and volumes, and is currently working on *Mutiny in South India, 1806–1809* and on *History and Religion: A Comparison of Major Historiographic Traditions*.

KENNETH W. JONES completed his Ph.D. from the University

of California at Berkeley and is currently Professor of South Asian History at Kansas State University. He has written extensively on social, cultural, and religious change in British India including regional studies and more recently on such change in the entire subcontinent. His books include *Sources on Punjab History*, edited with E. Eric Gustafson (1975), *Arya Dharm: Hindu Consciousness in 19th-Century Punjab* (1976), and *Socio-Religious Movements in British India*, forthcoming in the New Cambridge History of India. His articles have appeared in the *Journal of Asian Studies*, the *Indian Economic and Social History Review*, *The Indian Archives*, and numerous edited volumes. Professor Jones wishes to thank his colleagues Sandra Coyner, Robert Frykenberg, Gail Minault, Barbara Ramusack, and Lynn Stoner, whose comments aided in preparation of this article. The final product, however, is his own responsibility.

SURJIT MANSINGH is currently with the School of Advanced International Studies, Johns Hopkins University, Washington D.C. doing research on United States policies in the Indian Ocean region. She has held teaching positions at the American University (Washington D.C.), the University of Delhi (Delhi, India), and Trinity University (San Antonio). Before taking up an academic career, she was a member of the Indian Foreign Service. Her degrees are from the University of Delhi in History, and from the American University in International Studies. Dr. Mansingh has authored *India's Search for Power: Indira Gandhi's Foreign Policy 1966–1982* (1984) and coauthored *Diplomatic History of Modern India* (1971) with her late husband, Charles H. Heimsath. She has also published numerous other papers in journals and edited books. She thanks the editor of this volume for insisting that she venture into a new field.

KULDEEP MATHUR has his M.A. from Rajasthan University and Ph.D. from the University of Hawaii. He has taught at the Universities of Rajasthan and Himachal Pradesh and at the Indian Institute of Public Administration as well as headed the research division of HCM State Institute of Public Administration, Jaipur. Currently Professor at the Centre of Political Studies, Jawaharlal Nehru University, New Delhi, Mathur has many publications to his credit including *Bureaucracy and the New Agricultural Strategy* (1982) and edited a volume, *Survey of Research in Public Administ-*

ration (1986), on behalf of the Indian Council of Social Science Research. The author would like to thank the Corporate Studies Group of the IIPA for the use of its computer facilities and for providing technical support for analyzing the data for this paper. This paper is part of a larger study supported by the Indian Council of Social Science Research, New Delhi.

LLOYD I. RUDOLPH and SUSANNE HOEBER RUDOLPH earned doctorates at Harvard University in the 1950s and are now Professors of Political Science at the University of Chicago. Their numerous joint publications on South Asian politics include *The Modernity of Tradition: Political Development in India* (1967), *Education and Politics in India* (1972), and *The Regional Imperative: US Foreign Policy Towards South Asian States* (1980). With the kind permission of the University of Chicago Press, their contribution is a slimmed selection from *In Pursuit of Lakshmi: The Political Economy of the Indian State* (1987); complete documentation and elaborate arguments are available in the original chapter called "Centrist Politics, Class Politics, and the Indian State."

PAUL WALLACE, who holds a Ph.D. from the University of California, Berkeley, is presently Professor of Political Science at the University of Missouri, Columbia. He has served as Department Chair and as Director of the Center for International Studies and Programs. He has twice chaired the North American Research Committee on Punjab and is on the editorial boards of *Asian Survey* (U.S.) and the *Punjab Journal of Politics* (India). He is editor of *Region and Nation in India* (1985), and co-editor of *The Political Dynamics of Punjab* (1981) and *The Punjab Press: 1880–1905* (1970). His articles have appeared in *Asian Survey*, the *Journal of Commonwealth and Comparative Studies*, the *Indian Journal of Political Science*, the *Punjab Journal of Politics*, and as chapters in several books.

Contents

1

The Dark Side of the Force: Notes on Religion and Politics

JAMES WARNER BJÖRKMAN

'Religions are not meant for separating men; they are meant to bind them.'

'Those who say that religion has nothing to do with politics do not know what religion means.'

M.K. Gandhi

These two statements by the greatest South Asian of this century may in themselves say more than all the pages which follow. Yet if the Great Soul could again be conjured into corporeal form, he would find an entire subcontinent in ferment as religious militancy, under the facade of orthodoxy, rises on all sides. Tragically, a cyclic action-reaction is underway which feeds upon itself. In the wake of terrorist acts, the victims lose faith in government to maintain lawful order and begin to arm themselves in self-defense. Private armies are organized in order to protect religions which otherwise preach love, compassion, harmony, concern, commitment, and detachment. From the shores of Sri Lanka to the jungles of Assam to the mountainous wastes of the Hindu Kush, the countries of South Asia are riddled with militant groups ready, willing, and able to employ violence. Against this backdrop of militancy and religious intolerance, new political forces are emerging amidst dangerous scenarios of hate and bigotry.

New terminology has appeared to describe these political phenomena, or at least old labels are applied to new events. "Fundamentalism," sometimes referred to as "revivalism," is the effort by the interpreters of religions to hark back to what they consider to be pure, original codes of belief and behavior, no matter how long ago the era when a text was written or its message preached and no matter what the changes that have since over-taken human society. Although any religion may (rightly) regard itself to be eternally and universally relevant to human affairs, social context is particularly important for the emergence and maintenance of fundamentalist attitudes. Social change, whether development or decay, disrupts the predictable patterns of community living so that the individual loses his roots, his sense of identity. Without roots and without a sense of identity, individuals clutch at any straw for support and solace. In such a situation, religious fundamentalism replaces questions with answers, doubts with certitudes, rootlessness with stability. The psychological appeal of revivalism is enormous for it promises restitution of an earlier, better age. Under conditions of disruptive modernization, it is no surprise that people succumb to the temptations of fundamentalism.

In terms of personal outlook, fundamentalism is characterized by a comprehensive and absolutist belief system capable of generating intense aspirations and total commitment to precepts. It involves a totalistic definition of reality in order to revitalize authentic values, usually by restoring the spirit and commitment of a past era. Such an all-encompassing outlook does not leave room for toleration of others. Being in possession of truth, fundamentalists can ignore and do discard democracy and the rule of law. Indeed, in principle fundamentalism is intrinsically undemocratic although it will, when convenient or necessary, use democracy to achieve its ends. More significantly, fundamentalism does not leave room for civil rights of anyone outside the community of the elect. The conviction exists, although rarely articulated, that "the notion of universal human rights is a foreign ideal" (Sprinzak 1986:12). Non-believers may be denied their rights since they do not belong. Clearly this formulation makes it morally possible for the individual to justify killing and terrorism, especially since the end—usually the establishment of a specific homeland like Israel, Khalistan, or Eelam—justifies the means. All those who hold contrary viewpoints, whether as critics or outright enemies, are demonized. Most important of all, the fundamentalist cast of mind simply refuses to acknowledge the constraints of political reality. "The danger of the fundamentalist mind is its conviction that reality is bound to follow ideology and not vice versa. Facts can simply be disregarded. . . ." (*ibidem*: 26).

The aim of fundamentalists is explicitly *to preserve continuity with an original formulation*, whatever that original revelation or formulation may have been. Fundamentalism is easier to utilize by those whose faith is based on a single sacred book although as a descriptive term it applies to all religions. Frykenberg (chapter 2) points out that the label itself derives from turn-of-the-century American protestantism when a wealthy believer, by financing the publication of a series of twelve texts, sought to pin down *The Fundamentals* of the Christian faith. That effort was notably unsuccessful, at least in terms of the numbers of those adopting or even utilizing those principles of faith. Quite clearly, pluralism or diversity is incompatible with "true" religion.

In order to maintain coherence and momentum, fundamentalists require an enemy—or rather two enemies: one within their ranks, the other outside. Since the internal enemy might betray the "cause," periodic purges and purifications of members become necessary; since the external enemy threatens to destroy the "cause," ranks must consolidate. In Christianity the respective roles of Judas and Caiaphus are well-known. Disastrously for durable government, however, fundamentalists often are more interested in ideological purity than in winning elections or maintaining coalitions, a point richly illuminated by Wallace (chapter 4) and Mansingh (chapter 9).

But can "fundamentalism" apply to religions like Hinduism which are not based on a single book or a single lawgiver? According to some pundits, Hinduism should not be called a religion at all, at least if a religion requires well-defined fundamentals (RGK 1986: iv). "It is a corpus of philosophical thought, involving explanations of the cosmic and the spiritual, held together by the belief that each human being is part of a divine consciousness, sovereign to the point of giving each individual the power to decide what is right and wrong" (Thapar 1986: 8). Basham's definitive summary (cited in Banerjee 1987: 17) notes that "in principle Hinduism incorporates all forms of beliefs and worships . . . [and] is then, both a civilisation and conglomeration of religions with neither a beginning, a founder, nor a central authority, hierarchy, or organization. . . ."

Again, socio-political context is all important. When confronted by the proselytising faiths of Islam and Christianity, Hindus—whatever their individual configurations of belief—panicked. At first they turned "inwards" by evolving endless private rituals; then they turned "outwards" in aggressive self-assertion through public rituals and "in processions around this and that god or goddess. . . ." (Thapar 1986: 8). B.G. Tilak's use of the Ganesh festival was an early, mild example. Current fundamentalism—at least its politically relevant variant—requires ritualistiç assertion in public places, particularly aggressive assertion. The devotee or believer cannot just go to the fundamentals, but must be seen going to those fundamentals; public witnessing, claims, and announcements are mandatory acts which explain the frequency in South Asia of religious processions, amplified loud-speakers, and other visible or audible evidence of one's faith. These public exhibitions of militant faith, in turn, excite fears among other religious groups, and the vicious cycle continues.

There are, of course, alternative views. Girilal Jain (1987: 13) insists that Hindu revivalism can never become a reality because Hindus have neither a vision of the future nor a "Golden Age" to revive. "'Hinduism' is an arbitrary imposition on a highly variegated civilisation, which is truly oceanic in its range. Such a civilisation cannot be enclosed in a narrow doctrine. . . . To put it differently, Hinduism has refused to be organised. By the same token, it has refused to be communalised." Rajni Kothari (1986: 16), however, disagrees by arguing that Hindu revivalism is an upper-caste phenomenon. Deprived of their traditional privileges over the lower-castes, upper-caste Hindus seek to re-establish the fundamentals of proper belief and behavior. These twice-born Hindus resent being left out of the benefits of a secular society where everyone else (Muslim, Sikh, Christian, ex-Untouchable) gets privileges. Indeed such pioneer Hindu organizations as the Arya Samaj, the Brahmo Samaj, and the Ramakrishna Mission have sought and obtained court orders declaring them to be non-Hindu and therefore qualified for the benefits and protection granted to minority communities under Articles 29 and 30 of the Constitution (Banerjee 1987: 17). Yet these organizations spearheaded the various reforms of Hindu society in the nineteenth century (Jones, chapter 3). Issues of confessional identity and political consequences are discussed by the Rudolphs (chapter 5).

Given such subtle and infinitely "fissiparous" complexity, the notion of a majority community as well as the very term "Hindu" seems alien to Hinduism. Rather "Hinduism" is a series of social communities stratified along caste lines, with different rituals and different gods. Indeed, the term was initially a geographical label for anyone from the subcontinent, such as the now oxymoronic "Hindu Muslims on haj to Mecca." As Jones (chapter 3) reminds us, what distinguishes Hinduism from Christianity or Islam is its intrinsic pluralism. It has neither a monolithic church nor a single text nor a centralized clergy. Rather it is a descriptive label for a dispersed society, with its series of local elites. These local elites— particularly the brahminical castes—derived benefits of British education, controlled the nationalist movement, and manned the services after independence. However, the democratic revolution upset the hegemony of the upper castes who were simultaneously deprived of traditional privileges without being compensated by the modern state. These elites now seek restoration of the *status quo ante* which, if achieved, would not victimize other religious minorities so much as the lower-caste Hindus! In this respect even Hinduism, or at least a select set of Hindus, is not immune to the appeal of fundamentalism.

Historical accuracy is a weapon that can do much to deflate fundamentalist passions. Despite the relative accessibility of holy books and interpretative texts—an accessibility enhanced by rising literacy, however, a great deal of fundamentalism is built on distortion, half-truth, and falsehood. These exacerbate religious cleavages that present particular dangers to civil society because few other political controversies (except, perhaps, language) can dismember a country quite as conclusively as communal politics. The British Raj itself was partitioned between two successor states, one of which again split apart in 1971. Claims for other "independent homelands" have been pressed in the past four decades, the most recent being Eelam and Khalistan, but their number is potentially legion.

All South Asian states, even the Hindu kingdom of Nepal, display the evident institutions of liberal democracy, including elections and parliaments. Even otherwise thinly-disguised military regimes orchestrate periodic plebiscites in order to legitimize their political arrangements with the stamp of popular approval. Yet despite liberal trappings and constitutional clauses the post-colonial states of South Asia remain marked by the absence of separation of religion and politics. Despite the hopes and claims of liberals (Björkman 1984), secularism seems an insufficient basis for sustaining national identity.

Since religion has such entrenched roots in the subcontinent, nationalists have regularly appealed to religion to mobilize support for the nation-state. In its simplest form, such an appeal provided and provides the ideological basis of Pakistan. In a somewhat more subtle form, the same appeal applied to India and Sri Lanka respectively. Mahatma Gandhi certainly saw nothing wrong in combining the religious and the secular. On the contrary, he openly argued the religious basis of ethnic tolerance in India and he employed specifically religious symbols—drawn, it might be noted, from *all* faiths—to mobilize support for the independence movement. Unfortunately, Gandhi's simultaneous concern for "personal" or "internal" independence in addition to "mass" or "external" independence, often irritated and confused Nehru as well as many other nationalist leaders. Yet today the Mahatma still might see Hindu revivalism in India or Buddhist revivalism in Sri Lanka as expressions of nationalism rather than religion per se. From the vantage point of statescraft and the need to mobilize collective identity plus assure loyalty to the state, religion provides a readymade albeit sometimes unpredictable tool.

Even in self-labelled "secular" India, the legacy of history mixes religion with politics. Certainly the major religions of India have historically had intimate links with politics. Islam is particularly clear about this linkage since submission to God's will not only regulates the spiritual conduct of Muslims but also permeates every facet of human activity (Rodinson 1980: 41). The *Koran* along with the *Hadith* contain very specific injunctions on how to conduct daily life. The universe of a Muslim is therefore circumscribed by his or her religion. Islam is a complete way of life where politics and religion are inseparable.

The resurgence of Islam over the recent decades appears to be a manifest result of self-perceived non-achievement. In comparative terms, South Asian Muslims are regularly described as educationally backward, economically poor, and politically less conscious. Their backwardness makes them cling to the security of religious belief and makes them intolerant of anything which threatens these beliefs. Broadly speaking, the pressures which characterize most developing societies—population growth, industrialization, urbanization, growing literacy, spread of Western habits or at least Western models—have added to Muslim disenchantment with the contemporary world and its problems. The result has been a fervent search for social meaning and for roots which, in the case of Islam, means the golden age of the seventh century when the Prophet Mohammed guided human affairs. A return to a simpler, purer, more authentic Islam is seen as a remedy for societies tormented by the pace of change. For some Muslims this return requires or necessitates the worldwide unity of the *Umma* or community of believers, a pan-Islamic position which conflicts with nationalistic sentiments and other local identities. Frequently the fundamentalist dissent therefore manifests itself in violence.

Ironically one interpretation of Islam opposes any form of restricted rule like autocracy or hereditary monarchy and instead emphasizes consultation, consent, and consensus. Yet as long as the traditional theologians support and reinforce the ruling elite, the fundamentalists regard violence as an important vehicle towards establishing a "true" Islamic society. True Islam is often equated with the adoption and application of Islamic law, a process sometimes labelled "Islamicization." That simplistic formulation begs the question—though to a fundamentalist, it provides a sufficient answer—since the *Shariah* is not set down in the *Koran* alone. It is a system of law derived from the *Koran* which embodies the word of God, the *Sunnah* or practices of the Prophet, the *Ijma* or consensus of Islamic jurists, and *Qiyas* or analogical reasoning (Dil 1980: 165 citing Rahman 1979: 68). Collectively the latter three comprise the *Hadith* or tradition. No less than four main schools of *Shariah* codification and interpretation vie for attention and supremacy. Therefore, what Islamic activists seek to impose on their societies is not so much *Shariah* law per se as their interpretation of *Shariah* law. The *Koran* and the *Hadith* are ambiguous about many matters. Therefore, in no sense do liberal interpretations somehow stretch the intent of the law. *Shariah* law is not conservative law by definition; it is its interpretations, reflecting other biases, which can be either conservative, literalist, or modernist.

Political problems arise because religious law and civil law can and do overlap, and a decision must be taken as to which has precedence in a particular case. The 1985 Shah Bano judgment of the

Indian Supreme Court ruled that the secular civil code would apply in an area [alimony or maintenance after divorce] formerly under the jurisdiction of Muslim personal law, and the issue quickly became a *cause célèbre*. This ruling was quickly countermanded by the Congress(I) government through new parliamentary legislation which restored the authority of the Shari'at. But protests against the Shah Bano judgment are seen as evidence of growing Islamic fundamentalism. There is a sense among Indian Muslims that their "personal law" has been subverted and they are about to be engulfed and assimilated by the amorphous Hindu majority. When added to the February 1986 district court ruling that the 450 year old Babari Masjid near Lucknow be opened to Hindus as well (who claim the site as the birthplace of their deity Rama), Muslims fear they will lose their identity and distinctiveness (Ali 1986: 32).

The same fear, expressed somewhat differently, infects many Sikhs. In terms of belief, Sikhism is strictly monotheistic and closer to Islam. But in social practice, Sikhs tend to identify with Hinduism and observe a number of similar festivals and customs, including the tenacious social order of caste. There is considerable diversity, not to say confusion, among Sikhs as to how they relate to Hinduism (Fox 1985; Kapur 1986). Some explicitly deny that they are Hindus; others see little difference (Swarup 1986: 8). But contemporary terrorism has brought this fear into renewed consciousness. The psychic wounds and humiliations of Operation Bluestar (June 1984), when the Indian Army forcibly cleared armed Sikh fundamentalists out of that holiest of Sikh shrines, the Golden Temple in Amritsar, followed by the anti-Sikh carnage after Mrs. Gandhi's assassination (November 1984), have reinforced these fears of subjugation and assimilation. Yet the empirical record indicates that the pro-Khalistan terrorists in Punjab are killing both Hindus and Sikhs. Between October 1985 and June 1986, 283 persons were killed in the Punjab of whom 180 were Hindus, 100 Sikhs, and 3 from other communities (*Indian Express*, 11 July 1986).

Sikhism itself originally appeared in the 15th century. Its pietistic founder, Guru Nanak, sought to draw the universal best from the two contending religions of his era—Islam of the conquerors and Hinduism of the subjugated—and thereby reconcile them. Two of his successors, however, lost their lives while defending the basic political rights of Hindus, and the warrior Guru Govind Singh waged a life-long battle against the Mughal state. Indeed, as Wallace (chapter 4) observes, the two swords of Guru Hargobind Singh symbolized the close relationship of *Peeri* and *Meeri*, the spiritual and the temporal. Over time the Sikh tradition came to emphasize the unity of Church and State; and in this unity of religion and politics, the pursuit of power eventually over-shadowed the religious quest per se. Sikh polities appeared in the eighteenth century, and until well into the nineteenth century an independent Sikh kingdom flourished with only indirect British influence, much as in the princely states of Rajputana. This king-dom collapsed in 1846 and British rule was extended throughout the Punjab.

Unlike the sprawling presidencies of Bengal, Bombay, or Mad-ras, however, the Punjab experienced western impact all at once—and in all spheres of social, economic, and political life. And "like the Muslims who, in a similar situation of loss of political power, had earlier turned to the 'purification' of their religious life," Sikhs after the loss of Ranjit Singh's kingdom sought to revive orthodox practices (Madan 1986: 269). The genesis of cur-rent Sikh identity is rooted in the religious reform movement of approximately 1870–1920, at the tag-end of which Gandhi got involved in helping Sikhs gain control of their gurudwaras. These temples had fallen under the hereditary control of *mahants* or priests who often were thoroughly Hinduized. The massacre of Indians at Amritsar (Jallianwallahbagh) in 1919 turned the religion into a political movement and reinforced the importance of martyrdom. The Akali Dal, the Sikh political party which has been central to twentieth century Punjab politics, began as a result of the massacre. In particular "the Akalis repudiated any notion of the separation of the Church and the State. This repudi-ation became the basis for the demand for a Sikh homeland" (*ibidem*: 271).

The recent and rapid revival of Sikh fundamentalism was facili-tated by factionalism within both the ruling Congress Party and its regional rival, the Akali Dal. This revivalist fundamentalism raised issues of identity, psyche, and community insult, all ironi-cally exacerbated by the phenomenal success of the green revolution and the profound changes in social relation-ships which it entailed (Critchfield 1984:4). Almost perfectly epitomized by the behavior of Jarnail Singh Bhindranwale, "Sikh extremists denied cultural change and sought to preserve the old ways by force and violence" (*ibidem*). Violent expression of political disagreements went out of control, and now threatens the viability of the Akali Dal as a political party as well as the civil order of Punjabi society itself. These dilemmas, their origins and consequences, are sharply etched in Wallace (chapter 4).

In contrast to Islam and Sikhism, Hinduism lacks a central orthodoxy or a mandate to spread its message. Indeed, its messages are multiple and Hinduism has been marked by almost amorphous plurality and openness which have unintentionally provided a supportive milieu for politically democratic institutions. But does this mean that Hinduism, as an umbrella concept spanning many interpretations of method and content, is itself apolitical? Perhaps in comparison to historical Islam and historical Sikhism, Hinduism appears to lack political focus and political organization. Yet the *Arthasastra* (*c.* 300 BC) had a well-developed theory of statecraft at which Machiavelli would have marvelled; and the caste system, which stratifies Hindu society, is one of the most enduring human institutions created anywhere in the world. While the 1950 Constitution of India may forbid and thereby deny its existence, the caste system manifestly organizes the daily life of almost all Hindus. As Gill (1987: 8) observes, "It is a great tribute to the sophistication and finesse of the Brahmins that the scaffolding they designed to uphold their class interests was made to appear as a part of the natural order of things—a constraint ordained at the time of creation of the world. In fact the social universe of a Hindu is wholly permeated by his religion." It is no accident that one of the most durable of opposition parties (whatever its changing nomenclature) draws its inspiration from Hinduism much as Christian-Democrats in Europe utilize the wellsprings of the Church.

It is also not insignificant that, except for Jawaharlal Nehru, most of the pre-eminent leaders of the independence movements in India and Ceylon maintained prominent religious profiles in public and made frequent use of religious imagery. Mahatma Gandhi is the automatic example who, being one of the greatest mass communicators in history, spoke to the people through images and symbols which lay deeply embedded in their consciousness. Most of his imagery was derived from Hindu scriptures and mythology, but he systematically encouraged similar politico-religiosity among Muslims, Sikhs, and Christians. Other South Asian notables throughout this century also displayed staunch religious identities, at least in public: Gokhale, Tilak, Jinnah, Maulana Azad, Rajendra Prasad, Rajagopalachari, Dharmapala, Senanayake, Jayewardene, Bandaranaike, *et aliter*. The point is not that these nationalist leaders were communalists in deceptively democratic attire; it is rather that with the best of intentions, these men of integrity used religion for political ends.

Unfortunately, such public displays of religious faith produced divisive as well as integrative results. Fears of domination, submergence, and assimilation appeared; and charges of obstinacy, self-centeredness, and exploitation were heard. In the post-British era, politicians in all South Asian states have succumbed to the easy alternative of mobilizing support along religious lines and have thoroughly mixed religion and politics. Whereas political leaders during the pre-independence era had usually used religious imagery and metaphors only to establish rapport with the masses, their post-independence successors have regularly used religion to rouse communal passions and thereby bargain with other centers of political power.

In contemporary South Asia, therefore, an intense struggle is underway between the spirits of liberalism and dogmatism. The former spirit is generous, moderate, compassionate, and focused on real men and women; the latter is uncompromising, power-hungry, and finds inspiration in religious dogma, ethnic pride, or words like Motherland. The Enlightenment took the individual as the measure of all things and resists abstractions that go beyond the dimensions of man; it cannot justify cruelties to individuals for the sake of a faith or an ideology, nor justify pain in the present for the sake of a utopian future or a paradisical hereafter (Björkman 1984:44–45. And yet such cruelties and pain are intentional tactics in communal conflict. The terrorist [or freedom fighter] seeks to provoke repressive reactions which will drive moderates out of the political arena and simultaneously bind those who remain more tightly to the "cause." In their fervor, fundamentalists condemn moderation as a crime.

The traditional conception of religion in South Asia embraces all aspects of human life. Neither politics nor economics is autonomous of religion; they are simply encompassed by religion

(Dumont 1970). Another basic feature of Indian life for millenia has been the acceptability of religious diversity. This was not secularism in its modern connotation, but it meant that "cultural pluralism within the state was an accepted fact and the Hindu king was everybody's protector within the kingdom. The basis of a common state was the recognition of the legitimacy of cultural difference" (Madan 1983: 12).

Secularism as a political principle stands for the separation of church and state as well as for the essentially private, inward-dwelling, individualistic nature of religious faith. Contrary to popular misconception, secularism does not stand for the abolition of religion but for its banishment from the public sphere of political affairs. There is, however, an alternative view of religion-plus-politics which is positive rather than negative. With a clearly acknowledged debt to Mahatma Gandhi, Nandy (1985) argues that religion "rightly understood" respects the views of others and thus supports democracy and pluralism. He notes that of the three great practitioners of religious tolerance on the Indian subcontinent over the past 2500 years the Emperor Ashoka was a devout Buddhist, the Emperor Akbar derived his tolerance from Islam, and Mahatma Gandhi was deeply rooted in folk Hinduism. In short, tolerance derives not from the abolition of religion from the public sphere but from its vital presence.

Nandy (1986: 14) further argues, in full agreement with the observations of Dumont (1970) and Madan (1983), that "to the faithful, . . . religion is religion precisely because it provides an over-all theory of life, including public life, and because life is not worth living without the theory." Indeed, in a near parody of socio-psychoanalytic analysis, he suggests that "much of the fanaticism and violence associated with religions come today from the sense of defeat in the believers, from their feelings of impotency, anger, and self-hatred while facing a world which is mostly secular and nonbelieving. . . . Thus, we are at a point of time when old-style secularism can no longer guide moral or political action. All that the ideology of secularism can do now is to sanction the absurd search for a modern language of politics in a traditional society which has an open polity" (Nandy 1986: 14).

In an earlier work entitled *The Intimate Enemy: Loss and Recovery of Self under Colonialism*, Nandy (1983) notes how polarities like masculine–feminine and hard–soft shaped 19th century efforts of Indians to revive Hindu traditions. Under the influence of British

stereotypes the balance among three elements of Hinduism—
purusatva (essence of masculinity), *naritva* (essence of femininity),
and *klibatva* (essence of hermaphroditism)—was altered so that
the masculine and aggressive aspects of Hindu mythology could
be asserted against the "virility" of British culture. He shows how
texts were reinterpreted to emphasize martial valor plus morally
coherent monotheism, thus masculine divinity consistent with
the Aryan qualities shared with the Christian rulers.

In order to develop his "anti-secular" argument, Nandy (1985:
5) posits four ideal-types of political response to the clash between
religious traditions and modernity. The western-man-as-the-
ideal-political-man has a "managerial attitude" toward religious
groupings which ultimately will face cultural extinction because
of successful social engineering. The westernized native has inter-
nalized this western ideal and turned against his own cultural self.
His aim is to modernize his own culture by emulating western
standards and ideals, whether of Marxist or bourgeois persuasion.
The semi-modern zealot, however, proclaims otherwise—even
though he has unconsciously accepted the western-model-as-best
and thus been culturally defeated. "If such a zealot is a Muslim or
a Sikh we call him a fundamentalist; if he is a Hindu we call him a
revivalist. . . ." Finally there is the nonmodern majority who do
not keep religion separate from politics but, as peripheral believers,
practice their traditional ways—which include tolerating other
faiths. They draw on "the experience of neighbourliness and co-
survival which characterises the relationships among the
peripheral believers of different faiths." The Mahatma embodied
as well as nurtured this latter nonmodern ethnic outlook.

Of particular relevance to political activity is the strength of
identity within these groups and their capacity to adapt to changing
circumstances. Ironically, distance from the scene of political
action appears to be inversely related to courage—that is, overseas
co-religionists are much more uncompromising than those who
have to live in daily society (Björkman 1988). This observation is
true whether describing Croatians, Sikhs, Irish, or Tamils for this
"overseas dimension" supplies money, material, and morale to
those terrorists (or freedom-fighters) on the front lines. Of
course, an alternative and probably more common posture overseas is total neglect or lack of concern. This issue merits additional
research.

Nandy reserves his richest scorn for the third ideal-type who is politically active while simultaneously unaware of his cultural defeat. A single example of his evocative prose will suffice as he writes about ". . . the zealot and the so-called revivalist move-ments modelled on the zealot's concept of religion. Take Hindu revivalism. Actually, whatever the revivalist Hindu revives, it is not Hinduism. The pathetically comic, martial uniform of khaki half-pants which the RSS cadres have to wear tell it all. Uncon-sciously modelled on the uniforms of the colonial police, the khaki shorts are the final proof that the RSS is an illegitimate child of western colonialism" (Nandy 1986: 14).

The strength of Nandy's argument is its creativity, especially in describing the political utility of religion in terms of both public and private lives. His analysis contains an implicit four-fold chart, with exemplary entries for the matrix cells:

Public Sphere

		Believer	Nonbeliever
Private Sphere			
Believer		M.K. Gandhi	Indira Gandhi
Nonbeliever		M.A. Jinnah	Jawaharlal Nehru

Jinnah, for example, like his heirs in Pakistan and Bangladesh, tried to "encash the appeal of Islam" and thereby mobilize popular support for his political goals. Unfortunately Jinnah, a "wester-nized ethnic," could not differentiate between a Hindu zealot like D.V. Savarkar and a spokesman of the nonmodern majority of Hindus like Gandhi. Interestingly, Nandy (1985: 4) notes that "the experience of Islam in this respect has been the experience of every religion of the subcontinent. It is the experience of being often reduced to the status of a handmaiden of politics, subservient to the needs of a nation-state and the class interests of the zealot and the westernized secularist, both of whom hold the vast majority of the people of their own religion in contempt. . . ."

Clearly, democratization and politicization have not eliminated religion from politics but rather have given xenophobic and anti-democratic forms of religion new power and salience. Con-sequently, the problems of religion have found political expression whereas its strengths have not been available for checking violence in public life. Not surprisingly, therefore, data on religious violence throughout the subcontinent indicate that most riots take place in urban and semi-urban areas. In rural precincts, however, believers from different faiths display little or no violence motivated by religious antipathies—although Mathur (chapter 8) reports ample amounts of other types of violent behavior in the rural hinterland.

In a very perspicacious observation several decades ago, Harrison (1967: 291) noted that ". . . liberal Indian nationalism has nothing in reserve to deal with the irrationality of particularist appeals, no larger symbolism of its own to bring forth in competition with the parochial symbolism of its opponents." It was sheer good fortune, plus the adroit political tenacity of Gandhi, that Hindu extremists like D. V. Savarkar of the Mahasabha or M. S. Golwalkar of the Rashtriya Swayamsevak Sangh remained a marginal force throughout the freedom movement. In fact, the political miracle in retrospect is that Gandhi could insist on nonviolence when Arjuna in the *Bhagavad Gita* symbolized the righteousness of violence in a righteous cause. With equal foresight, Harrison (*ibidem*: 298) predicted that although "Nehru [had] given a secular cast to the political landscape [it] might not last long should bedrock forces come to the surface in future upheavals and realignments."

Of course, the ideology of Pakistan, as Ahmad (chapter 6) reiterates, was originally and continues to be based on religion. The Pakistani state owes its existence to the successful claim for a separate homeland comprising the Muslim-majority areas of the Indian subcontinent. In 1968–69 the Muhajirs [refugees or displaced Muslims from India] of Karachi, particularly the more disadvantaged sections, played an important role in the movement which overthrew Ayub Khan. In the late 1970s, the Muhajirs again supported fundamentalist elements and helped to create the disturbances that led to Bhutto's downfall and the military takeover by General Zia-ul-Haq. Today, a decade later, these Urdu-speaking immigrants from Uttar Pradesh, Bihar, and Hyderabad (Deccan) object strenuously to the dominance of Punjabis and Pathans in Pakistan's power structure. In 1983 these Urdu-speakers formed the Muhajir Qomi Movement (MQM) which seeks recognition as a fifth distinct ethnic nationality in Pakistan [in addition to Punjabis, Pathans, Sindhis, and Baluch] as well as their 'due share' of opportunities. In late 1986, savage inter-ethnic battles in Karachi and Hyderabad (Sind) suggest once again that Islam by itself cannot forge indestructible bonds of nationhood—the myth on which the State of Pakistan was founded in 1947. The same

lesson was evident on the secession of its East Wing in 1971 which
became Bangladesh.

Furthermore, although born and brought up in Pakistan, many
descendants of the Muhajirs are not as obsessed with religion as
were or are their parents and grandparents. One is tempted to
generalize that religion alone cannot and does not provide sufficient
social cement for a nation-state in South Asia—or perhaps, for
that matter, anywhere. Religion is only of value for mobilizing or
creating solidarity when one religion is opposed to another— particularly if there is an asymmetrical bipolarity between two religions, a point elaborated by de Silva (chapter 7) in the Sri Lankan
case. One is reminded that, in political affairs, internal unity
requires [as a necessary, if not sufficient condition] an external
adversary. Units do not unite, nor remain united, without the
existence of an external enemy—a political point central to fundamentalism as well.

It is also patently evident in South Asia that not all communal
conflict pits one religion against another. Sects within one religion employ violence againt one another; likewise specific
ethnicities. In Darjeeling's present Gorkhaland agitation, Hindu
Nepalis and Hindu Bengalis are in conflict. Tamil militants in
pursuit of Eelam terminate one another as well as Sinhalese
(Björkman 1988). Episodic violence occurs in Karachi and
Hyderabad (Sind) between Muslim Muhajirs and Muslim Pathans,
the latter Pushto-speaking migrants from the Northwest Frontier
and Afghanistan. Often language becomes a label for ethnic solidarities, as when Punjabi speakers divide between Gurmukhi
script (for Sikhs) and Devanagari script (for Hindus). Since the
linkages among religion, language, and ethnicity are causally
multi-directional, one cannot automatically predict the results for
integration or for conflict. But as Surjit Mansingh argues
eloquently in the concluding chapter, religion remains a powerful
force for both good and evil.

To sum up, what factors underlie the growth of fundamentalism and the appeal of revivalists? Certainly the pressures of
modernization are among the most potent forces which intensify
the search to define and retain both individual and group identities.
"Who am I?" "Who are we?" and "What are we doing here?" are
eternal human questions about self and society which religion

tries, in part, to answer. As long as change occurs and as long as social relations are disrupted, humankind will seek some mental or spiritual solace from those who at least pretend to know. In twentieth century South Asia, fundamentalists plow fertile ground and sow the dragonteeth of future violence.

The connection between religion and violence is definitely not casual for it involves the basic question: "who can kill and who cannot!" Many theories and theorists argue for an authorized, permissible spilling of blood which includes the concept of a just war. Certainly to the believing Nazi, Hitler's extermination camps were justified; likewise these newest of political murders are justified by their perpetrators, whether called terrorists or freedom-fighters. One's choice of term or label invokes cognitive affect and suggests one's implicit answer to the basic question. The freedom-fighter has a just cause; the terrorist is a common criminal. In almost every South Asian country there are people who are ready to kill in order to achieve their goals. They consider themselves to be honest men and they defend their acts by citing an increasingly general view that killing can be justified as self-defense through pre-emptive action. In July 1985, the Adam Sena was founded by Syed Ahmed Bukhari, son of the Shahi Imam of Delhi's Jama Masjid, as a Muslim counterpart to militant Hindu groups like the Shiv Sena, the Hindu Manch, the Shiv Shakti Dal, and dozens of others. The growth of private armies bears ominous resemblance to political events of the 1930s or, more recently, to confessional Lebanon with its descent into anarchy.

Sometimes, of course, the mobilization of people along lines of religious solidarities is useful; it can elicit votes, share welfare, bolster group demands, or otherwise generate support for particular activities; however, "communal conflict is destructive in India because it is pathological. The Hindus and Muslims in India do not organize themselves against each other to win anything substantial for the welfare of their communities. . . . They organize themselves against each other to settle the residue of psychological hurts from earlier battles" (Naidu 1982: 10–11). There is a distinctly historical dimension to religious violence in South Asia because stories of past hurts and humiliations are regularly invoked. Sri Lanka's Sinhalese Buddhists grimly recall the inexorable waves of South Indian Hindus invading over the millenia (de Silva 1981). "The Hindu has for decades stored within his unconscious, rages against the Muslims for humiliating memories they evoke, for their conquering role in Indian history, for their role in dividing the subcontinent, for their special status today as a political pawn during elections, and the pseudo-privileges which these generate, such as the retention of their personal laws. . . . The Muslim too rages within himself, for the loss of his political position, the erosion he suffers culturally and for his limited economic opportunities" (Naidu 1982: 11).

To compound matters, the historic memories of past conflicts, conquests, humiliations, economic competition, cultural antipathies, and religious animosities are all reinforced by modern political processes. These transform the individual subject into a citizen; make him conscious of his rights; and encourage him to press his rights through electoral mechanisms. Older mechanisms of adjustment through conciliation and adaptation give way to rule by numbers. Those in the minority must submit to those with a voting majority.

The concept of "majority" is particularly important in discussions of religion, politics, and violence. Frykenberg (chapter 2) argues that the concept of a majority is both fictional and pernicious in South Asia. At best it is mischievous since context is all-important in deciding whether "X" is a majority or a minority. Indeed if geographic boundaries are drawn broadly enough, everyone is in the minority! Hence a sense of context as well as of identity is essential. Historically the best-governed states were pluralistic, with no claim of majority rule. Both Wallace (chapter 4) and de Silva (chapter 8) describe for the Punjab and Sri Lanka, respectively, how each community sees itself as disadvantaged. Even when in a privileged position locally, it can refer to a larger context in which the community is beset by enemies.

In a liberal state each person and community is given freedom of religion as a private activity while the state itself does not participate in any religion. The state exists as a political power in order to organize temporal and social affairs; by contrast, religion in essence is an entirely private matter in which the individual pursues the meaning of life. Religion remains essential for grounding ethical behavior and morality, but it does not loom large in the public sphere. In pluralistic liberalism, both state and religion exist for the individual, for his or her convenience, help, guidance—but the individual does not exist for either state or religion. Yet many South Asian political leaders, including those of secular India, regularly attend religious functions. Some, like President Jayewardene of Sri Lanka, even hold religious office; and the presidents of Pakistan and Bangladesh are frequently photographed at prayer. An exception to prove the rule was Jawaharlal Nehru who also dissuaded his reluctant contemporary, President Rajendra Prasad, from engaging in public religious activities. Nehru was one of the few authentic secularists who argued that it was not desirable for public figures to be involved in religious functions, even if only as a display of tolerance for all religious communities. His counsel is, however, rarely heeded throughout South Asia as religious fundamentalism, revivalists, and violence continue their relentless growth. And few understand, much less practice, the Mahatma's message about the meaningful linkage between religion and politics.

2

Fundamentalism and Revivalism in South Asia

ROBERT ERIC FRYKENBERG

Extreme forms of fundamentalism and revivalism not only hold the interest of intellectuals but also, throughout the world of our own day, are at the very forefront of contemporary public consiousness and concern. Yet, in historical terms, the phenomenological manifestations of extreme revivalism and fundamentalism have always been closely linked. So inextricably have they intermingled that one cannot consider one without the other. Historical understanding of the close relationship between revivalism and fundamentalism, as conceptualizations of social phenomena, prompts a closer examination of the origins of these terms as such. This is important because the terms are so widely applied to movements all over the world. Indeed, Buddhist revivalism and fundamentalism, Hindu revivalism and fundamentalism, Muslim revivalism and fundamentalism, Sikh revivalism and fundamentalism, and other forms of revivalism and fundamentalism in South Asia cannot be fully or properly understood, without reference to the historical context out of which such movements have come. Moreover, many scholars using such conceptualizations do not know that both terms have their roots in the crises which have beset evangelical Protestants in North America since the middle of the nineteenth century and especially in conflicts which arose among such Christians during the years from 1870 to 1925.

By 1925, a profound change in social climate had occurred. America's evangelicals, once among the most respectable of the country's citizens—once among those who had set many of the intellectual, moral, and social standards for American culture as a whole—no longer mattered. They had become despised and.

worse, ridiculed. William Jennings Bryan's behaviour at the Scopes trial in Tennessee, in 1925, served to symbolize that change. Those events made evangelicals a laughing stock across the country and the epithet "fundamentalist" came to characterize an especially militant and obscurantist brand of anti-modernism, anti-liberalism, and anti-secularism. Evangelicals had virtually become strangers in their own land.

How and why this came about has been brought to light through the penetrating and thorough scholarship of such historians as Ernest Sandeen (1970) and George Marsden (1980). In a comprehensive study entitled *Fundamentalism and American Culture: The Shaping of Twentieth Century Evangelicalism: 1870–1925*, Marsden (1980) explored the earliest use of this term among revivalist evangelicals and carefully traced the growth of the fundamentalist movement in North America. He followed its tortured path, from its sunlit heyday in the time of Dwight L. Moody, through crises engendered by the First World War, and found that the terms "fundamentalist" and "fundamentalism" came from the name for a series of books which were published in defense of "*the* faith." These works constituted an attack upon what were considered to be the excesses and foibles of higher criticism (upon Scripture), of modern science (in evolutionism and scientism), and of "liberal" or anti-theistic theology. The books condemned any public practice or preaching which might be seen as a hidden danger or an overt threat to that popular American culture which was by then so often described as "the faith once delivered to the saints," a phrase lifted out of the Epistle of Jude (1:3), the context of which (*c.* AD 68) was a warning for believers to beware of apostasy, an exhortation for them to "earnestly contend for the faith which was once delivered to the saints."

The Fundamentals, in short, were a series of twelve paperback books published between 1910 and 1915, which came out of the imaginative inspiration of a Californian oil magnate. They were edited by popular evangelists and teachers whose intentions were to mark down those basics of "*the* Truth," those essential and irreducible absolutes which constituted *the* foundations of *the* faith. An attempt was made to distribute free copies of these books—"some three million individual volumes in all"—to every Protestant religious worker in the English-speaking world.

While this distribution failed to bring the great public response which had been hoped for or even to arouse more than passing notice in either serious journals or popular periodicals, the books did produce one important long-term consequence. *The Fundamentals* not only became a symbolic point of reference for identifying a "fundamentalist" movement as such; but, perhaps more significantly, they and the movement they represented also unwittingly served to spawn a new concept.

This concept has served ever since as a neat, although somewhat simplistic instrument of social analysis. Indeed, in the course of time, the term has come into common (and even popular) usage. It has been applied more generally to other social phenomena and to ideological, political, religious, or social movements in every corner of the world. As such, the term itself has become widely if inexactly used for assessing, naming, and measuring all sorts of movements.

Just as fascinating is the relationship of this term to that of revivalism, a concept which also has roots in radical conversion movements and in their periodic millenarian reawakenings. More specifically, the origin of the term and its use in modern times can be traced back into the evangelical "revivals" of the seventeenth and eighteenth centuries (Stoeffler 1965, 1971, 1973). From these came the Great Awakening in America, the Evangelical Awakening in Britain, and the Methodist revivals which periodically thereafter have swept various parts of the English-speaking (and European) world—and which still continue so to do. So profound were the impacts of these revivals that, even today in the colloquial language of the American South (and also occasionally in the so-called "Bible Belt"), regular or periodic "revivals" are held. As a form of populistic religious rally or evangelistic campaign (or what was once called a "tent meeting"), these are no longer merely forms of spontaneous social combustion, but are planned and scheduled, if not staged (Ahlstrom 1972: 263–329; McLoughlin 1959; Sweet 1944). It is out of such traditions as these that, during this century, the great nationwide campaigns of Billy Sunday and the greater world-wide campaigns of Billy Graham have come. It is also out of these traditions that many of the current weekly appeals and programs of radio and televisions preachers—composing the so-called "electronic church"—have arisen. Commencing a half century ago with the wide-ranging network radio programs of Charles E. Fuller, this phenomenon is now most manifest in regular weekly programs of such fundamentalist (and populist) television preachers as Jerry Falwell, Pat Robertson, Jimmy Swaggart, Oral Roberts, Robert Schuller, or Herbert Armstrong.

Thus, there are strong historical grounds for linking revivalism and evangelicalism. There is both an intimate and a legitimate connection between these two concepts. Revivalisms, especially those which are most extremely radical, have almost invariably been, and in some particular and predominant way continue to be, fundamentalistic.

Several semantic classifications are essential in order to differentiate concepts more exactly and use them more finely since everyday language often confuses the usage of some of our most common concepts (Riggs and Dahlberg 1982). In much of our common language, and in the language of the public media, ideological kinds of concepts are often confused with institutional kinds of concepts. There is no conceptual reason, for example, why "conservative" and "liberal" should necessarily or always be antithetical. Such concepts as "conservative" and "radical" and "reactionary" are, in fact, essentially institutional. In their intrinsic character, these concepts are ideologically contentless or neutral. But, like receptacles, institutions to which they refer can be ideologically loaded. The only ideologies inherent within such concepts pertain to whether what exists in institutional form should be kept (*status quo*) or eradicated.

In other words, conservatives seek to "conserve" *what exists* whatever it may be and regardless of its content (culture, ideology, etc.). Radicals and reactionaries, on the other hand, are determined to remove altogether or destroy what exists, considering it to be without redeeming value. That what actually exists, institutionally, may indeed possess—in fact, almost invariably does possess within it—the quality or ideology of being liberal or authoritarian is not relevant to the concept. That institutions which do exist—and which their upholders may which to conserve—may actually happen to have ideological content should not cause confusion. On the other hand, such concepts as "liberal" and "authoritarian" are intrinsically ideological or value-laden. As such they are without any inherent or intrinsic "institutionality." Purely metaphysical, nothing but abstractions of world-views and values concerning ethical or moral or religious or issues, such ideals could conceivably remain without institutional embodiment, always and ever aspiring and never becoming embodied or institutionalized (Bjorkman, in Riggs and Dahlberg 1982: 14–19).

Nevertheless, within the common conceptual nomenclature of our culture these two kinds of concepts are constantly being confused. Without defining precisely the grounds on which they differ, "conservatives" and "liberals" constantly and perennially talk past each other. They are commonly seen to be inherently at odds. But, unless clarifications are made about what it is conservatives actually wish to conserve and what exactly liberals wish to keep or make "free" (or "liberated"), confusions multiply and Babel is rebuilt. One occasionally finds that conservatives are actually more liberal than those who, in the name of liberalism, wish to exchange what actually exists for something more authoritarian and autocratic. Of course, liberals will often piously claim that they do this "for greater *equality* between men" or "for the good of the common man"—who is helpless and cannot do for himself what he needs. On the other hand, conservatives are often heedless of how much so-called "liberty for all" becomes unrestrained liberty for a few to the detriment of the liberty of many and how much such liberty under law may undermine that "equality" between people within a society which is so necessary to their liberty.

Therefore, when we say that revivalist movements have been radical in a particular way, we often mean that such movements have not only been "anti-conservative" but that they have also been radical in a special direction. That is, they have been "radical-in-reverse" or "reactionary." They have sought to "recreate" something which once was thought to be but which, in actuality, never existed. Moreover, if "*romantic*" (as distinct from but very similar to "*utopian*"), they have actually sought for something which can never be, something chimeric from a golden age. To be reactionary, in other words, is to be radical backwards. Such radicalism is sometimes also confused with conservatism. Any attempt to alter profoundly the *status quo* is inherently anti-conservative. Going backwards to "*the* roots;" backwards to the rediscovery of what once was; backwards to the recapturing or to the trying to recapture past glory; backwards to preserve the sense of what was there before what looks dangerous appeared; backwards to the time before some present sense of danger or threats to security came into existence: that is fundamentalism. That is what "Going back to Fundamentals!!" means. It can be, and usually is, extremely radical (or reactionary, as the case may be).

Curiously and paradoxically, fundamentalists are invariably doctrinaire and, as such, altogether uncompromising. Fundamentals of doctrine will admit no contradiction, no qualification of "*the* Truth," no betrayal of *the* essentials, and no compromise with "*the* enemy." This characteristic, in one way or another, can make fundamentalists anti-intellectual and even anti-political, often to the point of self-destruction. Fundamentalists can go so far as to argue that it is "Better to die than to live in this utterly corrupt and evil world!!!"

A typology of conversion movements (Frykenberg 1980) suggests that, although there are many kinds of fundamentalist and revivalist movements, all such movements are, at least in some measure, connected to some sort of "reconversion" or to some sense of "radical reconversion." In other words, fundamentalist movements are almost invariably *revivalistic*. Many such movements, moreover, seem to have been highly contagious. They have been of such a nature that, regardless of the actual content or internal quality of any given movement, they have always tended to ignite or provoke further movements, either proliferating or reticulating out of the original movement or reacting to it. Indeed, fundamentalisms as a kind of phenomena can be seen to have been contagious in direct proportion to the presence of all of the essential ingredients which made up such movements and in direct proportion to the intensity with which many such ingredients were manifest within any given movement.

Following this logic, it is further suggested that many such movements of radical conversion, revivalist reconversion, and fundamentalism have produced phenomena and have drawn upon concepts which, by and large, might be traced to some common historical root. Many of them, indeed, can be seen to have been affected, in one way or another, by a contagiously "prophetic" tradition of radical conversion movements, the roots of which go all the way back into the ancient Middle East—back to what, for want of better metaphor, might be called "the seed of

Abraham." By this line of argument, connections by means of some sort of cultural contact can be traced among sub-sub-branches and sub-branches and branches and so forth, which can be seen to stem from this one root. In modern times, such prophetic movements could be divided into two categories—those which have been theistic and those which have been non-theistic (even anti-theistic). If one goes back far enough, they all hark back to prior Judaistic, Christian, and Islamic kinds of theistic models, together with all of their manifold offshoots, both orthodox and heterodox. These offshoots, in more modern times, then developed non-theistic counterparts—most notably, different kinds of nationalisms, socialisms, and Marxisms (not to mention certain kinds of "scientisms"). From the Law (Truth) of Moses down to the Law of Marx, one might suggest, there have been movements which, in one way or another, are connected to each other by contagious chains of causal reaction. Each of these variant forms has been capable in turn of generating its own intrinsically unique kinds of revivalism and fundamentalism. Non-theistic forms of fundamentalism have generated *all* of those characteristics, including various kinds of struggles (and witchhunts), which normally accompany any fundamentalistic movement.

Given the preceding epistemological framework, more specific observations can be made about the four studies of fundamentalism and revivalism in South Asia which follow.

First, there may be some overlap or confusion between what are essentially reformist movements and what are revivalist. While one may not wish to quibble, there *is* a difference between completely and radically re-creating something anew and merely reasserting, recapturing, re-defining, rediscovering, or even revivifying something from out of a forgotten past. What, for example, was the "Hinduism" which emerged into self-consciousness and generated an All-India identity during the nineteenth century? Was it the awakening of something old? Or, was it perhaps the creation of something altogether new, albeit out of ancient materials? If the latter, was it radically new in reaction to other radical movements which had become so powerful during the Victorian Age? Was it a reaction to an aggressive Christian evangelicalism and to mass conversion movements generated therefrom? It might be useful, on such questions, to separate out those elements which have been, in fact, wholly new—new ideas and techniques taken

out of (or used as backfires to counter) radical conversion movements—from those which were, in fact, reformist attempts to
recapture vital elements taken out of an older, long forgotten (or
lost) past. Not as extreme as "revive," the term "reform" denotes
a mending process or a restoring to previous form elements
which were once a part thereof. A reformation need not be
revivalistic; it need only be restorative and melliorative.

Occasionally both reformist and revivalist features might be
found in a socio-religious movement. More often, the two
become one and the same when that which is being "recreated"
from the past (and thus reactionary) is just as radical as that which
is being made entirely from scratch and hence truly and entirely
new. Revivalists will often say that they are bringing back what
once existed; but in fact they too may be creating something
which is as altogether new as what utopian radicals claim they are
trying to create.

In other words, there are plenty of grounds for considering that
what emerged in India during the late eigheenth to the twentieth
centuries under the label of "Hinduism" was, in fact, the
emergence of an almost entirely new religious system within the
context of indigenous cultures, a religion the likes of which India
had never before seen. Moreover, it was this new and "syndicated"
kind of religion, this phenomenon now so loosely and vaguely
lumped together and called "Hinduism" which, by borrowing
much from the prophetic and radical conversionist traditions,
became radical, revivalist, and eventually, even fundamentalistic in
ways hitherto unknown. Perhaps the earliest glimmerings of
what may be called "Hindu fundamentalism" are those which
were stimulated by fundamentalistic missionaries at Serempore
(Young 1981). It is this kind of phenomena, as epitomized in such
terms as "*Arya Dharm*" and "*Sanathana Dharm*" and as organized
by such fundamentalist movements and parties as the Vibuthi
Sangam, the Arya Samaj, the Nagari Pracharini Sabha, the Hindu
Mahasabha, and the Rashtriya Swayamsevak Sangh (RSS), and
the Jana Sangh, which Kenneth Jones has so brilliantly brought to
light. In similar fashion, the explosive new forms of Buddhism,
Sikhism, and Islam which have arisen in South Asia—as characterized respectively by de Silva, Wallace, and Ahmed and as
epitomized in such revitalized agencies as the *Buddha Sasana* for
some Sinhalese, the *Singh Sabha* for some Sikhs, and the *Jama'at-i-*

Islami for certain Muslims of Pakistan—have all had varying shades of extremist fundamentalism within them.

Second, there is the issue of that hoary and now rather shop-worn historiography on the denigration of "Hinduism" which is charged against Europeans. This kind of caricature, as found at the beginning of Jones' essay (and often parroted in much of the literature), may not only be less than fully accurate or complete but, indeed, may also be all too simplistic. It is important to note, in this connection, that during the eighteenth century few of the gentry among "Hindus" or "Native Indians" or "Indians" (or "East Indians") were uniformly looked down upon by the British, certainly not in the same way as would later occur more generally by the middle of the nineteenth century. Indeed, the term "Hindu" often meant "Indian" and, for a while (as sometimes even now), the terms were virtually synonymous. Nathaniel Halhed and William Jones, not to mention their mentor (Warren Hastings who was Governor-General), were frank and open admirers of cultures which they found in India (Marshal 1970; Mukherjee 1968; Rocher 1983). Fascinated by the complexities of this ancient and high civilization and anxious to learn more, these servants of the Company were the founders of Oriental studies, Orientalism, and the whole ethos of the Asiatic Society of Bengal. The climate of discovery, excitement, and wide-eyed wonder at what they found never disappeared—nor, for some, has it yet. Thereafter, there have always remained a coterie of admiring, even wonderstruck Europeans (and Americans) who, to this day, have devoted themselves to learning more about "Hindu" India. Rarely if ever defined with precision, the concept "Hindu" is applied vaguely to cultures, peoples, and religions of India which are neither Muslim, Christian, nor Judaic—yet, even this consistency breaks down because references to "Hindu" Christians, "Hindu" Muslims, and such abound in early writings. Many of the early nationalist leaders, indeed, first gained their knowledge of the cultural heritage of their own civilization from these fascinated Europeans. Gandhi, Nehru, and many others read their Hindu classics in the English translations of such scholars as Max Mueller and Edwin Arnold. The ironies of this circumstance did not escape the notice of many among the more perceptive nationalists.

Thus, to dwell too exclusively upon the position that Euro-

peans had a denigrating view of Hindu culture—seeing India as
hopelessly if not totally degenerate and depraved—without indi-
cating that there was also a strong opposite tendency among
Europeans, is to miss the whole picture. There is a danger, in consequence, of grossly oversimplifying and even distorting that
picture. How representative of European views these different
kinds of expression and influence were is a subject which scholars
have yet to address adequately. Indeed, the very idea that the
"Hindu degeneracy" view was really a reaction to Hindu India by
only two forces, however accurate this idea may be, *as far as it
goes*, is also too simple. Utilitarianism and Evangelicalism certainly were two streams of influence which were flowing out to
India from Britain during the nineteenth century. But by the time
this reaction took place among Europeans, some sort of a Company raj—first a micro-raj and then a macro-raj of imperial
dimensions—had already been in place for over a century.
Moreover, by the third decade of the nineteenth century, the
Company's larger imperium had itself been established for several
generations. Thus, justification for the Raj in terms of its "civilizing" mission and its "rescuing" the benighted from darkness—
justification of rule by denigration of what is ruled, so to speak—
must be seen as a much later development.

Inherent contradictions in justifications for the existence of the
Raj were certainly manifold. For example, some of those who were
later to use the "civilizing" ("Hindu" degradation and European
moral-superiority) argument were among those pamphleteers
of the Anti-Idolatry Connexion League (*c.*1833–1845) who
attacked the Indian Empire precisely because of the excessively
"Hindu" and "Heathen" (and hence, by implication also "cor-
rupted") character of the British Raj. These pamphleteers saw the
Company's Raj itself as a "Heathen" empire. In this, they were
merely responding to their own belated discovery of such things
as Madras Regulation VII of 1817, which put the care of all religious
institutions under Government (Frykenberg 1977: 37–53). What
business did the British Nation have, they asked, in helping the
Company to construct and maintain an empire which was so
completely pagan and idolatrous and, hence, so diabolically evil?
Why should those of the Company's civil and military officers who
were Christians (even if only a minority) be obliged, against their
own private consciences, to attend and serve temple ceremonies,

rituals, and festivals (*pujas, abhishekams, melas, tirnals,* and such)? During the 1830s and early 1840s, the Anti-Idolatry Connnexion League sent petition after petition and lobbied members of the British Government. Their purpose was to force the Company into disassociating itself, its Raj, and its local governments in India from having any connection with "Heathen" worship and into ending all maintenance of Hindu temples by the Company's officials. They demanded a complete separation of the Company's rulership from indigenous religion. Yet, these same pamphlets never advocated complete removal of Western missionaries, any prohibition of their proselytizing activities, nor any cessation of other forms of interference and meddling with indigenous religious institutions in India (for context, see Kaye 1859:387–474; Frykenberg 1985c:21, 34).

The Company's Raj had, in fact, always been deeply involved and could never have extricated itself from such involvement (Frykenberg 1979). Indeed, recent research indicates that there may have been a pro-Hindu Raj or a Hindu-exalting phase long before there was an anti-Hindu campaign or a Hindu-denigrating historiography. The issue certainly requires much more investigation, more sophisticated questions, and a thorough revision.

The same kinds of questions also need to be addressed to the interactions of religion and state in Sri Lanka. Admittedly complex in ways entirely different from conditions in the subcontinent itself, there are nevertheless some factors relating to the very logic of power on the island which might have required certain kinds of responses from any regime, whether Sinhalese, Tamil, Portuguese, Dutch, or British. Furthermore, the very fact that, at least initially, it was the Company rather than the Colonial Office which succeeded to rulerships over Sri Lanka prompts us to enquire whether initial policies with respect to indigenous religious institutions may not have been similar to those of the Madras Presidency. If so, then what are called "Buddhist temporalities" would have enjoyed much more state support than now supposed and what identity there may have been between Christianity and the state would have been minimal, if not initially hostile. The East India Company itself, it should be recalled, remained implacably opposed and profoundly suspicious of all alien missionary activities within its domains, even after admission of such agencies was imposed upon its Raj by Parliament as a price for the Charter renewal of 1813.

Likewise, therefore, our assessments of European missionary activities and attitudes must be no less exacting and free from reductionistic or simplistic elements. One must look carefully at the programs and styles of both Catholic and Protestant missionaries who had been working in India long before the arrival of the British (and American) evangelicals. Those groups which had been active in India long *before* the arrival of European evangelicals and reformers of the early nineteenth century and long *before* the Indian reformers who worked with these late arriving Europeans (e.g. Raja Ram Mohan Roy and others) were still in India. Danish-German pietists, for example, seem to have been rather more irenic and intellectual in their missionary enterprises, more sensitive to existing social sensibilities. Their work emphasized a more contextualizing and indigenizing approach to local institutions. In their day, such concepts as "Hinduism" or "Indian" had not yet been coined; and, even after the words emerged, the concepts were as yet far from clear in value, meaning or content. To them all "Hindoo" institutions were not necessarily antithetical to Christian institutions. They refrained from attacking caste or from attacking many of the other institutions which they found already existing in India.

Again, the older the Christian communities in various parts of South Asia were and the longer different kinds of missionary agencies had been active in one region or another, whether they were indigenous or alien (European and American) and whether Nestorian, Syrian ("Mar Thoma"), Catholic, or Protestant, the more complex and compounded were the different kinds of local relationships which developed. While it is certainly true that some peoples of Sri Lanka experienced over four centuries of "colonial" rule and almost as long a period of sometimes aggressive intrusion and expansion by various Christian communities, it is no less true that extreme differences of approach, method, and style between and among some of these Christian communities can be found. In struggles between the Padroado of Goa and the Propaganda Fides of Rome, as now revealed in recent research (Boudens 1978), there were far greater resonances of Sinhalese and Tamil cultures with the Catholicism of South India than with that of Europe. And the brilliant and cogent analysis of the place of one Christian caste, the Paravas, on both sides of the Palk Straits as well as in the Gulf of Mannar shows us something altogether new and far more complex (Kaufmann 1981, 1979). Instead of the simplistic old story of conquest and imposition by an alien civilization, fresh elements were introduced into an already intricate mosaic of reciprocities, with participants rather than conquerors rendering services and receiving benefits. In short, in neither India nor Sri Lanka can elements of "Christian" culture be studied either exclusively or merely as as "alien" imports (Neill 1984; Frykenberg 1985a).

Third, studies of fundamentalism and revivalism in this volume suggest something which Rothermund (1965) has labelled the "differential impacts" of the Raj. Impacts upon India by elements from various European movements cannot be lumped together but must be chronologically and geographically differentiated. Different movements coming out of Europe, coming at different times, or taking root or growing up within different parts of South Asia, either simultaneously or at different times, not unnaturally produced very different consequences. All movements were not equally radical, either in their origins or in their impacts. Movements which began in the seventeenth or early eighteenth centuries and which germinated slowly and developed gradually did not have effects which were as radical or disruptive as movements which arrived much later and which struck much more suddenly and much more disturbingly. Older movements may even, in fact, have generated strongly conservative and indigenous features.

In short, we must ask to what degree we are talking about parallel or synchronic processes, to what degree we are dealing with non-synchronic or sequential processes. We must discover in what measure we are concerned with processes the impact of which can be seen to have been, both in qualitative or quantitative terms, "differential." To what degree are we talking about the impact of events which were prior in Europe or prior in India? To what degree were processes and their impacts almost being felt both in India and in the West simultaneously? How synchronized or dissynchronized were impacts of the same movement in India and other parts of the world?

For example, the Great Awakening in America, the Evangelical

Awakening in England, and the Tranquebar Mission in Tanjore and Tinnevelly were closely parallel and simultaneous events, with all three having origins which can be traced back to Herrenhut, Halle University, and influences of the Moravian diaspora. Likewise, what happened in Punjab was very different in its impact from what had happened earlier in the original "down country" presidencies. The late arrival of the Raj in Punjab, from 1846 onwards, was very sudden. It came all at once, all in a rush, and all in its most radical forms. Moreover it was accompanied by the entire panoply of the Company's huge Imperial system, with its extensive entourage. As such, it was a Bengali-British phenomenon, a cumulative system which had taken two centuries to develop before it struck Punjab. This system included, in addition to the tiny elite of British mandarins, hosts of Bengali bureaucrats and civil servants, along with hosts of sepoys from various parts of India; the latest and most recent technologies of the West; and the latest and the most radical manifestations of British (Anglo-Saxon or European) culture. Such an arrival—with roads, bridges, canals, postal and telegraph services, railways, schools, and much more—was bound to be profoundly disruptive to local institutions and disturbing to local elites. More disturbing still was the policy victory of John Lawrence over his brother, Henry. Henceforth, measures aimed at social "levelling" would prevail over more cautious attempts to work with the old aristocracies of Punjab, thereby removing that buffering of cultural and social cement between the different communities by a modicum of domestic tranquillity which had been secured under previous dynasties. In such circumstances, one can begin to imagine how severe and sudden the impacts of changes upon the entire social fabric of Punjab have been. Perhaps in no other part of South Asia were impacts of sudden change so drastic. And, once the aristocratic culture was removed, or at least weakened, certainly no other region in South Asia possessed such an explosive combination of fundamentalist communities and movements. In Punjab is where the heart of Jama'at-i-Islam and of Pakistan now lies. In Punjab is where the heart of Khalistan, the Sikh Subha, is to be found. And in Punjab is where one also finds the heart and root of Arya Dharm.

Thus, when we look at what Kenneth Jones has learned about the radical impacts of Western culture upon "Hindus" (Non-

Muslims and Non-Sikhs of high caste) in the Punjab or when we look at what Mumtaz Ahmad and Paul Wallace tell us about those same impacts upon Muslims and Sikhs, it is not difficult to understand how each scholar has come to his position. To repeat, in the Punjab, the Raj and Western influences came all at once and all in a rush, and all in their most radical and sometimes most rank forms. Some of these ingredients were often not just imperialistic but blatantly "colonialistic" in a classic sense. In Punjab were what in the Bible Belt of America would be considered "redneck" preachers railing against degenerate "heathen" and "native" customs, arousing antagonism and controversy by the very confrontational manner in which they assailed their adversaries.

By that time, meanwhile, the influences of Western culture in Bengal were nearly two centuries old and had been pervading the countryside slowly and steadily for much of that time. Bengal had already been the very heart of the Raj for a century; and Bengalis had long collaborated with Britons in the cumulative building of a common Indo-British civilization. If this were the case for Bengal, it was even more so for the upper caste gentry of Madras where mutual collaboration had been profound from the very beginning. Even for Bombay Island, where its previous history as a Portuguese enclave and overwhelming Maratha power had produced a kind of defensive isolation, there had been a long and slow incubation before the Company's Raj gained its final paramountcy in 1818. Thus, the original growth of the Company's first city-states had been cautious and slow: the micro-raj at Madras which began in 1639; that of Bombay which began in 1661; and that of Calcutta which began in 1692. And slow also had been the early impact of the Danish-Halle-SPCK missionary enterprises at Tranquebar and Thanjavuru (Tanjore) which began in 1706. The impacts of ventures which grew gradually and which drew substantially upon indigenous manpower and partnerships for their successes, were not as disruptive as the impacts of what happened in Punjab. It is no wonder, under the circumstances, that Punjab became and has remained such a seething caldron.

Buddhist Revivalism in Sri Lanka, while it parallels what happened elsewhere in South Asia, is in many ways quite obviously different and unique. Yet many of the observations made about the clashes of antagonistic fundamentalisms in the Punjab (Christian, Hindu, Muslim, and Sikh) can be applied with equal validity to what K. M. de Silva has described as clashing fundamentalisms in Sri Lanka. The successive phases of Buddhist-Christian confrontation have been revealed in rich detail. Yet, as in the case of India, we cannot too easily jump to hasty conclusions about the nature of the connections between British rule and religious institutions. Special relationships there may have been with each religious community, but whether these were nearly as monolithic as one might first assume seems far from clear.

If anything, one is forced by what we have learned to ask whether the rulers of Sri Lanka did not face some of the same kinds of dilemmas or experience some of the same kinds of inner contradictions which one finds within the subcontinent. The long-established linkage between state and religion which had existed before the arrival of European power and the continuance of this linkage by the Portuguese, the Dutch, and the early British (Company) finds its parallels in India. The fact that certain radical (Protestant) missionaries sought, with limited success, to bring about a dissociation between religion and the state also find its parallels in India. Total disestablishment of traditional religious institutions never occurred.

The explosive blending of Buddhist revivalism with Sinhalese nationalism has produced a religious nationalism which is clearly fundamentalistic. In some sense, when people undergo radical reconversion to "*The Truth*" insomuch that they see themselves "*The Select*" whose destiny it is to achieve "*The New (or Perfect) Order on Earth,*" when people perceive that there is threat to what they hold most dear and most basic, and when people are prepared to die before they give up "fundamentals," essentials from which they will not budge, then a situation occurs in which violent struggle and martyrdom are not only acceptable but mandatory and sacred. Incarnate evil may then be identified as consisting of all alien elements, whether Colonial rulers, Non-Buddhist (Burgher, Christian, Muslim, or Hindu) communities, or secessionist Tamil (Eelam) Tigers, together with the cultures which they represent. Attainment of an ideal "Pure Land" may then require a drastic cleansing and scrubbing away of all impure remnants, at whatever cost. Such feelings explain how monks, feeling betrayed by Bandaranayake, could resort to assassination and how military forces can turn upon the entire population of Jaffna Tamils.

The necessary logic of power in India is not like that of Pakistan or Sri Lanka. For any larger state, but especially for an All-India political system, whether imperial or national, no single religion, certainly no religion with a fundamentalist ideology, can be afforded. The ancient symbol for state power, the *Mahachakra* or Great Wheel, was no accident. *Mahachatra* ("Great Parasol" or "Great Umbrella") for State Authority, *Chatrapati* ["Lord of the Parasol (of Authority)"] and *Chakavartin* ("World-Conqueror"), are symbolic variants of this basic logic (Spellman 1964: 170–174). Without giving balanced and equal tension or treatment to each of the many (thousand) spokes of social diversity, how could the peripheral rim of many peoples and religions be bonded to the hub of central power? If one were to favor any one revivalist movement to the exclusion of others, whether Hindu or Sikh, Christian or Muslim, the state itself would find itself in dire trouble. The very notion that there can be a Khalistan, or a Pakistan, or even a "Hindustan," for that matter, becomes, by this logic, altogether intolerable. Yielding to such a notion opens a Pandora's Box of "fissiparous tendencies." By this logic, there never could be any such thing as a "majority community." The very nursing of such a notion is profoundly dangerous (see below).

Whether or not, or in what degree, the same logic may be true for Sri Lanka remains to be seen. It is something about which we need more information. Quite obviously, the situation in Pakistan, where state ideology has intimately linked Islam to very survival of the state, raises the same question. Here, close identification of the state, rulership over the state by any regime, and fundamentalist religion are perceived as being essential to Pakistan's continued existence. Such close identification may eventually, in fact, sound its knell.

Yet, within India itself, Sikhism has generated all of those ingredients which are so essential in a revivalistic fundamentalist movement. Elements of radical reconversion to a fundamentalist ideology—namely, *the* Truth, *the* Prophet(s) or Messengers (who are Instruments) for carrying this Truth, *the* (Chosen, or Select) People, *the* (Promised, or Sacred) Land, *the* Locus of (Sacred and Central) Authority (within the Akal Takht of the Golden Temple in Amritsar), and *the* (Utopian) Ideal Solution of Khalistan (as a completely independent Sikh State)—are all present. Thus, when one looks at the struggle which developed between the Akali Dal under Longowal and the militantly extremist forces of the Damdani

Taksal led by Bhindranwale, it becomes clear that all of the established lines of external (state) authority were perceived as having failed. Having endangered the Sikh *panth* by falling away from *the Truth* as defined by the fundamentalists and having betrayed the Sikh community, all established Sikhs institutions—such as the Akali Dal and its dissident branches, the SGPC (Shiromani Gurdwara Prabandhak Committee), and the High Priests—became stigmatized as *the enemy within*. For fundamentalists there has got to be both *the enemy within* and *the enemy without* which together are hindering fulfillment of that destiny, that ultimate arrival in "the promised land" which alone can usher in the expected millennial utopia. All apostates, like dirt, must be scrubbed away if the true faith is to be purified and made worthy of its destiny.

Thus, as *all* authority systems in Punjab began to break down after 1978, one might well ask for greater specificity. What authority systems were breaking? Did the commitment of many peoples from many religions to a larger Common Wheel with many spokes leading to its hub begin to crumble? Was such a commitment replaced by commitment to smaller wheels which might be defined in narrower and more fundamentalistic terms, whether Hindu or Sikh? Had the great Humpty Dumpty now and forever fallen, never to be put together again? Notwithstanding Operation Bluestar, communal riots, and the assassinations of Indira Gandhi, Sant Longowal and others, attempts to repair and restore the balanced spokes of the *Mahachakra* in Punjab have not ceased. The fires of extreme fundamentalism, both Hindu and Sikh, have yet to be quenched, or even (as of this writing) brought under control. This crisis, requiring astute management and extreme restraint at the Centre, through the assuaging of fears and the granting of concessions, is still far from over. Neither Barnala nor Rajiv's ministers have found ways to gain control.

As for the position of Islam in South Asia, there remains a continuous if not chronic tension between the Islam of India and the Islam of Pakistan. The more successfully that India can manage to assuage the fears of various Muslim communities within its borders, the more it can find ways to provide security and satisfaction for its Muslims, the more India remains as a standing threat to Pakistan and all that Pakistan stands for. On the other hand, the more successfully that Pakistan, with its prophetic religion and its military rulership, can combine fundamentalism with economic security and social tranquillity, the more its continuance and strength can pose a threat to India. This is both the dilemma and the irony. The stability and strength of either serves, by that very fact, to threaten the other. India with its ideal of secularistic anti-fundamentalism and Pakistan with its ideal of religious fundamentalism are, by their very natures, at war with each other. Yet, further compounding this irony, is the fact that India itself, quite apart from Bangladesh, holds more Muslims than Pakistan. Moreover, India's Muslims not only have grounds to consider that they possess the strongest Islamic institutions of South Asia (i.e. Deoband as well as Aligarh) but also grounds to feel that Pakistan was founded by modernistic and apostate "winebibbers and porkeaters" who were anything but devout. ("When we Muslims first came into India a thousand years ago," goes the argument, "we were but few. Look how God has increased our numbers! Is God still not Great?")

Again, for Bangladesh, Bengali culture provides a focus for a regional nationalism which is quite distinct and which competes with its Islamic identity. Yet, the very nature of this Bengali appeal poses a different sort of threat for India, in which the lure of a Greater Bengal for all Bengalis, some kind of a Maha-Bangladesh, has an attraction all its own.

Finally, there is the vexing and mischievous issue which keeps rising to the surface in almost every confrontation and in almost every debate: the issue of *majority* as against *minority*. Perhaps no single concept during the past century has done as much damage to political stability in South Asia as the concept of "majority." Surjit Mansingh, while far from the first to emphasize the essentials of the central fact which underlies this crucially important point, puts it aptly. In her words, "It is clear from recorded history that *no single group became all-engulfing in number, or uniformly dominant in power, either throughout South Asia, or in constituent elements of it*" (emphasis added; see chapter below). In other words, no country nor region of South Asia has ever had a "majority" as such. Neither in terms of caste, community, ethnicity, or religious identity, has there been such a thing as a "majority."

The cogency of this crucial factor can be argued and demonstrated in a number of ways. One can look at the sense of being a beleaguered "minority" which, according to Kenneth Jones (1976), afflicted the high caste leaders of the "Hindu" revivalists of North India during the 19th century (see also King 1974; Sender 1974). Nor were such feelings confined merely to the Punjab. There is hardly any region in the subcontinent in which "Hindus," as they defined themselves before Gandhi attempted to co-opt or incorporate all Untouchable communities into the "Hindu" fold, represented a cohesive or clearly identifiable "majority" community. Perhaps no study has done more to show the sinister implications of this notion than that produced by Saraswati (1974); *Minorities in Madras State* effectively destroyed the historical validity of "majority" as anything but a mischievous, if inadvertent, invention of modern times. It demonstrates that, within a highly complex socio-political mosaic of "minorities"—where there had never ever been anything but minorities but where some elite minorities had always succeeded in dominating the rest, albeit under circumstances which minimized polluting contact (whether in streets, temples, or anywhere else) and where devices for control had necessarily had to be more discontinuous than direct—the conjuring up of this concept can be seen as nothing more than another attempt by one elite minority or coalitions of elite minorities to dominate all others. In this connection, the profound "*discontinuities*" between castes and communities of the incredibly fractured and pluralistic and segmented populations of each region had, until modern times, prevented both the formation and the mobilization of "majorities" among them (Frykenberg 1985b: 64–85, 74).

3

Socio-Religious Movements and Changing Gender Relationships Among Hindus of British India

KENNETH W. JONES

During the nineteenth century a variety of socio-religious movements swept through the South Asian subcontinent in all religious communities. Among Hindus each movement attempted to rediscover the pure and proper past and thus to remove its degenerate and decadent present. These movements demanded various changes in social, religious, and customary behavior. Their programs were legitimized by appeals to religious authority, through reinterpretation of existing scriptures, the teachings of a new charismatic leader, or through a combination of the two. All sought to return to the fundamental principles of Hinduism, as they conceived them, and thus to create a purified future in which Hindus would regain their lost honor, their dignity, and their role as spiritual leaders in the world.

Central to these efforts to reconstruct society was a series of changes in the social position and role of women. Movement after movement pointed to the inferior status of women and called for a dramatic transformation in their condition. "The crusade for emancipation of Indian women became the first tenet of the social reform movement everywhere in India" (Heimsath 1964: 14). In the past, historians have accepted the central role of women's "emancipation" as an obvious and dramatic example of nineteenth century progress. It has been pointed to with pride and satisfaction by Hindu leaders as clear evidence of the regeneration of society and of its march toward "modernity." It is the intention of this study to re-examine social change in the nineteenth century as it related to the role of Hindu women. It will focus on two aspects of this process of change: first, the degree of actual change achieved; and, second, the motivations behind such changes. More questions will be raised than answered, but it is hoped that a new understanding will result along with a different and more sophisticated dialogue on the nature of social change during this century.

Religious ferment among Bengali Hindus started with Ram Mohun Roy in the nineteenth century. As did later religious leaders, he considered contemporary Hinduism to be degenerate, filled with superstition and errors. He used this critical stance to justify the rejection of a wide range of Hindu beliefs: idolatry, Brahmin priests, elaborate rituals, polytheism, numerous established customs, and female deities. Roy maintained that the worship of Kali and Tantric Hinduism encouraged immorality and debauchery through "human sacrifice, the use of wine, criminal intercourse, and licentious songs. . . . " (Ghose 1885: 177). Roy's message was a strongly puritanical one that asked for a purging of social sin and a restructuring of social behavior.

Many of the elements Roy condemned directly affected the treatment of Hindu women. The custom against which Roy fought the hardest with dramatic personal conviction was sati, the immolation of widows on their husbands' funeral pyres. In 1829, after years of agitation, Roy and his Hindu and resident English allies succeeded in persuading the government to outlaw sati which became a criminal offense and was treated as a form of murder. Roy also spoke against polygamy and child-marriage. He favored education for women, but did not define its extent, and little was done prior to his death in 1833.

Roy described the source of the secondary status of women as arising from their physical characteristics. "Women are in general inferior to men in bodily strength and energy; consequently the male part of the community, taking advantage of their corporeal weakness, have denied to them those excellent merits that they are entitled to by nature, and afterwards they are apt to say that women are naturally incapable of acquiring those merits" (*ibidem*: 343). The writings and work of Ram Mohun Roy became the basis for later Brahmo Samaj attempts to restructure the social role of women. He instigated a wide ranging debate over the value of education for women, women's status, child marriage, and widow remarriage among the upper castes. This debate, however, was conducted by men and the prime subjects of this controversy remained largely excluded. Actual change was slow to take place. Rhetoric rather than action dominated during the first half of the nineteenth century (Borthwick 1984: xi).

By the 1850s and 1860s, a more radical activism entered the Brahmo Samaj as a new generation of young, educated Bengalis began to aspire to leadership in the Brahmo Samaj. The rise of a social radicalism was centered on the figure of Keshab Chandra Sen, who joined the Samaj in 1857. Sen was a Vaidya, a member of the doctor caste, and thus lower in status than the Brahmins who had provided leadership in the movement until then. He demonstrated a willingness to attack social beliefs and to strive openly for greater women's equality. In 1860, Sen founded the Sangat Sabha, a subdivision within the Samaj, composed of individuals who pledged to put their religious ideology into action. One of their concerns was the encouragement of women's education. In 1863, a group of Sen's disciples organized the Bamabodhini Sabha and it in turn published the *Bamabodhini Patrika*, a women's journal with a greater circulation than any other (Borthwick 1984: 50–51). In 1865, another organization was established, one dedicated to "female improvement," the Brahmika Samaj (Brahmo Ladies Prayer Meeting), a society intended only for Brahmo women. This was a radical step and produced immediate opposition from orthodox Hindus even to the extent that Brahmo supporters found themselves excommunicated by their orthodox relatives (Shastri 1911: 151–152, 158–160 and 166–167). In 1862, K. C. Sen had faced similar reactions in his attempt to break the tradition of seclusion by taking his wife with him to the home of Debendranath Tagore.

The issues of "female emancipation" and "improvement" covered a variety of social practices. Emancipation meant an end to *purdah*, the exclusion of women from public life and their seclusion in a section of the family home. Improvement included a wide variety of efforts to educate women, change marriage customs, and expand the sphere of acceptable activity for women. In 1864, Sen and fellow radicals dared to celebrate an inter-caste marriage that was also a widow remarriage. This action shocked orthodox Hindus and older members of the Samaj (*ibidem*: 151–152). By the 1870s, issues of female emancipation divided many of the Brahmos into radical and moderate members, as one issue after another arose, was debated, and then transformed into organizational policy. In 1872, Durga Mohun Das, one of the younger Brahmos, demanded that women be allowed to sit with their families in the weekly services. Previously all women had remained behind a screen so that *purdah* was maintained. After considerable heated debate Sen allowed women of the "advanced" families to sit with their relatives (Kopf 1979: 35–36). Similar issues flared up and on occasion died down with little aftereffect. In 1856, champions of change led by Pandit Vidyasagar had won a victory with the passage of the Widow Remarriage Bill, but enthusiasm for this cause then waned and few such marriages were actually performed (Borthwick 1984: 49–50). The education of women, however, remained a concern for Brahmos throughout the latter half of the nineteenth century.

Although Ram Mohun Roy had advocated educating girls, little was done by the Brahmos prior to the 1860s. Christian missionaries and a few Hindu proponents of education attempted to establish schools for women. They were frustrated by shortages of trained teachers, appropriate texts, apathy, and hostility. There was considerable confusion about what such education might entail and whether it should mirror the schooling of boys. England provided a ready model for women's education in the nineteenth century. A textbook for girls published in 1849 included needlework, popular in England, but not part of women's culture in India (*ibidem*: 81). Brahmo interest in women's education was strengthened after K. C. Sen returned from a trip to England. In February 1870, he founded a Native Ladies' Normal School to train teachers and then added a girls primary school later that same year (*ibidem*: 86).

This concern for women's education was also demonstrated by the Sadharan Brahmo Samaj after its formation in 1878. They strongly supported the equality of women and proudly opened a Brahmo Girls School complete with a boarding house as a concrete expression of their ideals. The Victoria Girls School, founded by Keshab Chandra Sen, did not seek equality, but taught a domestic arts curriculum described in a statement by the school administrators:

With a view to avoid masculine training and meet the special requirements and develop the softer susceptibilities of the female mind, special
subjects were included in the curriculum besides the ordinary course of
studies, such as domestic economy, drawing, music, cookery, needlework, and laws of health (quoted in *ibidem*: 98–99).

The Adi Samaj, the conservative wing of the Brahmo movement, carefully advocated an "education for intelligent wifely
companionship and motherhood" (Kopf 1979: 127). By the last
decade of the century, women's education had gained sufficient
acceptance that the orthodox leaders of Hindu society established
their own school, the Mahakali Pathsala, opened in 1893 (Borthwick 1984: 100). Debates then turned to whether women should
be educated at the collegiate level or whether this was inappropriate
for them and would lessen their effectiveness as wives and
mothers. By the end of the century, literate Hindus had accepted
primary education for women. A small group of women were
educated to an advanced standard and a few had even achieved a
degree of economic independence.

As the first of the nineteenth century Hindu social reform
movements, the Brahmo Samaj articulated an ideology of social
change in female gender roles as a major part of its vision of a
purified and rationalized Hinduism. These "reforms" included a
number of issues: sati, widow remarriage, education of women,
the custom of child marriage, inter-caste marriages, and the
removal of immoral religious and social customs. These issues
were not limited to either Bengal or the Brahmo Samaj, but concerned a variety of movements and individuals throughout the
subcontinent. An examination of other struggles to change social
behavior will provide a clearer understanding of the motivation
behind these attempts to restructure the role of women in Hindu
society. The two customs that received the earliest and most vigorous attention were sati and female infanticide. They were the
first to be outlawed and thus transformed into criminal acts rather
than questions of social custom.

After conquering a new territory British officials and missionaries attempted to end the practice of female infanticide. In
these campaigns they sought and generally received the active
support of religious and secular leaders. In Gujarat during the
early 1800s, Sahajanand Swami, founder of the Swami Naryana
Sampradaya, rejected decadent Hinduism, including religious

rituals that contained elements of sexual practices, superstition, magic, self-torture, and elaborate rituals. His was a puritanical ideology that also attacked all forms of immoral and improper behavior. Sahajanand Swami condemned adultery, the use of bawdy songs at marriage celebrations, and the lewd customs of Holi. He banned the use of alcohol and drugs instructing his disciples to follow a life of discipline and purity. To Sahajanand, the Hindu worshippers of the Shakti cults and the mother goddesses represented the worst elements of Hinduism, elements which should be purged. He attacked the worship of tribal deities and condemned infanticide and sati, which he considered to be errors within Hinduism. He equated both with the murder of women. Sahajanand stressed the right of women to shave their heads and become ascetics, thus providing an acceptable social role for widows and unmarried women (Williams 1984: 14–15 and 19–22.)

The initial concern over sati and infanticide did not lead to the advocacy of further changes in the social position of women. Instead, Sahajanand Swami articulated a return to the traditional role of women as subservient to their husbands and subject to the rules of purdah. He stressed the necessity of separating women during all rituals and created temples solely for his female followers. He warned his male ascetics to refrain from seeing or even thinking of a woman. Should they touch one, they were required to fast on the day of their transgression. Within this socio-religious movement then there were two distinct trends in regard to women's role in society: first, a concern for sati, female infanticide, and the plight of widows; and, secondly, a reinforcement of the traditional role of women including the institution of purdah. There were no further "reforms" in regards to women. The reasons for this pattern may well result from Sahajanand's contacts with English officials and missionaries who opposed sati and female infanticide.

A similar pattern of interaction between the English and local leaders was manifest in the Punjab where, in 1853, a large gathering was assembled in Amritsar at the instigation of British officials. This gathering included local chieftains, landlords, merchants, and representatives of the ruling Punjabi families. It was dedicated to the eradication of female infanticide and to limiting both the cost of dowries and general marriage expense. Other meetings took place throughout the province and resulted in tracts and pamphlets on the custom of infanticide and the need to limit dowries.

In Gujarat and Punjab the British publicly condemned sati and infanticide. In the Punjab this was done as part of government policy with the result that these customs became an acute embarrassment to Hindu leaders. A willingness to attack these customs publicly offered an opportunity to gain approval from the English. Other "reform" issues also won similar positive reactions from the new rulers of South Asia; however, this was only one of several possible reasons for advocating change in the role of women. The question of education stemmed from a wider variety of motivations, as was to be demonstrated by leaders of the Arya Samaj, a reform and revival movement centered in Punjab.

Founded in 1875, the Arya Samaj championed women's education. As with many of the socio-religious movements of the nineteenth century, its followers were expected to find the proper forms of belief and behavior from scriptural sources. If unable to read the scriptures themselves, they should turn to the literature written by leaders of the movement. Thus literacy was a necessity and a religious virtue. All Aryas should be literate, but in practice Aryas focused on the education of males through the creation of the Dayananda Anglo-Vedic (D.A.-V.) College and its associated schools. The earliest and for some years the only girls school was located in Ferozepore as an adjunct of the Arya Samaj orphange founded in 1877. The drive for expanded education of girls began in December 1890 with the establishment of the Arya Kanya Pathshala of Jullundur. This was an elementary school that taught basic literacy and some general knowledge along with "sewing, stitching, drawing, doing of Havan and singing of Bhajans" (Kanya Mahavidyalaya, *Annual Report, 1891*). Leadership in the field of women's education rested with two Aryas: Lala Dev Raj, for whom this became a personal crusade; and Lala Munshi Ram, a dynamic exponent of radical Aryanism who later became President of the Jullundur Arya Samaj.

Lala Munshi Ram recorded in his diary an event that sparked his entry into the campaign for women's education.

On my return home from Court, Vedakumari [his daughter] came running with this newly learnt message, 'Christ is the Prophet. No price is required to mention his name. Christ is my anchor. He is my

Krishna. . . .' I was startled to hear this and, on enquiry, I learnt that they were taught even to detest our holy Shastras. I realized then that an Aryan Girls School was an absolute necessity (Jambunathan 1961: 101–102).

Munshi Ram moved quickly to gather support and won other Aryas to his cause with the result that they founded the Pathshala. This school in turn evolved into the Kanya Mahavidyalaya, a girls high school, opened in 1896. The attempt to provide more advanced education for women met with stiff resistance from the Hindu community in general and from the Aryas who were involved in the D.A.-V. schools. They claimed that such education was unnecessary and feared competition for the limited resources available within the Hindu community. The Aryas who advocated women's education did so on the grounds that "a country can never rise high without giving high education to its women. No reform can be brought in any field without bringing reforms in your women." The arguments that swirled around this new education discussed what was, in fact, a rather limited form of schooling. "In addition to basic literacy, the girls learned sewing, embroidery, drawing, cooking, some music, poetry, games, arithmetic, hygiene, and the religious literature of the Samaj (Jones 1976: 216–217). The Kanya Mahavidyalaya was at most a parochial finishing school designed to provide wives with a minimum academic education and a set of social and homemaking skills.

Education was not intended to prepare girls for careers outside the home or to an independent existence except in one area, namely, teaching. All efforts to open girls schools collided with an almost total lack of teachers. Since women were uneducated, they could not teach; and given the social taboos of Hindu society, men could not teach young girls. The Kanya Mahavidyalaya became a source for new teachers who began their own schools. Thus a respectable profession for women, perhaps the sole such profession in the Punjab of the nineteenth century, grew out of the movement for women's education. A majority of those studying to be teachers were widows, women who remained longer in school and who were free to accept a career (Kanya Mahavidyalaya *Annual Reports 1895–1897*). Girls often left school at young ages, usually when they were called upon to fulfill the role of wife and mother.

By the end of the nineteenth century, the education of young women was just beginning to affect the literate classes of Punjabi Hindus and had also established a new female role, that of teacher. A teaching career provided a few widows with dignified positions in Hindu society. The Arya Samaj then demonstrated the importance of communal defense against Christian missionaries as an initial driving force behind efforts to educate girls. There was, however, another set of motivational forces that stimulated efforts at social reconstruction. These are most clearly demonstrated through the records of the Amritsar Dharm Sabha.

Under the leadership of Rai Bahadur Bihari Lal, a group of the leading citizens, both Hindus and Sikhs, founded the Amritsar Dharm Sabha and held their first meeting on 30 September 1872. The Sabha was dedicated to "the betterment and cultural uplift of the whole of the Hindu community. . . ." Its purpose was to remove all "evil practices . . . which are opposed to the Shastras and to intelligence, which are in vogue among the Hindus. . . ." Although general in its stated aims, the Sabha concentrated on the customs and behavior of women as major problem areas within Hindu society. Munshi Kanhayalal Alakdhari summed up this situation as one in which

The women becoming free of all proper and necessary restraints, gave up all their duties, and all initiative was lost. Whoever threatened or flattered them, they became his followers, and they fell at the feet of anybody who was stronger, while they became lions for the weak. Nobody was born with good intentions, and bad ways led to worldliness and license. (All Information on the Dharm Sabha has been taken from the annual report, *Tajawiz Kameli Dharm Sabha* prepared by Pandit Bihari Lal and published in Lahore in 1873).

Alakdhari's sentiments were shared by other speakers and reflected in the issues considered by the Sabha and by their actions.

One of the first customs attacked by the Sabha was the use of dowries. Alakdhari condemned it, stating that "marriages of girls are performed in exchange of money, which other people call the sale of girls." He claimed that dowries were against the teachings of the *Dharma Shastras* and also a humiliation for the girls involved. His remarks led to a decision by the Sabha to ban all acceptance of money at the time of marriage and to threaten excommunication of anyone who defied this ban. The Sabha moved on to consider other customs, primarily among women. Extended periods of mourning by women were rejected because they produced a "hellish life" for all the male members of a family. One Brahmin attending this meeting complained that he was 41 years of age and "this mourning was not lifted for a single day and he had not known one day of happiness and had passed all his life in sorrow. . . ." The Sabha quickly moved to limit mourning to 17 days; after which women were expected to attend to "all worldly affairs without restraint of any kind." From its concern with marriage and death rites the Sabha moved on to examine questions of social morality.

As did many moral crusades, the Dharm Sabha condemned prostitution, an institution already under attack from the Amritsar Municipal Government. Houses of ill fame had been closed and, in discussing this achievement, the Dharm Sabha demonstrated the reasons for its opposition to prostitution. With a sense of relief, they declared "that during the last four months or so, no respectable woman became a public woman, although formerly about four or five women from respectable families used to become prostitutes in the past every month." Not morality as such, but concern over the status and honor of middle and upper class families lay behind this campaign against prostitution. A similar motivation led to attempts to end various forms of public nakedness such as the occasions when women bathed at ponds, wells, and along the river banks, and in the process exposed parts of their bodies much as they did in various rituals of public mourning. Also condemned were certain customary festivals at which women sang bawdy and obscene songs. These activities were deeply resented and perhaps feared by male members of "respectable" families. To control such social behavior, the Dharm Sabha passed a series of resolutions that declared:

Firstly, no woman belonging to the Hindu community would bathe naked at any ponds, wells, rivers or canals, but she would take her bath in her own home behind a curtain, and if no such bathroom with curtain be available, then she would take her bath with a chadar or dhoti on her body; secondly, no love songs or obscene words would be uttered by any women at the time of marriages, etc., in market places or streets and lanes, openly or from behind a curtain; thirdly, no women would carry out mourning in market places and tourist resorts etc., with naked heads or breasts; fourthly, the mourning period of three years, practiced at present would now be reduced to seventeen days only, and after that one day every six months and one day on the death anniversary of a dead person would be permitted for the performance of religious rites connected with the dead . . . , fifthly, women would not put on shameless dresses, and their dress in the future shall be: first, a ghagra with a wide girth; second, a pyjama under it; third, a kurta; fourth, a dopatta; fifth, a chadar made of long-cloth.

In this way the daily life and customs of women were reordered by a male group according to its ideas of morality, its concern for maintaining family honor, and its own needs.

Attempts to control the female members of society led to criticism of the institution of the guru, the initiation of women by a holy man, a rite conducted when one finds a religious preceptor, is given a mantra or sacred verse, and accepts his authority over their life. Clearly the person of a guru provided a rival and threat to the authority of a husband over his wife: ". . . for a married woman, who has her husband living, her husband is like her guru, according to the Shastras. When any man gets for his wife a guru mantra from some other person, such a woman becomes a most debauched person." The acceptance of a mantra and the authority of a guru threatened not only to degrade a woman, but to harm her husband. "Any woman who takes a Mantra by herself in the lifetime of her husband reduces the life span of her husband, and ultimately goes to hell." This institution struck partly at family honor but more directly at the power and privileges of the Hindu husband.

More directly related to respectability were three women's festivals, *Kanagats, Moh Mahi,* and *Sada Talla,* which degraded male society and were, as a result, condemned by the Dharm Sabha. The orthodox leader, Pandit Shraddha Ram Phillouri, described this custom with disgust and some degree of apprehension: " . . . during the period of *Kanagats,* the women of one Mohalla, or locality, after putting on their best clothes and jewelry, according to their position and status, collect together as a group and take their stand at any road crossing or other place of importance and start hurling insults and abuses on the women of another Mohalla or area near by and start quarrelling." The women did not abuse each other, but taunted each other's husbands, parents, or relatives. According to the Pandit this form of public abuse expanded and "now, the situation has become such that nobody of any consequence in the city, i.e. nobody of position and status and respect in the city or town, is spared, even though women of these families might be present there...." This form of public ridicule dishonored "the wives and daughters of such a family, and if by chance any woman of one mohalla or locality happens to pass another mohalla... within fifteen days of *Kanagats*, her clothes are torn and she is badly belabored...." *Kanagats* often degenerated into "hand fights and even wrestling," much to the amusement of the hundreds of men who collected to watch.

Kanagats exemplified the "bad and evil" customs that plagued Hindu society. It was also a ritual occasion on which women could vent their accumulated frustrations and strike back at the male members of their world; so too was *Moh Mahi*.

The festival of *Moh Mahi* was celebrated during mid-winter. On this day little girls and even grown-up adults and young women, both rich and poor, put on costly dresses and ornaments, as they move about the various localities and market places in group. As soon as they come across any miserly person or stranger, they tease and harass him to such an extent that they even tear off his clothes. Until and unless he pays pice or two, he cannot secure his release, and this uncultured way of begging is called *Moh Mahi* by name.

The Dharm Sabha also rejected the festival of *Sada Talla*, a fertility rite performed by the Hindu women of Amritsar.

Hundreds of women, both from rich families as well as from poor families, put on their best dresses and jewelry and go to the Tek Chand Garden and the Guru Bagh, and gather together, while there are in front of them thousands of men of all classes, collected together to see this entertainment or drama, and these women bare their bodies up to their breasts and then start rolling on the ground with great zest and enthusiasm, shouting with their mouths in loud voices: 'I have laid down on a wheat field, may my womb become fertile.' During this action of theirs almost the whole of their bodies become naked. The women believe that by this action of theirs, they become pregnant immediately thereafter.

As with the other women's festivals, this was proclaimed as "shameless" and "evil" and the Sabha declared it would bring it to a swift end, as they asserted control over their female relatives.

The Sabha passed resolutions, organized committees to supervise their neighbors, threatened social boycotts to enforce its decisions, and took steps to draw up new "proper" rituals and rites to replace those considered decadent. In addition to the standard ideological explanations of irrationality, uselessness, or actions that are contrary to religious texts, the Sabha expressed its concern for respectability, especially in relation to the English ruling class: ". . . you can get honor only when you have modesty first. Our rulers, who are Englishmen, also feel happy on seeing good characters and respectable persons. What I mean to say is that this great shamelessness and immodesty has spread among the women folk of this city, on seeing which other people ridicule us. Let us adopt measures, by means of which this blot giving us a bad name might disappear." The motivation that undergirded the Amritsar Dharm Sabha centered on the desire of a male-dominated society to protect its sense of worth in general and the honor of each family in particular, and to do that through a restructuring of women's customary behavior. In order to accomplish this, male authority was extended in areas previously beyond its jurisdiction, as men sought to extinguish festivals conducted by and for women.

Attempts to curtail "bad customs" were not limited to the Punjab, but had been articulated by numerous religious leaders from Ram Mohun Roy in Bengal to Swami Narayana Guru in Kerala. As with other Hindu "reformers," a number of the "bad customs" that Swami Narayana condemned were part of female culture. He called for his followers to cease celebrating *Thalikettu*, an expensive festival held at the time of a girl's marriage; *Thirandukuli*, a bathing ritual conducted on the occasion of a daughter's first menses; and, *Pulikudy*, a ritual celebrated when a woman became pregnant for the first time, all festivals held by women for women (Samuel 1973: 91 and Rao 1979: 38–39).

A century of progress and social change witnessed the end of sati and female infanticide, since these customs were defined as criminal acts and outlawed by the British Indian Government. The only other legal step taken was raising the age of cohabitation from ten years to twelve years of age. All other changes derived from social pressure by individuals and socio-religious movements or by a general change of attitudes on the part of Hindu society. The age of marriage gradually rose throughout this century as least among the educated classes. Accompanying this was a demand for education for both men and women, but for different purposes. Boys were educated as preparation for a career and girls were educated to increase their value within the system of arranged marriages. For members of the literate Hindu classes an

educated girl was considered prepared for marriage and motherhood (Borthwick 1984: 55–56, 64–65, 74, 83, 114–115, 149 and
334). Widow remarriage made some limited gains, but only for a
virgin widow. On the question of elaborate marriage rites and
expensive dowries, there seems to have been very little progress,
although many movements struggled against the use of dowries.
Little evidence exists on the fate of women's rituals and festivals,
but it is likely that their popularity was restricted among women
of the educated classes. The nineteenth century then was a period
of conflicting trends and limited results, a period that cannot be
understood by simple, one-dimensional explanations.

The evidence presented here points to a variety of aims among
those who advocated modifications in the social behavior of
women and in the institutions that gave form to that behavior.
This search for motivation, however, must be conducted within
half of society, the male half. The debates over the proper role of
women were between men, and only rarely did a woman participate. In northern India the literature of discussion was written in
languages unknown to most women so that even in theory tracts
were written by men, for men. This was especially so prior to the
last two decades of the nineteenth century. Organizations were
created by men with a male membership and consequently the
programs they created served male interests and responded to
male sensitivities.

Most movements of social change had within them a strong
desire for approval from the English community. Meredith
Borthwick has noted that the educated elite of Bengal was
extremely sensitive to English criticism of the status of Bengali
women and had absorbed the idea that the position of women
was a gauge of a civilized society. They also had uncritically
accepted an idealized vision of the English woman (*ibidem*: 29–30
and 35–37). The Amritsar Dharm Sabha openly stated its desire
for general social respectability and specifically for English
approval. This concern for status in the eyes of the Hindu and
English communities ran through many of the reform movements.

The attempts by male organizations to remove "bad customs"
and replace them with "proper" social behavior must be
examined with more than one dimension in mind. First, many of
the "evil" practices that were attacked were general in nature and

were not associated with either sex. Lying, cheating, stealing, adultery, and the use of intoxicants had been rejected by socio-religious movements for many centuries. Other "bad customs," however, were rituals and festivals that were part of women's society. The Amritsar Dharm Sabha and similar "reformist" organizations spent much of their efforts to end such ceremonies. Women's society was, within its limits, more openly erotic and contained behavior that both embarrassed men and also attacked their sense of superiority.

The removal of "bad customs" then meant that men were extending their control over women by entering areas of social life that previously had been beyond their authority. This expansion of male control over women ran in two directions. First, it meant diminishing and, perhaps, removing completely all traditional practices that were disapproved of by men, and that caused inconvenience to them or that threatened the status and authority of the Hindu husband. Secondly, male control was extended by "reformers" who defined the new areas of women's activity and their place in the changing world. Where she could go outside of the house, what she was allowed to do, her role as a "modern" mother and wife, the type of education she was given, and even the nature of her clothing were all debated and specified by men. Women remained subservient to their husbands and to males in general.

Women's education illustrates the variety of motivation that lay behind such questions. Lala Munshi Ram and his fellow Arya Samajis reacted to fear of Christian missionary influence and of conversion. For them education had to be Hinduized as a means of communal defense. Similar dynamics existed among those Muslims who advocated the education of girls (Minault 1982: 85–87). For members of the English educated elite, and especially for those who worked directly under the British, a wife who could socialize and who possessed a degree of education was a distinct advantage. They needed women who could travel with them, as they were posted from town to town. Such a wife was an asset to an official's career. Initially women's education was structured to serve the interests of men and their social needs as they perceived them. In time, however, education created a class of women who could and did begin to articulate their own priorities and programs for social change. Such developments did not take place until well into the twentieth century.

The social changes in the role of women within Hindu society were legitimized by appeals to reason or logic and to various forms of religious authority. The former, however, could not be the only basis for advocating new social or religious practice. The authority of a reinterpreted religious text, the teachings of a new religious leader, or a combination of the two were needed to gain the acceptance of new ideas. Ram Mohun Roy spoke of reason and used rationality to judge numerous Hindu customs, but then he turned to a reinterpretation of scriptural texts for the final authority needed to legitimize his arguments. This appeal to religion was framed in terms of a return to proper practice and to the "fundamentals" of Hinduism. Within Hinduism and other religions of South Asia movements of return constituted "the fundamentalism" of the nineteenth century. At this time, there was no other type of ideology that could provide legitimization for social and cultural change. By the end of the century and into the next, new secular ideologies began to appear with the emergence of nationalism, then socialism and, after World War I, the arrival of Marxism. For the nineteenth century and the centuries preceding it, religion constituted the source of legitimization for social and cultural movements.

The degree to which this was a period of "progress," of "liberalism" and positive change for Hindu women remains an open question, one that depends as much on the attitudes and suppositions of those who provide answers as on the data now available. Two things stand out, however. First, our knowledge of social change in this century is still fragmentary and somewhat superficial, largely through the limited use of non-English language sources and the tendency to accept the statements of various movements at face value. Secondly, if Hindu men actually extended their power over Hindu women during the nineteenth century, then what does this tell us of the relationship between technological and cultural change, on the one hand, and on the other, the goals of political and social development? Perhaps "progress" should be understood as change that is advantageous to a particular group rather than some all encompassing step toward an undefined and undefinable "modernization." A similar rethinking may be needed for such favorite terms as "liberalism" and "rationalism." There is no immediate answer to this question, but it is evident that we must re-examine, if not simply reject, many of the suppositions that lie beneath the standard historical interpretations applied by numerous scholars. With this we may also have to rethink the developmental theories that have become popular in the last two decades. Such theories generally imply that technological and associated cultural changes, so often called "modernization," somehow have a positive effect on all members of a society and thus are an unquestionable "good."

4

The Dilemma of Sikh Revivalism: Identity versus Political Power

PAUL WALLACE

Religious revivalism is not simply a response of anachronistic social and political forces seeking to maintain an inevitably decaying position in an increasingly modern context. Tradition, including religious and caste elements, is not necessarily antithetical to modernization, as has been amply demonstrated (Rudolph and Rudolph 1967; Kothari 1970). This chapter examines the thesis that the Sikh community in the state of Punjab, India, is confronted with a dilemma that pits religious revivalism against the achievement of political power. More specifically, the long-term process of distinguishing between Sikh and other types of identification has taken a direction since 1979 which reduces Sikhs to the status of a threatened minority.

Fundamentally, this political problem involves intra-Sikh and intercommunal patterns of authority. Four major political parties in Punjab—the Akali Dal, Congress, and two communist parties—contest for Sikh support. The other significant party, the Bharatiya Janata Party (BJP, erstwhile Jana Sangh) relies on a Hindu support base. The BJP has also been allied with the major Sikh political party, the Akali Dal, during important periods since 1966 when the northwest region was reorganized into three successor states (Punjab, Haryana, and Himachal Pradesh) plus the Union Territory of Chandigarh. At other times, the two parties are major antagonists. Overlaying and interpenetrating the play of religion and politics at the state level is the Union

Government and, in particular, Indira Gandhi's Congress Party, now led by her son, Rajiv Gandhi.

Two contrasting patterns of political behavior emerge for the Sikhs from the complex context provided by Punjab. One pattern emphasizes accommodation of intra-Sikh differences and careful attention to nurturing alliances with non-Sikhs. A second pattern centers on a narrow definition of Sikhism and a felt need to defend the community against perceived threats, both internal and external, to the *Panth* (religion). This second pattern began to reassert itself in 1978, became a systematic campaign in 1981, suffered the consequences of severe repression in 1984, and regained momentum in 1985.

OPERATION BLUESTAR

Operation Bluestar, launched on 1 June 1984, was a watershed event for the Sikh community. Approximately 70,000 troops from the Indian army and paramilitary forces sealed off the state of Punjab and the city of Amritsar. Fighting began around the Golden Temple on 4 June and ended with a final assault on 6 June. Approximately 1,000 people were killed including almost 100 soldiers and about 400 pilgrims (*India Today*, 30 June 1984: 8–21ff); Weaver 1984: 7; *New York Times*, 9 June and 29 July 1984; GOI 1984). One report states that 55 women and 15 children were among the people killed (*India Today*, 15 August 1984: 33). Simultaneously, Indian military units moved against other Sikh temples throughout Punjab to root out the widespread Sikh terrorist movement.

Within the Golden Temple complex, more precisely within the Akal Takht, the three major leaders of the terrorist movement were killed. Jarnail Singh Bhindranwale, often described as the Ayatollah Khomeini of Punjab, provided the charismatic leadership for a movement which rapidly seemed to be assuming dominance in the Sikh community. Amrik Singh was the second most important figure due to his leadership of the All India Sikh Students Federation and his close relationship to Bhindranwale (Joshi 1984: 5–7). Former Major-General Shahbeg Singh provided technical knowledge of military training and fortifications. He was a hero of the Bangladesh liberation war having trained the Bengali guerrilla force, the *Mukti Bahini*, but was subsequently sacked for corruption just before his expected retirement.

These three individuals had directed the growing terrorist movement in Punjab during the preceding three years. A convenient inaugural date for the movement is September 1981 when Lala Jagat Narain, a Hindu newspaper baron in Jalandhar, became the first prominent victim. His son, Mahesh Chandra, assumed control of the *Hind Samachar* group of newpapers and was, in turn, assassinated in May 1984 during the height of the killings shortly before the assault on the Golden Temple. In all, over 300 people were assassinated by terrorists as the situation became increasingly worse. From the government's perspective, attempts at negotiation were not productive and terrorism increased until extreme measures were essential. Most Sikhs believe that the Congress government did not bargain in good faith, undermined possible agreements, and assisted in the rise of Bhindranwale in order to exacerbate differences within the Akali Dal and further divide the Sikh community.

Even moderate Sikhs charged that communalism was pitting Hindus against Sikhs. The noted writer, Khushwant Singh, in an interview with a New Delhi journal, declared:

I said for once that I was not living in a secular India but in a Hindu India. Because, for once I discovered from the reactions, that the entire reaction— the adverse reaction—was almost entirely Hindu, that the favorable reaction was almost entirely Sikh. . . . And this is what I feared that this kind of army action would result in—a total polarisation of views between the Sikh and the Hindu and that has taken place (*Choice*, September 1984:8).

A similar reaction was registered by Kuldip Nayar, a respected Punjab Hindu journalist, who wrote dramatically that "Punjab's tragedy is that there are no Punjabis any more in Punjab—only Sikhs and Hindus." Even Punjabis outside the state, he maintains, are in the process of "getting divided according to their religion." Despite these pessimistic conclusions, he nonetheless expresses some "hope" that "this endangered species," the overarching concept of Punjabi, can be saved (Nayar and Singh 1984:7).

Jarnail Singh Bhindranwale, along with the others who died in June, will enter the Sikh memory pool of martyrs which extends back to the periods of Mughal persecution. It encompasses those who fell in the massacre at Jallianwalla Bagh in 1919, the dead of the revolutionary Ghadr Party, the legendary Bhagat Singh, and the heroes of many *morchas* for Sikh causes. These individuals and movements represent a spectrum from disciplined non-violence to terrorists engaging in assassination. Their common feature is identification as Sikhs, particularly by the Sikh community.

SIKH BACKGROUND: RELIGION, MILITANCY AND POLITICAL INSTITUTIONALIZATION

Sikh militancy as expressed in the extremism of the Bhindranwale terrorist movement has its roots in the lengthy history of developing Sikh identity. Guru Nanak founded the Sikh religion in the fifteenth century essentially on a pietistic, pacifistic, non-violent basis. In 1699, at Anandpur Sahib, Guru Gobind Singh culminated the process of transforming Sikhs into a militant and physically distinct community. Sikhs were enjoined by the tenth, and last, Guru to observe the five Ks (*kes*, unshorn hair; *kangha*, comb; *kach*, shorts; *kara*, steel bracelet; and *kirpan*, sword). Thus, amidst repression from the Mughal rulers, they were not to slide into Hinduism or Islam, nor to be inconspicuous by blending in with fellow villagers from the other faiths.

Militancy earlier had been institutionalized in a symbolic and physical manner by the sixth guru, Guru Hargobind (1606–1645). He constructed the *Akal Takht* (seat of immortal power, throne of the immortal) and wore two swords which represented spiritual and temporal authority (*piri* and *miri*) (Dilgeer 1984:18–21). For two years prior to the June assault by the Indian military on the Golden Temple, the *Akal Takht* served as headquarters for Bhindranwale and as his major fortification. Religion and politics were intertwined.

Sikh identity in the 1980s stresses the period of political independence under Ranjit Singh as a political golden age. The "Sikh Kingdom" in fact encompassed the social diversity of Punjab, including Hindus and Muslims, as well as adventurers and military specialists from other countries. British conquest in the 1840s resulted in the Sikhs becoming a major, and probably the single most important, component of the British Indian army.

Hinduism posed a more subtle and pervasive danger to Sikhism than the clash of arms. The two communities maintained linkages which reinforced a common sense of identity but also threatened the reabsorption of Sikhs into Hinduism. Prakash Tandon, in *Punjabi Century*, describes the similarity of castes and customs and notes the frequency of intermarriage (Tandon 1962:10–11). Hindu influence could be seen most dangerously in the control of Sikh *gurdwaras* (temples) by *Sahajdhari* Sikhs and particularly the Udasi sect. These *mahants* or priests were not *keshdhari* Sikhs as formulated by Guru Gobind Singh in 1699, but frequently cut their hair, followed Hindu practices, and were seen as corrupt and outside the mainstream of the Sikh community. Social practices and control of religious institutions by Sikhs perceived to be Hindus or close to Hinduism, coupled with a *de facto* alliance with Hindus against first the Mughals and then the majority Muslim population during the British period, posed a serious problem. The most extreme view regarding Sikh absorption by Hinduism is set forth by Khushwant Singh (1953:185):

If the present pace of amalgamation continues, there is little doubt that before the century has run its course Sikh religion will have become a branch of Hinduism and the Sikhs a part of the Hindu social system.

Considering the time of his research and writing, he overstated assimilationist tendencies. What is especially significant is that the fear of assimilation continues, even from the pen of someone seemingly as secularized as Khushwant Singh. An early response to these concerns surfaced in an organized form in the 1870s with the establishment of the Singh Sabhas. These elite and middle strata Sikh groups, centered in Lahore and Amritsar, were part of the broader Indian renaissance or revivalism (Kopf 1969). Examples include the Brahmo Samaj, Arya Samaj (Jones 1976), Prarthana Samaj, and Anjuman-i-Islamias. All stressed re-examination of their respective religious communities.

Specifically, the foremost goal of the Singh Sabhas was to restore Sikhism to its pristine purity. A contemporary British account summarized the Sikh demands as follows: "The gist of their demand (to the Viceroy) is that they be no longer confounded with the Hindus but treated in all respects as a separate community" (*History of the Khalsa College Amritsar* 1949:2). Teja Singh, an eminent Sikh scholar, sums up the Singh Sabhas' contribution by citing their emphasis on education and:

the inculcation of the belief that the Sikhs were a separate community, which should have separate rights, separate institutions, and separate provisions in the law to protect them (Teja Singh 1944:140ff; Narang 1980:157ff and 1981:67–81).

A communal tract of the period captures the essence of Sikh revivalism at this point in its title, *Hum Hindu Nahin* which translates as "We are not Hindus" (Jones 1973).

A leap from elitist and middle class mobilization occurred with the largely rural based movement for reform of Sikh temples. Beginning about 1895 and involving the Singh Sabhas, the efforts at temple reform became a mass movement under the direction of the Akalis by 1921 (Teja Singh 1922:87). Despite firings by the police, this essentially non-violent movement resulted in a compromise in 1925 favorable to the reformers. The movement achieved its primary goal of obtaining control of the temples. It also mobilized Sikhs in large numbers since government figures during the five-year period report 30,000 Sikhs arrested, 400 killed, 2,000 wounded, and Rs. 1,500,000 assessed in fines (Mitra 1925:90).

Control of the temples by what are categorized here as mainstream Sikhs established an institutionalized identity for Sikhs encompassing the religious and political spheres. Inauguration of the *Shiromani Gurdwara Prabandhak Committee* (SGPC) on 12 December 1920 (Mohinder Singh 1978:92) provided a precise center for Sikh politics, legitimacy for contending Sikh groups, and a virtually unassailable base for the Sikh group or groups which control the SGPC system. The SGPC is more than a committee of Sikhs elected every five years by adult Sikhs in Punjab. It is a political system mediating a wide range of Sikh affairs including the revenues of Punjab's gurdwaras which totalled about US $8 million in 1980 (*The Tribune*, 20 November 1980). This compares with a total budget of about $1.3 million in 1964 [interview with Arjan Singh Budhiraja, Akali Dal Secretary (Sant Group), SGPC headquarters, Amritsar, 24 April 1964], $2.6 million in 1970 (*The Tribune*, 27 November 1970), and $4 million in 1977 (*The Hindu*, 11 July 1977).

The SGPC comprises a communications network through its varied publications and, more importantly, through the temples. In brief, the SGPC is the physical manifestation of Sikh identity in control. This hub of Sikhism is the scene of bitter contests between contending Sikh groups as symbolized by the Teja Singh Samundri Assembly Hall in the SGPC headquarters directly across from the Golden Temple complex. Opposing rows of benches based on the British House of Commons model accommodate the ruling and opposing parties.

In fact, the Akali Dal has controlled the SGPC as the ruling party since its inception. Sikh conflict for control of the SGPC accordingly, with one major exception in 1984, revolves around the struggle for control of the Akali Dal. Religious leaders of the Golden Temple and the major *gurdwaras* of Punjab, often termed the "five high priests of the Sikhs" (*India Today*, 31 October 1984:7), constitute a seldom used basis of authority who normally limit themselves to confirming the majority group or engaging in conciliation. Bereft of other leadership, the high priests emerged as an independent authority only in the period following Operation Bluestar, and particularly in September and October 1984.

THE COMMUNAL CONTEXT

Sikh revivalism encompassing both a clearer and institutionalized sense of identity has taken place over a period of time during which its political and geographical parameters have markedly changed. Each time the communal calculus has also been altered. Leaving aside the Mughal and Ranjit Singh eras, the British period up to 1947 is probably the most germane. Beginning in the late nineteenth century, intensified ethnic and religious identification and religious revivalism occurred not only among the Sikhs, but also among all major groups in Punjab. Religious and political conflict between Mughul rulers and their Hindu and Sikh subjects form the context of deepening communal orientations with the Sikhs emerging as the major antagonists of the Muslim rulers. Thus arose the phrase that has become a cliché: Sikhs are the "sword arm of the Hindus." Britain introduced a fourth religious presence, Christianity, notable for its missionary zeal, modern organizational methods, and governmental support. A process ensued which in a fission-like manner mobilized each of the major communities in response to internal and external stimuli.

Jones (1979:6) argues convincingly that an essential catalyst for the process in Punjab and elsewhere in India could be found in "the alienation and marginality of the English educated classes." English education and new educational institutions combined with professional opportunities under the British Raj to produce the new classes, many of which, in fact, were not new in the sense that the same castes had traditionally provided the human infrastructure for whoever ruled. Marginality, alienation, and perhaps also a dash of self-confidence and superiority about their role in what can be construed as the dynamic part of society resulted in communal self-examination, revivalism, and renaissance (Kopf 1969; Jones 1979).

In Punjab under the British, all four major communities engaged in a competitive process in which each could be seen and saw themselves as disadvantaged. Hindus, a majority India-wide, were a minority in Punjab with 35 percent of the population and felt themselves threatened by proselytizing Christianity. Muslims, a bare majority in the province, were and felt disadvantaged by their educational backwardness as compared to Hindus and Sikhs (GOI 1923:292). Numerically, Sikhs were number three in Punjab (12 percent) and pressed for communal recruitment targets from the government which would reflect what they perceived as their contribution to the province rather than their numbers. Sikhs were able to increase their recruitment percentage from 17 percent in 1932 to 20 percent in 1941 as against 50 percent for the Muslims and 30 percent for the Hindus (GOP 1945:v).

More significantly, with the advent of the Pakistan movement, a communal axis combining Sikhs with Hindus against Muslims reconfirmed the communal configuration of the earlier Mughal period. Despite some exploration and posturing by Akali leader Master Tara Singh in the immediate pre-independence period, Sikhs never genuinely considered an independent Sikh state. Partition fully activated the communal calculus in 1947 with virtually all Sikhs leaving or being driven out of Pakistan and all but a statistically insignificant number of Muslims abandoning the Indian half of Punjab.

From independence in 1947 to the creation of Punjab's present boundaries in 1966, Sikhs remained a 33 percent minority in Punjab. The communal divisions, moreover, had been reduced from four to two with the forced departure of most of the Muslims and the loss of special consideration for the small Christian community. Sikhs dominated the rural areas while Hindus, with a 64 percent state-wide total, had marked majorities in all urban areas, including Amritsar. This demographic feature heightened the differences between the two major communities but also provided an opportunity for cooperation. Different social bases resulted in the Akali Dal and the Jana Sangh, the two communal parties, identifying each other as its major antagonist. As a consequence, the Congress party drew support from both communities and played off their mutual antagonisms so as to dominate state government during virtually the entire period. Alliances between the Congress and Akali parties, from 1948 to 1951 and, again from 1956 to 1960 placed the Akali Dal in an unsatisfactory position as the junior partner.

Sikh revivalism during the period took the political form of a *Punjabi Suba* movement (Nayar 1966). First, under long-time leader Master Tara Singh, non-violent *morchas* demanded a Sikh majority state. Sant Fateh Singh took control of the Akali Dal and SGPC from Master Tara Singh in 1960 with a new strategy. His tactic of transforming the demand for a Sikh majority state to one for a Punjabi speaking state somewhat masked the continued real intent of achieving a Sikh majority state. Whether galvanized by Master Tara Singh or Sant Fateh Singh, Sikhs marching under the banner of "the *Panth* in danger" certainly saw a Sikh majority state as a goal.

The tactics emphasized a broader Punjabi language identity and thus enlarged the possibilities of Sikh-Hindu cooperation. After the new boundaries in Punjab were set in place in 1966, Sant Fateh Singh followed through with an inter-communal strategy of allying with the Jana Sangh against the Congress Party. Alliances between the two were successful for a short period in 1967, for the 1969 elections, and for the Janata period from 1977 to 1979. Rural Sikh dominance was combined with Hindu urban support to create an alliance in which the Akali Dal served as the major partner. Communal interests and differences continued, but were moderated through a political bargaining system centered in the two major political parties and the context of state government.

THE PRESENT PROBLEM: IDENTITY VERSUS POLITICAL POWER

Control of the Akali Dal and the SGPC has been central to Sikh politics since at least 1920. The intertwining of religious and secular concerns, present at least since the sixth guru, became institutionalized through the SGPC system and provided the Akali Dal with a virtually unassailable political base among Sikhs. The party could and does use this base to seek political power in the state-wide system embracing both political communities.

A stark political fact confronts the Akali Dal in its efforts to win a majority of the seats in the Vidhan Sabha, the state assembly. It cannot do so on its own. First, it identifies itself as a party for Sikhs in a state which in 1971 had a 60.2 percent Sikh majority (GOP 1984:70), but which the press estimated to have dropped to about 52 percent. When the long delayed 1980 census data on religion became available in July 1985 Sikhs marginally had increased their majority to 60.7 percent (*Indian Express*, 21 July 1985:1). The disparity between the press estimate and the census figure has not been explained.

Second, there have always been groups contesting the dominant group in the Akali Dal. In 1986, the ruling group is headed by Chief Minister Surjit Singh Barnala who succeeded the assassinated leader Sant Harcharan Singh Longowal, in August 1985. Direct competition comes from several Akali factions. In May 1986 a group of Akali legislators went into opposition in reaction to Operation Search in which the State government used the military, as in Operation Bluestar, to break the militants' control of the Golden Temple (*India Today*, 31 May 1986:8–13). Former Chief Minister Prakash Singh Badal presides over this newest of the Akali Dal dissident groups in alliance with former SGPC president Gurcharan Singh Tohra. Veteran Akali leader, Jagdev Singh Talwandi, continues to lead yet another dissident Akali Dal faction. In the more extremist part of the political spectrum, Sant Bhindranwale's father, Joginder Singh, is the titular head of the United Akali Dal. A small Master Tara Singh Akali Dal also continues to exist even though his dominance ceased in 1960 and he died in 1967. In short, the Akali Dal is riven by factionalism. The Longowal-Barnala group is in fact a minority government which rules because the Congress Party legislators do not join the Akali dissidents in voting the "ruling group" out of power.

Third, major Sikh institutions, including the Akali Dal, are dominated by Jat Sikhs who are the landed element in the countryside. Non-Jat Sikhs, such as the approximately 20 percent of the Sikh population who are scheduled castes, tend to be anti-Jat and comprise an important element of the Congress party support base. Finally, both the Congress Party and the two communist parties (CPI and CPM) compete for the Jat base as well.

This is the Sikh dilemma. More appropriately it is the dilemma of the leading party among the Sikhs, the only purely Sikh party, the Akali Dal. The Akali Dal must moderate communal demands and engage in a political bargaining process if it is to secure an alliance which enables it to share political power in the state government. Sant Fateh Singh, a rural Jat, successfully developed this moderate approach and mediated Sikh and inter-communal differences until his death. Prakash Singh Badal, suave and skillful, served as the Akali Chief Minister of Punjab, most recently from 1977 to May 1980.

In Indian politics, endemic bi-factionalism afflicts a ruling party as the organizational wing presses the legislative wing. Chief Minister Prakash Singh Badal fought determinedly to preserve the alliance with the Hindu urban party. In July 1979, however, the Janata Party split at the national level partly over the issue of the role of the Rashtriya Swayamsevak Sangh (RSS) and the Jana Sangh elements within the Janata Party—i.e., charges of Hindu communalism. In Punjab, Akali Dal organizational leader Talwandi responded by successfully leading a fight to end the alliance with what his group characterized as the "Janata dominated by the RSS" (*The Hindu*, 4 September 1979). Results were predictable. In the ensuing parliamentary elections, active Akali intra-party sabotage occurred and the Congress(I) swept 12 of the 13 Punjab Lok Sabha seats (Wallace 1980). Similar circumstances led to the same result in the May 1980 state elections as the Congress Party won 63 seats to 37 for the Akali Dal in the 117 seat Assembly (Mehrottra 1980:130–133).

There is one more complicating factor. It always has been in the interests of the Congress Party to exacerbate the differences within the Akali Dal. Tactics have included contesting through a front group in SGPC elections and using the power of incumbency at the state and national levels (Wallace 1981:13–17; Anand 1975:237–250). It is widely believed in India that the Congress(I) assisted Bhindranwale from about 1978 in order to widen the differences within the Akali Dal (Kagal 1982; Sinha 1984:28–31).

Breakdown of Authority Systems

Revivalism as manifested in the Akali Dal Anandpur Sahib Resolution of 16–17 October 1973 stressed geographical concerns and markedly enhanced state autonomy. These resurfaced in a more communal version from the minority Akali Dal led by Talwandi in April 1981. Longowal's majority Akali Dal responded with a list of 45 demands in September 1981 and a revised list of 15 demands in October 1981 (GOI 1984:5–22, 67–84; 1984:88–97). Internal differences between Akali Dal groups, the lack of a superordinate leader such as Master Tara Singh or Sant Fateh Singh, and the presence of the rising extremist movement led by Sant Bhindranwale led to a breakdown of Sikh institutionalization constructed and nurtured so carefully from 1925.

The Akali Dal, its dissident groups, the SGPC and the high priests could not contain the growing whirlwind of the terrorist movement. At this juncture, from mid-1981, the state government of the Congress Party proved equally ineffective. Factionalism between a weak Chief Minister, Darbara Singh, and an equally ineffective Giani Zail Singh (first Union Home Minister and subsequently President of India) contributed to Congress weakness in Punjab. Changes of officials in the police and administration, President's Rule, and continuing efforts at negotiations all proved fruitless as negotiators lacked both authority and will.

Jarnail Singh Bhindranwale increasingly became the fount of authority for the Sikh community as he unfolded a new, violent reaction to the oft-proclaimed threat of the Sikh *Panth* in danger. Violence against the Nirankaris, a heterodox community of Sikhs who believe in a living guru, brought Bhindranwale to prominence in 1978, and he was implicated in the assassination of the Nirankari guru, Baba Gurbachan Singh on 24 April 1980. Subsequently, Charan Singh, Prime Minister in 1979 and leader of the opposition Lok Dal thereafter, criticized the government in Parliament for not taking any action against Bhindranwale's threats against Hindus even though "some 50 Nirankaris had so far been killed" (*The Times of India*, 25 August 1982:7). Bhindranwale assumed control of the *Akal Takht* and the Golden Temple, the physical center of the Sikh community.

In April and May 1984, Bhindranwale's forces and the Akali Dal engaged in mutual killings. His chief bodyguard and reputedly top hit man, Surinder Singh Sodhi, was killed, allegedly on Akali Dal orders. Bhindranwale retaliated. Sant Longowal then discovered, upon calling a meeting of his dominant Akali Dal and the SGPC, that about a third of the SGPC members and district Akali presidents had defected to Bhindranwale (*India Today*, 15 May 1984:30–31).

Sikh identity as reformulated by Bhindranwale became exclusive and violent. Paradoxically, this change may be caused by changing life styles in the prosperous Sikh community and its increasing secularization. The trimming of beards by mainstream *keshdhari* Sikhs and their enhanced mobility symbolizes the rapidity of change and consequent fear of straying from the *Panth*, the religion. Bhindranwale commanded his followers to buy weapons and motorcycles rather than refrigerators and television sets. "When the Hindus come to get you, are you going to crush their heads with your TV aerials?" he reportedly "screamed" (*Asiaweek*:16). By contrast, resolution No. 7 of the 18th All India Akali Dal Conference in October 1978 complains that the "poor farmers are unable to take to mechanization because of the enormity of the cost involved." The proposed solution is to "abolish the excise duty on tractors so that with the decrease in their price the ordinary farmers may also be able to avail of farm machinery and contribute to the growth of gross agricultural produce of the country" (GOI 1984:77; Sinha 1984:93). Obviously, this is an affluent Jat farmer view of the world.

In fairness to the Akali Dal, its various Anandpur Sahib demands increasingly related to Sikh issues. Bhindranwale represented the fundamentalist or revivalist thrust of religion and the felt need for a clear Sikh identity. Purity, sacrifice, and a panacea were presented to those parts of the Sikh population for whom religion and Sikh ethnic identity are paramount. Sikh youth represent a particularly important element. The All India Sikh Students' Federation constituted a major support group of revivalism for Bhindranwale. It supplanted communist student groups as the dominant element in Punjab institutions of higher education. Many of these students are rural youths competing unsuccessfully with urbanites on the latter's territory (Suri 1981:257–263). Badly educated, they formerly looked forward to marginal jobs in agriculture and in urban areas; but the motorcycles of the hit squads symbolized a new social freedom and exciting life style, and Bhindranwale assumed the mantle of the charismatic leader of the movement.

Other support groups, such as elements among the Nihangs, are marginal to the Sikh community. Ultimately, one must return to the major and dominant element among the Sikh population, the Jats. They provide a sea, a safe refuge, in which the terrorist fish can swim. Because of the importance of religion and ethnic identity among mainstream and successful Sikhs, large numbers have fallen under the revivalist spell, even in the violent form cast by Bhindranwale.

Approximately five months after the June 1984 assault, Sikh

politics began to flow once again into more regular channels. Even with the major Akali Dal leaders in jail, secondary leaders of the Akali Dal, the SGPC, and the high priests appeared to be regaining authority. This was partly in response to the shock of the assault, partly in response to Congress Party threats to the SGPC system and crude attempts to undermine the Akali Dal and SGPC further, and partly to the elimination of Bhindranwale, Amrik Singh, and Major-General Shahbeg Singh. The Union Government withdrew its threat to alter fundamentally the SGPC system. The army left the Golden Temple, thus averting a major reaction. The SGPC was credited for this withdrawal and negotiations were proceeding for release of the jailed Akali leaders.

Nonetheless, basic problems remained including continuing acts of terrorism. Many terrorists escaped from the Golden Temple and many more were neither there at the time of the army assault nor rounded up in the wholesale sweep of the state. Communal relations became embittered during the three years of terrorist action and reaction. They were further enflamed by the army assault on the Golden Temple and by unconfirmed rumors of military atrocities against Sikhs throughout the state.

Prime Minister Indira Gandhi's assassination by two of her Sikh bodyguards occurred in this mixed context on 31 October 1984. Communal violence, directed against Sikhs, resulted in the deaths of at least 2,700 people by 4 November when the military succeeded in restoring order and the violence abated. Half or more of the killings occurred in New Delhi (*The New York Times*, 5 November 1984:6). Charges of police complicity, *goonda* or hoodlum involvement, and the participation of some Congress(I) politicians in the riots became widespread (Mukhoty and Kothari 1984:1–26).

More than 1,900 people in New Delhi alone had been arrested by the police as of early January 1985. In addition, several police officials were suspended while inquiries continued. A special investigative cell headed by Additional Commissioner of Police Ved Marwah had primary responsibility (*Indian Express*, 11 January 1985:7). Nonetheless, considering the allegations of police involvement in the riots, Sikhs as well as civil liberties organizations strongly expressed the need for a high level special investigative body which would be completely independent of the police.

Further estrangement of Sikhs and Hindus stemmed from the riots that erupted as thousands of Sikhs left their homes for refugee camps in their own areas or in other states. Some approximation of the magnitude of the flight in the Delhi area can be gained from the government estimates of early January 1985. Approximately 4,000 "riot victims" had returned to their homes from "relief camps" in Punjab, Rajasthan, and Delhi. Another 2,000 remained in camps in Delhi and "would have to remain there for some time, till housing arrangements were made for them (*ibidem*).

Another report on Punjab estimated that 50,000 refugees had sought shelter in Patiala, Ludhiana, Jullundur, Amritsar, and other towns in Punjab (*The Times of India*, 23 December 1984:2). A projected relief fund of Rs. 10 million established by the SGPC had collected Rs. 21 million by early January. Donations in kind were forthcoming in such abundance that relief camps were described as "bursting with provisions and clothing." Government and Red Cross relief also contributed substantially (*Tribune*, 11 January 1985:1).

At this point it is problematical whether Humpty Dumpty can be put back together again. Sikhs and Hindus in the 1970s seemed to have achieved in Punjab the combination of strong communal identity *and* a workable sharing of political power. Cooperation has now been replaced to a marked extent by the negative aspects of what are perceived as threatened communal identities. In brief, communal self-confidence—at least temporarily—gave way to communalism.

Prime Minister Rajiv Gandhi, even before his landslide success in the December 1984 general elections, began cautiously to apply a healing touch to the Punjab situation. At the same time, his Congress(I) wave resulted at least partly from what was labelled the "Hindu factor" or the "Hindu reaction" to the Punjab problem and fear of secession (Sheth 1984:1,6). A series of dramatic events during the following two years, 1985 and 1986, continued this dualism in regard to communal tensions. Conciliation and accommodation on the one hand, and Sikh-Hindu tensions on the other continue to mark Punjab as a problem state.

Conciliation and mutual accommodation dominated in 1985. Prime Minister Rajiv Gandhi released major Akali Dal leaders from internment on March 11, announced an economic package for the state, and took a number of other measures designed to return Punjab to normalcy. A giant step toward conciliation resulted from the Rajiv-Longowal Accord signed on 24 July 1985 between the Prime Minister and the moderate leader of the Akali Dal. Sant Longowal's assassination the following month backfired against the terrorists and extremists who opposed the accord as well as the holding of elections to the state assembly. In September 1985, a sympathy wave for Longowal's Akali Dal propelled it into power with, for the first time, an absolute majority. An unusually high voter turnout of 67.58 percent further legitimized the moderate approach to Sikh and Punjab politics (Wallace 1986:372–375).

Moderate Akali Dal dominance led by Longowal's successor, Surjit Singh Barnala, and his chief lieutenant, Balwant Singh, proved to be relatively short lived. Difficulties in implementing the Rajiv-Longowal Accord coupled with renewed terrorism and revivalism returned Punjab to the forefront of India's problem list in 1986. Neither the Mathew Commission in January nor the Venkataramiah Commission in July were able to effect the transfer of Chandigarh to Punjab. Militant Sikh opposition to the Sutlej-Jamuna link canal receives less public attention, but is an equally explosive issue. Failure to implement the accord encouraged the extremists led by the revivalist Damdami Taksal and the militant All India Sikh Students' Federation to retake control of the Golden Temple complex on January 26. As the *Times of India* editorialized: "The inevitable failure of the Union government to implement the basically flawed Punjab accord has been overtaken by a renewed struggle for leadership of the Sikh community" (28 January 1986: 8).

Rooting out the extremists from the Golden Temple on 1 May 1986 in Operation Search resulted almost immediately in a split within the moderate ranks. Approximately 27 Akali Dal members of the Legislative Assembly formed a breakaway Akali Dal with former Chief Minister Prakash Singh Badal as the President and Amrinder Singh as the leader of the assembly party. Gurcharan Singh Tohra, former SGPC President, is the third major leader of the dissident group. Chief Minister Barnala subsequently had to rely on Congress(I) support because although his ruling Akali Dal remains the largest single party with about 46 seats, it no longer has a majority (*Times of India*, 3–5 May 1986). Badal's dissident Akali Dal joins the militants and extremists outside the assembly in charging that the center's treatment of the Punjab accord is a "betrayal" of the Punjabis (*Indian Express*, 25 July 1986: 7).

Hindu reaction to Sikh terrorism has resulted in the formation of militant Hindu groups such as the Shiv Sena in Punjab urban areas, and the migration of Hindus in the most affected areas to other parts of Punjab and to Haryana and Delhi. Hindu migration in 1986 appeared to be at a relatively low level, but does raise the spectre of partition as in 1947. One prognosis sees "the ghost of communal divide" providing "a blueprint for a civil war" between Hindus and Sikhs (*The Statesman*, 23 July 1986: 3). Another commentator describes the exodus of Hindus from Sikh majority areas as "only a trickle" but as "ominous" and suggesting "nightmarish visions of Ulster or Lebanon" (*Times of India*, 10 June 1986: 1).

Hindu reaction, moreover, is not confined to Punjab. Events in Punjab have combined with the Shah Bano divorce issue which stemmed from a case in Andhra Pradesh, Pope John Paul's visit to India, Islamic conversions of Hindus in the South, and the Ayodhya temple affair in Uttar Pradesh to stimulate what *India Today* in a major article headlines as "Hindus Militant Revivalism"(31 May 1986: 30–39).

India's political institutions, accordingly, once again face the task of moderating and channeling the powerful forces of revivalism while simultaneously attempting to suppress terrorism. Repression by the central government in the form of Operation Bluestar and martial law has been replaced by a mixed policy. Para-military forces, particularly the Central Reserve Police and the Border Security Forces, have been enhanced and reorganized in a more systematic manner under the command of the new Director-General of Police, J. F. Ribeiro, who maintains his own public hit list of terrorists. The veteran police officer from Maharashtra has been deputed by the central government in the past to troubled situations in Gujarat and Delhi. His reputation as "a one-man army" (*Statesman*, 22 July 1986: 1) faces its greatest challenge in Punjab.

Other institutions are even more important since force alone, no matter how effectively and judiciously applied, is not the answer. At the national level, Prime Minister Rajiv Gandhi's ability to maintain cooperative relations with the ruling Akali Dal and forego the temptation of President's Rule is a continuing test of the federal relationship. It also provides much needed time for implementation of the complicated provisions of the Punjab accord—if that is possible. (Editor's Note: President's Rule subsequently was instituted in May 1987.

Equally important, time is essential for rebuilding key Sikh institutions. The Akali Dal's role as the guardian of Sikh identity splintered before the onslaught of revivalist forces led by Jarnail Singh Bhindranwale. Central government actions before, during, and after Operation Bluestar complicated the isue. Tendencies became powerful movements which in 1986, with Bhindranwale dead, remain as a hydra–headed movement of many groups without a center. Sikh identity in this context does not flow through formerly authoritative institutions, premier of which is the SGPC with political control by the Akali Dal. Rebuilding the Akali Dal is a formidable task encompassing both religious and secular dimensions. Winning statewide elections to the assembly in September 1985 did not prove to be sufficient. Virulent Sikh revivalism challenges the ruling Akali Dal on the basis that the Sikh community is a threatened minority. Demand for an independent Khalistan is more of a symbol in this context than a deep-seated objective. Sikh apprehensions revolving around their own identity have to be assuaged.

At the same time, Akali Dal sensitivity to the larger Punjab context is essential. In particular, this translates into cooperative Sikh–Hindu relations. Balwant Singh Ramoowalia, Akali Dal parliamentary party leader, directly confronted the dilemma between religious and secular imperatives at a Gurdwara function in New Delhi on 19 July 1986. He called upon Sikhs to "scrupulously follow the teachings of the Guru Granth Sahib." His interpretation of the Sikh religion, however, is critical of "religious fundamentalism" which results in "communal tension and clashes." The Akali Dal, he maintains, is "a secular party" which could come to power only on the basis of Hindu-Sikh unity (*Times of India*, 20 July 1986:5).

In 1986, Sikh and Hindu revivalism flared dangerously in Punjab as elements in both communities acted and reacted from perceived positions as threatened minorites. Sikh and Hindu identities as a consequence are more salient than Punjabi identities; and continued terrorism—by both communities—has added a new dimension to Punjab. Restoring amicable relations is a formidable challenge to the state and national systems.

5

Confessional Politics, Secularism and Centrism in India

LLOYD I. RUDOLPH AND
SUSANNE HOEBER RUDOLPH

Centrist ideology in India includes secularism as much as it does socialism and democracy. If there are reasons why India does not have national class parties, why not confessional parties? Its South Asian sibling, Pakistan, was founded and initially governed by an explicitly confessional Muslim League. In a country like India whose population is over 80 percent Hindu, why not a national Hindu party? Because secularism as an ideology and as a constitutional arrangement has been controversial and difficult to define, opportunities for confessional politics would seem ideal. Nevertheless, national centrist parties, of which the Congress party has been the preeminent example, have retained their commitment to secularism despite temptations to adopt a Hindu confessional identity and program. To create a broad national base, a confessional party would have to challenge India's centrist ideological consensus, a formidable task in the face of India's founding myth as a secular state and its enormously diverse cultural and social pluralism.

The term "confessional politics" evokes European rather than American ideas and practice with respect to the role of religion in politics. The American constitutional doctrine of maintaining a wall of separation between religion and the state—of confining religious freedom to the private realm—is as alien to the Indian as it is to most Western European political systems. To confess a religion is publicly to acknowledge and express commitment to a religious identity. In Western Europe the roots of confessional politics go back to the Reformation in the sixteenth century which unleashed civil and international war. It also occasioned a secularizing process that, over several centuries, contributed to the separation of church and state and to religious tolerance. In Europe after World War II, confessional politics took the form of support for political parties that acknowledged a commitment to Catholic or Protestant Christianity, or to Christianity generally, and pursued policy objectives that implemented or at least were consistent with their religious commitment. Other parties, to a greater or lesser degree, advocated laicizing or secularizing politics, that is, freeing politics and the state from ecclesiastical control or religious influence. In this sense, an important political cleavage that can affect party competition is between confessional parties and nonconfessional or anticonfessional parties (Janda 1980). It is the European sense of confessional politics that we have in mind when we inquire whether in independent India confessional politics will again become, as it was prior to independence, not only an important but also a destructive cleavage in national politics.

The obvious candidate for national confessional politics is the "Hindu majority." But this majority, 83 percent according to the 1981 census, is an artifact of categorization. The Hinduism of the "Hindu majority" encompasses a diversity of gods, texts, and social practices and a variety of ontologies and epistomologies. Without an organized church, it is innocent of orthodoxy, heterodoxy, and heresy. Thus, until the transforming historical events and experiences that surfaced during the Janata government (1977–79) and crested in the early 1980s, the "Hindu majority" remained an illusory support base for a national confessional party. At the same time, minority religious communities—Muslims, Sikhs, and Christians—were able to play a role in state politics.

In addition to the 17 percent (115 million) of the population who are not Hindus, another 15 percent (105 million) are members of the scheduled castes or ex-untouchables. Their categorization as Hindus is as much a result of census enumeration as of their own choosing. Most are not susceptible to political appeals based on a Hindu identity or Hindu interests (Jurgensmeyer 1982). Similarly, it is questionable whether the 42 million of 52 million tribals classified as Hindus in the 1981 census share a Hindu identity. They too are not available for appeals to Hindu nationalism and interests.

Indeed, many are actively engaged in asserting a variety of cultural or subnational identities and defending their interests against "Hindu" encroachment and appropriation.

Together, Muslims, other non-Hindus (Christians, Sikhs, Buddhists, Jains, and others), scheduled.castes, and scheduled tribes counted as Hindus constitute 38 percent of India's population (11, 6, 15, 6 percent, respectively). Of the 62 percent of the population that is left after we deduct 38 percent, only a fraction of uncertain magnitude shared, until about 1980, a Hindu identity that had political saliency. More important, the Hindu majority was more fragmented and competitive along sect, class, caste, and regional lines of cleavage than were India's minority religious communities.

Prior to the 1975 emergency regime, it was the Jana Sangh and its sister organization, the Rashtriya Swayamsevak Sangh or RSS, that articulated the ideology of Hindu Rashtra (nation) and symbolic, cultural, and social policies that addressed Hindu interests and values. Hindu confessional politics thrived on partition and were sustained by the perception that an Islamic Pakistan posed an ideological and military threat to India. Even though these external forces were sometimes the occasion for considerable sound and fury, Hindu confessional politics prior to 1980 did not attract much political support.

A rough measure of support for Hindu confessional politics prior to Mrs. Gandhi's return to power in 1980 was the proportion of the vote captured by the Hindu nationalist Jana Sangh party before its merger with Janata in 1977. Its best showings were in 1967, when its vote share was 9 percent, and in 1971, when it was 7.4 percent. The fading away of the partition generations, particularly the Hindu refugees who migrated from Pakistan under violent conditions, and the fading away of the international threat after the breakup of Pakistan in 1971 as a result of India's military victory substantially reduced for a time the saliency of Hindu confessional politics.

India's founding myth of secularism is grounded in the traumatic circumstances of partition in 1947. Mohammed Ali Jinnah, the founder of Pakistan, insisted that Muslims in an undivided India would be oppressed by a Hindu majority. India was two nations, one Hindu, the other Muslim. A Muslim nation required an Islamic state (Merriam 1980; Wolpert 1984; Jalal 1985). Gandhi and Nehru, leaders of the Indian National Congress, spoke for a secular nationalism that tried but failed at partition to represent all Indians. Independence meant partition as well as freedom from British rule. Half a million died and ten million migrated. Pakistan became a Muslim state, India a secular state. Gandhi's assassin was a Hindu who believed that the Mahatma was betraying Hinduism in his efforts to be fair to Pakistan.

The lesson of partition that informed India's founding myth was that religious politics kills. What in India is called "communalism" destroys civil society and the state. As a result, India began its career as an independent state with a powerful commitment not only to a secular state but also secularism as an ideology. The Indian constitution declares India to be a secular (as well as a socialist and democratic) state, that is, one that is neutral and impartial toward all religions; it guarantees freedom of conscience and the right freely to profess, practice, and propagate religion. "Communalism," exclusive identification with and commitment to one's religious or social community, became a Congress party term of opprobrium, the antithesis of the inclusive nationalism and cosmopolitan secularism preached and practiced by Gandhi and Nehru.

The founding myth was constructed between 1885 and 1947 out of the experience of the nationalist era and the trauma of partition. It was sustained for thirty years after independence by Nehru's avoidance of the latent contradictions in the meaning of secularism as the nationalists had defined it. It was challenged after 1980 when mounting distrust and conflict among Sikhs, Hindus, and Muslims made the latent contradictions manifest.

The contradiction in India's concept of secularism was its simultaneous commitment to communities and to equal citizenship. The group component was rooted in the history of representation under British rule. Englishmen, who at home conceived of the political community in terms of equal citizens, in India saw it in terms of distinctive groups. This group vision of the political community, they thought, was an appropriate reflection of Indian society. Indian nationalists appreciated and sought to realize a political community composed of equal citizens but early on realized that they could not build a nationalist movement without recognizing cultural and territorial communities.

Political safeguards to minorities were a key element of British efforts to represent groups in Indian society. They were first elaborated in the Morley-Minto constitutional reforms of 1909.

then in the Montagu-Chelmsford scheme of 1919, and finally in the constitutional framework that received the royal assent in 1935 (Coupland 1944). Safeguards gave statutory recognition to communal representation by providing for separate electorates and reserved seats for religious and other minorities. Nationalists saw these provisions as a policy designed to divide and rule Indians.

For different reasons and in different ways, Mohandas Karamchand Gandhi, the dominant figure in the freedom movement, also recognized groups. He transformed Indian nationalism from a movement of the anglicized few to a mass movement by speaking the language of the people, including regional speech and religious idioms. By leading movements on behalf of saving the caliph, then the religious head of all Muslims (1920–22), and on behalf of reform and self-government of gurdwaras or Sikh temples (1920–25), Gandhi brought Muslims and Sikhs into the nationalist fold (Minault 1982; Akbar 1985: 134–143). Gandhi made Hindus self-conscious as a national religious community in 1932 when he turned a "fast unto death" against separate electorates for untouchables into a fast against the Hindu community's practice of untouchability. From jail and then in an extended nationwide tour he launched a massive campaign against untouchability that politicized Hindu India just as his caliphate agitation had politicized Muslims and his campaign for gurdwara reform had politicized Sikhs. Confessional politics for him was a vehicle for community reform that could bring communities together, not only as brothers who respected the truths of each other's religions but also as Indians whose unity could be found and maintained in diversity.

By contrast, Nehru, free India's first prime minister, could not take religion seriously or credit groups as valid components of the Indian nation. In his eyes, the Muslim League in the 1937 provincial election in Uttar Pradesh used religion as a cover to further the landed interests of its leading members. The political community of independent India was to be based on equal citizenship and committed to economic and social justice. But Nehru's commitment to scientific humanism and his confidence that the future lay with secularism, socialism, and democracy was tempered by a deep concern to insure that Muslims in secular India would feel not only safe but at home. They were to be not only citizens with equal rights but also a self-governing religious community in charge of its own personal law. The potential contradiction between Nehru's commitment to anticommunal secularism and to Muslim community autonomy, in other times and other hands, would be exposed in contradictory standards for action.

In the Constituent Assembly (1946–50), the nationalist leaders had to confront concretely how they would balance the claims of equal citizenship and of group identities and interests. After prolonged debate, members of the assembly eliminated reserved seats as well as separate electorates for Muslims, Sikhs, Christians, and other minorities provided for in the 1935 constitution, but not reserved seats for untouchables and tribal peoples. It was a decision that almost, but not quite, eliminated the group as a defining element of the political community.

Yet groups survived, not only in the provision of reserved seats for untouchables and tribals but also in the provisions of article 29, which explicitly recognized the rights of groups, including religious communities: "Any section of the citizens of India. . . having a distinct language, script [read Gurmukhi for Sikhs and Urdu for Muslims] or culture [a euphemism inter alia for religion] shall have the right to conserve the same." Article 30 established all religions on an equal footing by guaranteeing the right of religious minorities to establish and administer educational institutions and barring the state from discriminating against them when granting financial support to private educational institutions.

Paradoxically, the elimination of group safeguards was accomplished by a decision rule that gave groups the right to veto decisions affecting their interests. First adopted in the Congress party's constitution and later incorporated in the Lucknow Pact in 1916 that united for a time the Indian National Congress and the Muslim League on nationalist objectives, it held that no bill or resolution affecting a minority community should be proceeded with if three-fourths of the representatives of that community were opposed (Coupland 1944:48). The Muslim community was in fact deeply split on this issue. Partition had diminished their numbers and influence. Did they not need safeguards—separate electorates and reserved seats—more under a majoritarian Congress than under the British raj? But major Congress leaders in the convention "quietly and privately put a great deal of pressure on the minorities to relinquish special privileges." Also, partition had "altered the views of many Muslims, who now thought that they must drop this highly controversial point [reservation of seats] in order to ingratiate themselves with the Congress" (Austin

1966:151). Perhaps foregoing reservations in legislatures in order to create an at least politically homogeneous society would help to insure fair treatment from a Hindu-majority society. When on 11 May 1949 H. C. Mookerjee, a Christian, moved the resolution that reservations be abolished, he assured the minorities that all they needed for their protection was the fundamental rights of citizens guaranteed by the constitution. His resolution carried "with almost complete support" (*ibidem*: 154–155).

The challenge to centrist politics after independence and until the late 1970s came from linguistic movements and class conflict in the countryside, not from confessional politics. Selig Harrison (1960) foresaw authoritarian rule or the balkanization of India as a result of linguistic cleavages. But states reorganization in 1956 dispelled them, and repression and prosperity in time tamed Naxalite violence. These challenges, while extraordinarily threatening in their time, did not ultimately disrupt the effective practice of centrist politics by national parties. As Paul Brass (1985) has said of this period, most Indians comfortably accommodated "to recognition of themselves as member of two nations: a Sikh, Bengali, or Tamil nation at one level of identity and an Indian nation at another." With regional and local exceptions, of which the movement for a Punjabi Suba (created in 1966) was one, these identities rarely came into conflict with each other.

In the 1980s, the Hinduism that had been an "artifact of categorization" began to become a condition of national consciousness. This development signaled the possibility of a national Hindu confessional politics. Religious performances, celebrations, and demonstrations began to transcend localities and to acquire national dimensions. As they did so, they became more strident and militant. The agitations and *yatras* (pilgrimages) of the Hindu solidarity and unity movements, such as the Vishwa Hindu Parishad, were no longer the local phenomena they had been in the 1880s when Bal Gangadhar Tilak aroused Hindu political solidarity around the Ganesh festival at Poona. Aided by the proliferation of religious symbolism in the print and electronic media, Hindu themes and organizations crossed state boundaries and helped diverse sects, castes, and classes to acquire the consciousness of a popular and more homogeneous Hinduism.

Social mobility has contributed to the rise of popular Hinduism and Hindu nationalism. In the years prior to the Janata government of 1977–79 and Indira Gandhi's return to power in 1980, the support

base for Hindu confessional politics had been the traditionally
literate, spiritually initiated upper castes located for the most part
in the relatively backward "Hindi Heartland" states of northern
India and in Maharashtra (Baxter 1969; Rudolph and Rudolph
1967). But in the course of the 1970s, new generations of mobile
middle castes born after independence and partition and located as
often in the countryside as in the city were attracted to Hindu
revitalization movements and political appeals. As social moorings
gave way in a rapidly changing society and rapidly growing
population, these groups found that patronizing Hinduism and
practicing it in new ways not only earned respect but also provided
a familiar and satisfying world view and social identity (Babb
1986).

Patronizing Hinduism in order to acquire status and power
has an ancient pedigree in India. In the "old days," alien, newly
victorious, or ambitious rajas seeking to legitimize their power
patronized deities and temples, endowing them with land,
offices, and income. Landlords, merchants, and state servants
used religious patronage in a similar fashion (Eschmann *et aliter*
1978; Stein 1980). Today newly rich sugar barons and beneficiaries
of the green revolution have channeled their new wealth into
temples, *Ramayana* recitations, and more elaborate and expensive
ritual practices. What is a positive identity for socially mobile
groups, however, often becomes a controversial identity in inter-
community relations.

Economic competition that upsets received status and power
differentials has led to resentment and envy. In some communities in northern India and Kerala, investments in religion by
Muslims returning from lucrative employment in the Gulf countries
have spurred similar Hindu investments. Educated, prosperous
untouchables converted to Islam in and around Meenakshipuram
(Tamil Nadu) in 1981 to win as Muslims the respect and equality
Hinduism had denied them (Mathew 1982). In Maharashtra and
Gujarat, where there are large local concentrations of mostly
poor Muslims, communal violence became endemic as a result
of struggles between Hindus and Muslims over reservations,
employment, property, and business opportunities (Baxi 1985;
Rodrigues 1986; Engineer 1984).

Hindu confessional politics also became a forum of cultural
nationalism for the Hindi heartland states. Under certain conditions, such as those prevailing after 1980, Hindu nationalism was

exported to regions where Hindus are a minority, In Punjab and Kashmir, Sikhs and Muslims, respectively are the majority. In Kerala, Hindus confront large numbers of Christian, Muslim, and communist voters. In these states, minority Hindus resorted to defensive mobilization and sought outside support and protection. Hindu confessional politics was exported from the Hindi heartland to all three states. By contrast, the social structure and consciousness needed to support Hindu confessional politics are marginal in the southern states of Tamil Nadu and Andhra Pradesh, where regional nationalisms are the dominant ideology. These examples suggest that because Hindu confessional politics is weak in most of the periphery, it is dangerous for a national centrist party to become overcommitted to Hindu confessional politics.

The Janata party's victory in the 1977 national elections put proponents of Hindu confessional politics in the seats of power in Delhi for the first time. This was evident in the party's abortive effort to block conversions to Christianity through national legislation limiting the right of Christians to propagate religion and in its attempt to decertify textbooks that allegedly failed to depict Hinduism in a sufficiently favorable light and glossed over the flaws of Muslim rulers (Rudolph and Rudolph 1984).

After Mrs. Gandhi's return to power in 1980, Sikh extremism and terrorism in the Punjab entered national consciousness and politics at about the same time as the much publicized conversion of untouchables to Islam in Meenakshipuram. These Christian–, Sikh–, and Muslim–inspired events were used, by those who held that Hinduism was threatened by India's minority religions, to launch nationwide efforts to save Hinduism. The supporters of the Hindu backlash alleged that the minorities were privileged and pampered. Governments, particularly Congress governments, long accustomed to protecting and aiding the minorities in the expectation of electoral support, were charged with appeasing the minorities out of political expediency (Akbar 1985: 197–198).

The Indira Gandhi-led Congress(I) government that was returned to power in the 1980 parliamentary election was the first Congress government openly to court Hindu support. This was evident in the Kashmir assembly and Delhi municipal corporation elections in 1983 when voters who had traditionally voted for the Hindu-oriented Jana Sangh supported Congress(I) candidates. It was evident in Mrs. Gandhi's personal attention to Hindu temples, priests, and gurus. Most important was the crisis involving Sikhs in the Punjab that began to unfold soon after the Congress(I) government's return to power in 1980. Congress(I)'s attempt to recoup its position in the Punjab by patronizing Sikh extremists loosed a storm of communal politics. Mrs. Gandhi's subsequent attempts to crush the terrorism of secessionist Sikhs who were murdering moderate Sikhs led to the army's invasion of the Golden Temple, the Sikh's holiest shrine, an event that further alienated even moderate Sikhs and Hindus and triggered mini-mutinies by recent Sikh recruits. The spiral of distrust and fear wound its downward course from the 31 October 1984 assassination of Mrs. Gandhi by her Sikh bodyguards, through the retaliatory slaying by Hindus of at least two thousand Sikhs in the three days after Mrs. Gandhi's death, to the reciprocal violent "self-protection" among Sikhs and Hindus in Punjab, Haryana, and Delhi.

A parallel, if less dramatic, spiral of fear and distrust affected Muslims. The spiral included the national Hindu reaction in 1981 to the local conversion of a few untouchables to Islam; the killing (by Lalung tribals, not Hindus) at Nellie in Assam of more than one thousand Muslims during the 1983 state elections; the terms of Rajiv Gandhi's settlement in 1985 of the festering Assam regional agitation, which deprived some Muslim immigrants of their citizenship and others of their right to vote for ten years; a court ruling in 1985 that a disputed historic building in Ayodhya was a temple, not a mosque; and, finally and most important, the Shah Bano case of 1985, a supreme court ruling that Muslims perceived as depriving them of control over their personal law. These events in isolation might not have precipitated a crisis of distrust. But in conjunction with the Sikh-Hindu communal confrontations that had already agitated North India, they were construed as part of a larger pattern of Hindu revivalism and nationalism. Muslims became alarmed that in the name of secularism they would have to give up their religious identity. As Syed Shahabuddin, an aspirant for national leadership of the Muslim community and a Janata member of Parliament (MP) put it: "Ours is not a communal fight. It only amounts to resisting the inexorable process of assimilation. We want to keep our religious identity at all costs" (*India Today*, 31 May 1986: 55). The clearest indication of Muslim alienation was Shahabuddin's December 1985 by-election victory. By-elections in Assam, Gujarat, Orissa, and West Bengal told the same story: massive Muslim defection from the Congress.

In 1986, the Rajiv Gandhi Congress(I) government, in an effort to break and reverse the spiral of fear and distrust, forced through a reluctant Congress(I) party and national Parliament the Muslim Women (Protection of Rights on Divorce) Bill. The law preserved the independence and integrity of Muslim personal law that orthodox Muslims alleged the supreme court's judgment in the Shah Bano case (1985) had put at risk. The court had held that a divorced Muslim woman was entitled to support from her former husband. According to orthodox Muslim opinion, by contrast, the *shariat* held that when the marriage contract is terminated by divorce, the husband's financial responsibilities cease. It is the responsibility of blood relatives—fathers and sons—and perhaps Muslim religious bodies to see to the maintenance of divorced Muslim women. The decision had a national impact on Muslim consciousness because its challenge to Muslim personal law aroused a common concern in a community otherwise divided by region, historical experience, ethnicity, urban-rural differences, and language.

The bill passed on 5 May 1986 only by dint of a stringent three-line whip to enforce Congress party discipline. Prime Minister Rajiv Gandhi's initial response to the supreme court's Shah Bano judgment had been to accept it. He remarked in Parliament that he hoped in the twenty-first century Indians would be recognized as Indians and not as a collection of sects. But as orthodox Muslim objections mounted and the election returns confirmed massive Muslim resistance to the decision, he reconsidered his position. Equal citizenship, it seemed, was not a sufficient definition of secularism. Secularism had not only to take account of "sects" but also to allow them some measure of self-regulation. It was, he said, for the "Muslims themselves to look at their laws"; "it is not for us to be arbiter between" the traditional and westernized Muslims. Spokesmen for the government argued in Parliament that however regressive some might think the Muslim personal law, government was bound to respect what it believed to be the majority opinion of the Muslim community.

The Punjab crisis and the Shah Bano case became an occasion for confronting what secularism meant in an era of resurgent religious politics among Hindus, Muslims, and Sikhs. The Rajiv Gandhi government had reverted to a version of secularism implied by the Congress party's informal "rule," observed in the Constituent Assembly, that no act directly affecting a particular (religious) community should be taken without support of an extraordinary majority in that community. Like article 29 of the constitution, which protects the right of any group to preserve its culture, it is a rule that moves some way toward conceiving of the political community as constituted of distinctive groups as well as equal citizens. His concept of secularism, the prime minister said, was *sarv dharm sambhaav* (respect for all religions), a concept closer to Mohandas Gandhi's views than to those of Rajiv's grandfather, Jawaharlal Nehru.

By the mid-1980s the secularism of India's centrist consensus no longer commanded the understanding and commitment of the postindependence generations. With the rise of confessional politics, particularly its communal and violent version, these generations had to relearn the lesson of partition: in a diverse, plural society, communal politics can destroy civil society and the state. The Congress(I) had moved dangerously close to becoming a Hindu confessional party. Denying Christians the right to propagate their religion in the name of freedom of conscience, making war on Sikhs and their religion, and threatening to deprive Muslims of their law and their mosques were signs that centrist national parties, such as Janata and Congress(I), had been tempted by the option of Hindu confessional politics. Rajiv Gandhi's 1984 election campaign was based in part on Hindu backlash support: sympathy for a bereaved son whose mother had died as martyr to a Hindu cause and a campaign appeal for national unity that spoke to Hindu nationalism.

But there was another face to the possibilities of the mid-eighties. All of India's national parties remained nominally committed to a secular state. Only regional parties, in Punjab, Kashmir, and Kerala, had explicit confessional identities, and they were not new. Congress drew back from the prospect of confessional politics in the face of its consequences for the party's principles and electoral success. Many of Rajiv Gandhi's words and actions after the 1984 elections made it clear that he thought reliance on Hindu confessional politics was not a viable alternative for Congress(I) in the states or nationally. He made peace with the Sikhs in Punjab and with Muslims by reversing legislatively the supreme court's judgment in the Shah Bano case. Asked in May 1986 whether he had won the December 1984 election on the basis of a Hindu backlash vote, he offered a secular interpretation: "No, I don't.

Not at all . . . more than just Hindus voted [for the Congress] and in the same sort of percentages. "

For Congress to become a confessional party would not only threaten its principles but would also jeopardize its standing as a national party. The principal support for Hindu confessional politics is in the Hindi heartland, and even there Congress's comparative advantage over rivals who can compete effectively in the Hindu confessional mode lies with maintaining the support of the minorities. To embrace Hindu confessional politics would be to risk becoming a regional party.

Reliance on Hindu confessional politics is not compatible with Congress's legacy as the party of secularism. The meaning of that secularism historically has encompassed the celebration and constitutional protection of cultural diversity as well as the protection of equal rights of citizens in a secular state. The result has been an ambiguous and sometimes contradictory relationship between the confessional politics of the majority and the minority communities. The lessons of partition were there to remind the Congress, the opposition parties, and the country of their fate should they forget the consequences of allowing confessional politics to become a major cleavage in Indian national politics.

6

Islamic Revival in Pakistan

Mumtaz Ahmad

Islamic revival in South Asia can be studied from the perspective of three analytically distinct but not necessarily mutually exclusive theoretical approaches. The first approach emphasizes the intellectual base of Islam using Weber's conceptualization of world religions. The normative bases of the Islamic revival as enunciated in the Koran, the traditions of the Prophet, and the historical forms in which these norms were institutionalized are discussed. The second approach examines the Islamic revival in the context of world historical forces such as the rise of capitalism and secularism in the West; interaction between the Islamic world and the West; colonialism and its impact on Muslim societies; and the processes of social modernization and economic change which gave rise to new technologies, industrialization, urbanization, secular education, and new social classes. Thirdly, one can study the Islamic revival not as a monolithic, universal phenomenon characterized by homogeneous ideological and structural features throughout the Muslim world, but as a combination of diverse social, religious, and political movements produced by doctrinal and structural differences among Islamic societies.

The Weberian approach emphasizes the ideological vitality of Islam as an autonomous political force. It argues that Islamic ideology has often been a focal point in situations involving social and political conflict, foreign encroachments, and attempts to restore purity in dogma and rites. Invocation of Islam in times of crisis has numerous historical precedents in Muslim societies. The millenarian, puritanical, revivalist, and pre-modern religious reform movements which emerged in various Muslim societies after the beginning of the eighteenth century share features with the present movements.

The second approach situates Islam and the Muslim societies in the context of world historical forces and explains Islamic revivalism as one response to modernization and economic change. Some sociologists have related Islamic resurgence to the powerful comeback of religious ideologies, the worldwide re-awakening of religious identities, and the "re-enchantment" of the world as a reaction to modernity.

The third approach finds the basis for the variations in different Islamic revivalist movements in their relationship with the state and religious structures; their diverse doctrinal resource-base; their social bases of support, their constituencies, and their patterns of alliances; their relationships with the dominant power structures of society; and above all, the conjunction of forces that define the character of the regimes in specific Muslim societies.

Despite apparent similarities in their orientations towards problems of Islam and social change, revivalist movements in South Asia and the Muslim World are not unified and monolithic. Their differences are more important than their similarities. Although Islamic revivalist groups everywhere in the Muslim world strive for the restoration of the puritanical values and practices of early Islam, their programmatic emphases owe their origin to the local social forces. Each of these groups carries the distinctive marks of a unique social and political environment within which it operates. While intellectual developments in other Muslim societies and international events that affect all Muslims have their impact on South Asian Muslims, their influence is mediated by indigenous forces.

A case in point is the impact of the Iranian revolution in Pakistan. The Iranian revolution was enthusiastically supported by the leading revivalist group in Pakistan, the Jama'at-i-Islami, as a triumph of Islam over secular forces. Later, when this revolution encouraged Shi'ite militancy in Pakistan, which was perceived as an obstacle in the way of Pakistan's own program of Islamization, enthusiasm waned. In Bangladesh, where there are no Shias among indigenous Bengali Muslims, the attitude toward the Iranian revolution has remained indifferent.

The following discussion of the Islamic revival in South Asia, and particularly in Pakistan, will address two questions: what factors have contributed to the emergence of this revival? and in what specific forms has the revival been expressed in these societies?

In many other Muslim societies the experience with "political

Islam" is recent, but in Pakistan the experience with the interaction of religion and politics began with the idea of a separate homeland for Indian Muslims, an idea which took shape in the 1930s. Since then, and particularly after the creation of Pakistan in 1947, the history of this new nation has been influenced by Islam. Islam has played a very important role in the country's constitutional debates, political disputes, and ideological conflicts. At present, both in official rhetoric and policies, Islam is being projected as *the* state ideology; and along with the military, it is likely to remain a dominant feature of Pakistan's future political development. Furthermore, Pakistan is the most complex of the three South Asian cases. The Islamic revival in Pakistan embodies all the contradictions of Pakistani society. One witnesses the political authoritarianism of General Zia-ul-Haq, the economic liberalism of Mahbubal Haq, the cultural conservatism of the Jama'at-i-Islami, and the techno-logical modernism of the F-16 jet fighters and advanced nuclear programs, all coexisting.

Islamic revivalism in Pakistan has manifested itself in several areas of collective life. In politics, it has denied the legitimacy of Western parliamentary democracy and, instead, has sought to introduce a political system based on Islamic principles. One manifestation has been a referendum which sought a mandate for further Islamization and, by implication, the extension of the tenure of the President for five more years. Non-party elections have been held for the national and provincial assemblies (Ahmad 1985).

In economics, Islamic revivalism has expressed itself in com-pulsory collection of *zakat* and *ushr* taxes and the introduction of an interest-free banking and investment system. In the legal sphere, which held the top priority in the Islamization agenda of Islamic groups in Pakistan, revivalism has meant the reintroduction of Islamic penal laws which provide Islamic punishments for drinking alcohol, theft, adultery, and *gazaf* (false accusation concerning sexual offenses). Further ordinances have established a Federal *Shariah* Court as well as local *Qazi* Courts to hear criminal and civil cases under Islamic law. The Federal Shariah Court, in both its original and appellate jurisdictions, rules on whether existing laws are in accordance with Islam—except, of course, those issued under the authority of martial law. Another recent addition has been the introduction of the Islamic law of evidence under which, in certain cases, the evidence of two women is regarded as equal to that of one man.

In the cultural sphere, Islamic revivalism has manifested itself in the banning of dance clubs; the imposition of strict sexual morality; the observance of Islamic moral standards in the production and screening of television programs; the revision of all textbooks to express an Islamic orientation; increasing allocations for religious instruction; the establishment of an Islamic university in Islamabad; declaring Friday as the weekly holiday instead of Sunday; obligatory prayer breaks during working hours in government and private offices; emphasis on the Urdu language and national dress in government offices; and a kind of moral aversion, at least in rhetoric if not in substantive behavior, on the part of intellectuals as well as governmental authorities, against Western cultural symbols and institutions. One may also note an upsurge of international Islamic cultural exchanges and conferences as well as unprecedented enthusiasm and public display in celebrating Islamic religious festivals and holidays.

INCREASE IN RELIGIOSITY AS AN EVIDENCE OF ISLAMIC REVIVAL

The political activism of certain Islamic revivalist groups and the state-sponsored Islamic reforms may not reflect increased religiosity on the part of the Muslim masses. Although some correlation exists between religious practice and participation in religion-based political movements, these two dimensions of behavior are separate. The influence of religious groups in politics and society may expand irrespective of whether the number of people observing Islamic rituals is increasing. The mobilization of certain groups may be caused by factors external to religious consciousness.

Lynda Malik's linking of the Islamic revival movement in Pakistan to the frequency with which people pray misses the point of the Islamic revival. Based on her 1980 survey of 1,251 persons in Punjab, 60 percent of the respondents reported no change in their rate of prayer (Malik 1982). Others prayed less often (19 percent); some gave no answer (11 percent); and a small number prayed more often (10 percent). She concluded that "fewer than 10 percent of the sample would support the notion of revival in Pakistan" (*ibidem*: 41).

Evidence contrary to Malik's finding exists in a Pakistan Institute of Public Opinion survey, which showed that almost 40 percent of the people had become more religious between 1978 and 1980 (PIPO 1980). Most experienced no change (49 percent), but very few had become less religious (11 per cent) (*ibidem*: 25). The difference between Malik's findings and PIPO's is possibly significant.

Even if there has been no change in the observance of religious rituals, religion may play a larger role in public life. Sociologists of religion have demonstrated that the observance of rituals is only *one* of the many ways in which people express their religiosity. A person deficient in one dimension of religious behavior (in this case, the performance of rituals) may be more observant of other aspects of religiosity (Stark and Glock 1974: 11–21; Glock 1962; Glock and Stark 1965).

ISLAM AS AN IDEOLOGICAL BASIS OF THE STATE

Pakistan's political creation was intrinsically related to Islam. The leaders of the Pakistan movement demanded a separate homeland for Indian Muslims where they could practice their religion— both in their individual as well as collective lives—undisturbed by a Hindu majority. Although Pakistan was undoubtedly created by a nationalist movement (Malik 1980: 228–300), its nationalism was firmly anchored in the Islamic consciousness of the Muslim masses (Qureshi 1977; Sayeed 1968; Mujahid 1976; Naim 1979). The Muslim League's slogan, "Islam is in danger," proved to be a powerful stimulus for mass political action. The Two-Nation Theory of Mohammad Ali Jinnah reinforced the Islamic basis of the nationalist movement. Jinnah did not define "nation" in terms of shared language or common territory, history, culture, and customs; rather, he stated that Islam and Hinduism are not religions in the strict sense of the word but are in fact distinct social orders and thus cannot evolve into a single nationality.

Both Jinnah and the poet-philosopher Mohammad Iqbal perceived Islam at several interrelated levels. They saw: (1) Islam as a *faith* or as a religious system whose cardinal beliefs identify its adherents as Muslims; (2) Islam as a *culture* or a way of life that would integrate Muslims into a nation state; and (3) Islam as an *ideological system* whose set of values could socialize Muslims into a separate political community (Mujahid 1976).

To many Pakistani intellectuals, Islam constitutes the *raison d'être* of the Pakistani state and justifies its separate existence from

India (Hodgson 57–60). This understanding was articulated in the "Objectives Resolution" which was passed by the first Constituent Assembly of Pakistan in 1949 and later became an ideological preamble to all the subsequent constitutions of the country. This relationship of Islam to Pakistan has assumed such an orthodox status that secular and socialist political parties do not dare challenge it. The existence of a broad consensus on the inseparability of Islam and Pakistan—popularly known as the "Pakistan ideology"—has thus helped groups to press their demands and agitate for an increased role for Islam in public affairs. Islam is thought not only to be the ideological basis for the state of Pakistan but also fundamental to the nation's very existence. Without Islam the state would lose its identity, disintegrate, and perish. Propagation of an ideology other than Islam—be it secularism, socialism, communism, or Western liberal democracy—would be treason against the state.

ISLAM AS A LEGITIMATING FACTOR FOR EXISTING POWER RELATIONS

Since the very inception of the new state, Pakistan's rulers have used Islam to legitimize their authority which was, more often than not, derived from the coercive apparatus of the state rather than from popular support. Since the majority of the regimes came into power through extra-constitutional means, their claims to legitimacy were dubious. As a result, these regimes depended on Islam as a source of legitimacy. The chaotic parliamentary regime, Ayub Khan's development-oriented government, Yahya Khan's transient government, Zulfikar Ali Bhutto's populist corporatism, and Zia-ul-Haq's conservative authoritarianism—all benefited from the same tactics. In each phase, Islamic ideology was invoked, albeit with varying emphases, in order to legitimize not only the authority of the incumbents but also their contemporary policy goals. A degree of political stability was thus achieved at least in the short run (Ahmad 1981).

While the early parliamentary regime used a "liberal-modernist Islam," Ayub Khan a "developmentalist Islam," Yahya Khan a "nationalist Islam," and Bhutto a "socialist-populist Islam," to legitimize themselves, the present military regime under Zia-ul-Haq is using a "revivalist-fundamentalist Islam" to legitimize its continued grip on the political system of Pakistan.

Like several of its predecessors the Zia government has sought to elicit the moral commitment of the people by linking the destinies of Islam and Pakistan with that of the military regime. Zia maintains that the military rule has been vital for the preservation of Islam and Pakistan. Thus, the trinity of Islam, Pakistan, and the military regime become one and the same thing (Zia-ul-Haq n.d.). The new election law of September 1979 provided that no politician could propagate "any opinion or act in a manner prejudicial to the ideology of Pakistan" or would express views "defaming or ridiculing the... Armed Forces" (*Dawn*, Overseas Weekly Edition, 8 September 1979).

When a pro-government politician from Karachi was assassinated in 1982, Zia declared that the assassins were "enemies of Islam." The crux of Zia's case against his opposition is that since the elements identified with the opposition are ideologically leftist or secularly oriented, they have no legitimate claim to power in an Islamic state. In 1980, addressing the Councillors of Multan district, President Zia declared: "Pakistan was achieved in the name of Islam, and Islam alone could provide the basis to run the government of the country and sustain its integrity.... The present government would provide opportunity to others to serve the country after it achieved its objectives... (but) no un-Islamic government would be allowed to succeed the present regime" (*The Muslim*, 10 June 1980). The use of Islam has thus created a situation in which religious interests have become indistinguishable from purely political interests and the regime's need for legitimacy. The road to salvation has become the road to power as well.

This convergence of salvation and power is also evident in an ingenious argument about the ideological affinity and undifferentiated character of the institutions of an Islamic polity. According to this argument, the armed forces are not a separate corporate group. The ideological affinities that run through the civilian executive, the legislature, the judiciary, the bureaucracy, and the military transcend artificial institutional boundaries. If all the "load-bearing pillars" of the society are motivated by the same ideological considerations and adhere to the same *Shariah*, which is the "guiding and controlling spirit" of every section of the population, the distinction between civilian and military rule can not arise (Siddiqi 1980; Ahmed 1983).

Islam has been used to seek the support of the religious political parties and to create a constituency among the lower middle class of the Punjab, urban Sind, and the Northwest Frontier Province. This constituency participates in religious festivals and rituals; in the newly created religious institutional network of *zakat, ushr,* and the *islah-i-mu'ashra* (reformation of society) committees; and in government-organized religious gatherings such as the *Milad-un-Nabi* and the *qirat* and *na'at* competitions. Zia's policies and rhetoric have appealed to the religious sensibilities and economic interests of this stratum whose support is regarded as critical to the stability of the regime. His promise to protect the sanctity of *chador* (literally, "the veil") and *chardivari* ("the four walls of a house"), symbols of women's honor and private property, touches a vital chord.

Similarly, the introduction of *Shariah*, especially its penal laws; the organization of *zakat* and *ushr* systems; the establishment of a network of religious institutions in association with the *ulama*; and the recent legislation prohibiting the Qadianis (or Ahmadis)—a heretical group founded in early twentieth century Muslim India—have reinforced the regime's claims to political legitimacy.

Zia's Islamic revivalist commitment may be quite genuine but it is difficult to isolate the elements of personal piety and subjective commitment from the political benefits. Whatever degree of genuine religious enthusiasm and revivalist zeal one may be able to identify in Zia, he has used popular Islamic symbols to legitimize his continued grip on political power and to safeguard the interests of the social forces which constitute its bases of support.

ISLAM AS A VEHICLE OF PROTEST

One must not think that rulers have a monopoly over the instrumental use of Islam. The Iranian revolution is a prominent example of the use of Islam as a vehicle of protest. In Syria the Muslim Brotherhood is engaged in a fierce struggle against the Ba'athist regime in the name of Islam. Islamic groups in Egypt, Iraq, Turkey, Tunisia, and Indonesia protest the corrupt and un-Islamic character of the rulers.

The most outstanding example in Pakistan of this delegitimizing role of Islam is the 1977 Nizam-i-Mustafa (System of the Prophet Mohammad) movement. As a result of this movement, a militant alliance between the Jama'at-i-Islami and certain conservative *ulama* groups undermined the secularly-oriented regime of Zulfikar Ali Bhutto. At the time of the 1977 elections, various religio-political groups formed the Pakistan National Alliance (PNA) which campaigned on the central theme of the introduction of the Nizam-i-Mustafa and stirred up an unprecedented religious enthusiasm during and after elections.

The Nizam-i-Mustafa movement featured the effective use of Islamic revivalist ideals and symbols by discontented groups for whom religious concerns and material interests converged under the umbrella of Islamic fundamentalism. Even Prime Minister Bhutto during his last years had succumbed and introduced Islamic measures in order to widen his sources of legitimacy and to win support. In 1974, for example, Bhutto declared the Ahmadis to be non-Muslims. And his last bid to establish his Islamic credentials was to ban alcoholic drinks, gambling, dancing, horseracing, and dance clubs in May 1977.

As an incumbent, Prime Minister Bhutto enjoyed enormous advantages, including control of the mass media and the educational institutions. These enabled him to publicize widely the Islamic orientation of his government and the services he had rendered to the cause of Islam. He also had at his disposal—and to some extent used—the huge financial resources of the state to court the religious establishment, including the extensive network of the state-controlled *Auqaf* or religious institutions which had been taken over by the government during President Ayub Khan's rule.

The fact that the power to confer Islamic legitimacy was in the hands of those whose vital economic, status, and ideological interests he had earlier so vehemently challenged, however, proved to be a serious obstacle in Bhutto's search for Islamic credentials. Even if he had succeeded in winning over the orthodox religious establishment—and his Minister for Religious Affairs had in fact chalked out an elaborate program for Bhutto's second term to circumvent the militancy of the *ulama* using both persuasive and coercive measures—it would not have necessarily guaranteed automatic acceptance of his claims to Islamic legitimacy. The initial opposition to Bhutto, articulated in Islamic religious idioms by the Jama'at-i-Islami, came from the lay Islamic activists of the lower middle classes and not from the *ulama*. Given the relative lack of a structural hierarchy in Islam, incumbents have severe limitations in using the Islamic "card" (Hudson 1980:16–18). A Muslim ruler who has successfully incorporated the "professional" religious establishment into state structures may still be vulnerable to opposition by equally legitimate lay and popular Islamic forces. The relative success of General Zia in establishing his Islamic legitimacy can be explained in part by his strategy of seeking certification for his Islamic authenticity from both the "professional" religious establishment as represented by the *ulama* and the *Mashaikh* (sufi leaders), and the popular, lay Islamic forces as represented by the Jama'at-i-Islami.

ISLAM AND NATIONAL INTEGRATION

Another factor which has contributed significantly to the political salience of Islam in Pakistan is its role as a major source of national integration in a society characterized by considerable ethnic, linguistic and cultural diversity. At the time of independence, the constituent units of Pakistan (East Bengal, Punjab, Sind, Baluchistan, and the North West Frontier Province) had very little in common except Islam. It was Islam which became the basis for the Muslim League's appeal to the diverse Muslim regions of British India to join together in a common struggle for Pakistan (Khan 1951: 46–58; Khan 1967: 128).

The fact that Pakistan was not created in the name of ethnicity, language, or geography, but rather on the basis of Islamic solidarity, albeit expressed in the idioms of Muslim nationalism (Mujahid 1962: 14–24), was perceived as an important potential asset for the prospects of national integration by both policy makers and intellectuals. It was believed that an emphasis on Islam in official rhetoric and the incorporation of Islamic values in public policies, especially in the fields of education, culture and mass communications, would weaken the parochial loyalties of ethnicity and language. As a result, the bonds of unity among various regions of the new state would be strengthened. The historical experience of early Islamic empires was invoked as a paradigm for contemporary Pakistan to show how diverse ethnic groups and regions united into a single political community on the basis of over-arching loyalty to Islam (Watt 1966).

East Bengal—later renamed East Pakistan and now Bangladesh—was seen as a test case to demonstrate the effectiveness of ideological bonds in a situation where the differences in ethnicity, language, ecology, demography, and culture were acute. The two wings of the country, which were separated by over one thousand miles of hostile Indian territory, shared very little with each other except Islam (Quddus 1982:17). But the founders of the nation were convinced that the geographical remoteness and other differences would not in any significant way obstruct the processes of national integration if the people of both wings would continue to relate to each other on the basis of Islamic brotherhood (Syed 1979: 96–98; Ikram 1965; Tayyeb 1966; Chaudhery 1974; Ahmad 1964; Jahan 1972).

The emphasis on the role of Islam as the major integrative factor increased even more so in the 1960s when Pakistan witnessed a marked assertion of centrifugal, fissiparous forces based on ethnic identities and regional demands. The emergence of regional reverberations and separatist tendencies was seen as further reason to promote Islamic ideology as a basis for national solidarity (Sayeed 1967: 182–193). But as was evident from the subsequent developments, emphasis on the religious aspect alone to the exclusion of other more tangible ones could not ensure national unity (Quddus 1982: 17–18; Sayeed 1967: 183–184). As Nurul Huda, then Finance Minister of East Pakistan, put it in 1965:" . . . it would be unfair to expect that our spiritual bonds through Islam will be so strong. . . that we shall forget all our disparities and will still remain united. . . as a nation" (cited in Mujahid 1974: 9).

The secession of Bangladesh in December 1971 clearly demonstrated that Islam, although necessary for the creation of Pakistan consisting of two separate regions with distinct ethno-linguistic identities of their own, was still not a sufficient factor for sustaining their continued unity in the absence of other policy measures. The failure of the national political elite and the intellectuals to link Islam to more mundane issues such as the equitable distribution of economic resources among the various parts of the country and the enfranchisement of the politically alienated sectors of society, ultimately led to a situation in which Islam itself came to be seen by the deprived regions as an instrument of exploitation.

However one may interpret the experience, or rather the failure, of national integration in East Pakistan, the fact remains that it left an indelible mark, both before and after the breakup of the country, on the popular consciousness about the importance of Islam as a national political ideology. Before the separation of East Pakistan, it was the fear of the disintegration of the country which had acted as a propellent for Islam. In the aftermath of the separation, the faith in the efficacy of Islam as a basis for national unity for the remaining portion of Pakistan seems to have grown even stronger. It is in this context that one can describe the current wave of Islamic revivalism in Pakistan as a post–1972 phenomenon. The traumatic events of the 1971 civil war and the humiliating defeat of the Pakistani forces fighting for national unity at the hands of India had powerful psychologically unsettling effects for the people of the then largest Muslim state in the world, which often prided itself as the "fortress of Islam."

After the initial shock of the disintegration of the nation had been absorbed, there followed what may be called a period of introspection and soul–searching (Memon 1983). This renewed quest for authenticity and national identity coupled with self–criticism as a result of the mortifying encounter with the Bengali separatists and the Indians in East Pakistan, led to the reaffirmation of Islam as both a personal succor and a national ideology. The Islamic groups were quick to seize upon the opportunity and point out that East Pakistan was lost only because the people had not been good Muslims in their personal as well as collective behavior. They also accused the rulers of neglecting Islam as a source of public policy, a fact which, in their view, had led to the emergence of a wide variety of anti–national forces in the country. According to this formulation, the secession of East Pakistan was therefore not a failure of Islam but of the un–Islamic policies and conduct of the rulers.

The experience of East Pakistan thus became a rallying cry to return to Islam as an ideological remedy both to counteract similar developments elsewhere in the remaining part of Pakistan and to cultivate a new sense of religious rejuvenation. In many ways, one can compare this post–1971 rediscovery of Islamic identity in Pakistan with the experience of the Egyptian Muslims in the aftermath of their crushing defeat in the 1967 war with Israel (Dessuki 1981; Waterbury 1981; Haddad 1980; Jansen 1979; Esposito 1984: 153–155). In both cases, humiliating defeats in wars resulted in a return to Islamic roots and renewed public commitment to Islamic ideals.

INDIA AND BANGLADESH

Although this chapter focuses on Pakistan, it is instructive to make some brief comparative references to the Indian and Bangladeshi cases of Islamic revival.

Unlike Hinduism and Sikhism which are spatially confined to South Asia, Islam has transcontinental connections. Thus,

Muslims in Pakistan, India, and Bangladesh are not only affected by developments and experiences of one another but also by developments in the Middle East. Before the drawing of new political boundaries in 1947 and then again in 1971, the Muslims of South Asia had shared a common religio-political experience and had participated together in socioreligious and cultural movements of sub-continental scope. Even today, the majority of the Pakistani and Bangladeshi *ulama* in leadership roles consists of those who were trained in places like Deoband, Farangi Mahal, Rampur, and Baeli in India. The two major grassroot revivalist movements, the Jama'at-i-Islami and the Tablighi Jama'at, are truly subcontinental movements with their activities and branches spread all over Pakistan, India, and Bangladesh.

In an article entitled "India: Surprising Isolation," Imtiaz Ahmad argued in 1980 that "India has remained totally untouched by the recent developments in Iran and Pakistan as well as in other countries of the Muslim World. . . . The recent resurgence of Islamic revivalism has not struck a sympathetic chord among Muslims in India". If, however, one is not looking for those manifestations of Islamic revival in India which are usually identified with countries like Iran and Pakistan, the isolation thesis with regard to the Indian Muslims would become untenable. One cannot, obviously, expect the Indian Muslims who constitute only about 11 per cent of the total population, to launch an Islamic revolution (as in Iran) or make demands for the establishment of an Islamic state (as in Pakistan). Even from the perspective of the state, the political role of Islam is limited. Since India is a secular state, the Indian state authorities make very little use of religion as a legitimating force. Whenever they do feel such a need, they prefer to use Hindu symbols to legitimize their authority and programs. Islamic symbols are only used while dealing with the Arab world and at international Islamic conferences in order to authenticate India's Islamic credentials vis-à-vis Pakistan's.

The Muslim community of India—estimated to be 80 million in 1984 (Rahman 1986)—is probably the largest minority in the world. Despite its complex and highly differentiated structure in terms of socio-economic stratification, cultural, linguistic, and geographical dissimilarities, and diversities of political affiliations, the Muslim community has exhibited, over the years since the partition, an impressive unanimity of views on certain identity symbols derived either directly from their religious tradition or from the cultural history of the early British period. Among these symbols, Muslim Family Laws, the Urdu language, and the Muslim University of Aligarh have assumed considerable significance in the political and cultural life of Indian Muslims. It is primarily through these symbols that they are trying to preserve their distinctive Muslim identity in the wake of a secular constitutional framework and a communally-defined socio-political context.

The current wave of Islamic revivalism in India can be traced to four unrelated factors: (1) the failure of the old guard of Indian nationalism, both from the modern Muslim educated elite and from the traditional religious establishment of Deoband, to help solve the "communal" problems of the Indian Muslims in the post-independence era; (2) the 1971 Indo-Pakistan war and the break-up of Pakistan which finally brought home the truth to the Indian Muslims that they were on their own and could no longer look toward Pakistan for any possible help, even moral help; (3) the post-1973 oil boom and the subsequent migration of a large number of Muslims, especially from the south, to the countries of the Middle East, which brought substantial amounts of remittances to the families left behind; and, (4) the increasing militancy of the right wing Hindu revivalist movements, both cultural and political, whose slogans emphasized an integral relationship among "Hindi, Hindu, and Hindustan."

Unlike in Pakistan, the Islamic yearning in India finds expression in two types of movements. First, there are the more strictly religious movements such as the Tablighi Jama'at, Muslim Youth Movement (MYM), Students Islamic Movement (SIM), and the Jama'at-i-Islami. Within the community, their emphasis is on Islamization, i.e., to "purify" the beliefs and practices of their co-religionists in order to bring them closer to the teachings of Islamic orthodoxy as enunciated in the Qur'an and the *Sunnah* of the Prophet. With respect to the rest of Indian society, their activities are centered on the reassertion of Muslim religious rights and identity as represented by such issues as the Shah Banu case and the Babri Masjid case.

Second, groups like the Muslim League, the Muslim Union League, Itehad-ul-Muslimeen, Majlis-i-Mashawarat, the Muslim Majlis, Ta'amir-i-Millat, and the Islamic Council of

India, represent the increasing attempts of the Muslim political elites of various regions to find a focus for effective political mobilization and to enhance the economic autonomy of the Indian Muslim community.

With the exception of the Tablighi Jama'at which eschews politics and the "worldly" concerns of the community as a matter of policy, one can witness in recent years an increasing convergence of and cooperation between the purely religious revivalist movements on the one hand and the community-oriented groups on the other. The dominant thrust of their joint activities is building autonomous educational and economic institutions. Promotion of education is given the highest priority in the revivalist agenda. Funds from Middle East remittances and local sources are invested to create an educational infrastructure which combines Islamic and general education as well as technical education. The idea is to provide the Muslim youth with Islamic religious education which is not available in government schools and also to prepare them for gainful employment in various sectors of economy. The mushrooming of Muslim educational organizations in recent years is reminiscent of the great educational revival in Muslim India at the turn of the century. According to one estimate, educational organizations like the All India Muslim Educational Conference of Aligarh, All India Muslim Educational Society of Calicut, the *Al-almeen* Educational Society of Bangalore, the Hamdard Educational Society of New Delhi, the *Deeni T'alimi* Council of Lucknow, the Kerala Muslim Education Society, and dozens of other local organizations have established more than 500 educational institutions in recent years.

Islamic revivalism has also manifested itself in building autonomous economic institutions by the Muslims. Facing certain structural barriers in obtaining credit from the government controlled banks, many Muslim communities, especially in the south, are establishing their own cooperative banks, cooperative societies, *Bait-ul-Mals*, *zakat* funds, and interest-free (profit and loss sharing) credit societies in order to finance business initiatives by individual entrepreneurs as well as to invest in activities of collective economic benefits. In those cities of North India where there is a big concentration of Muslim artisans and craftsmen— such as Moradabad, Agra, Faizabad, Aligarh, Mirzapur, Varanasi, Lucknow, Tonk, and Jaipur—a large number of Muslim artisans' guilds and cooperative societies have been established both for generating credit and for marketing the products. As a result of these efforts—some of which owe their origin to the Bahuguna ministry in 1974—there is some evidence of the emergence of a Muslim petit bourgeoisie in these traditional centers of Muslim artisans. It is also interesting to note here that these are precisely the cities which have witnessed the worst and most violent communal riots in recent years (Mullick 1980).

The Islamic revival in India is not confined only to building parochial institutions and strengthening the religious moorings of the community. It is also related to efforts toward participating more fully in the political life of the country and sharing responsibility for its social progress and economic development. Only through participation in the national political process can Muslims face the problems and the discrimination to which they are subjected, bring them to national attention, and make them part of the national agenda. It was this realization that became the basis for the formation of the All India Muslim Majlis Mashawarat, a coalition of various Muslim political parties and religio-educational organizations.

At the level of ideas, the Indian Islamic scene also offers an interesting example of how a religio-political movement tends to articulate its ideology in two different political contexts. The case in point is that of the Jama'at-i-Islami of Pakistan and Jama'at-i-Islami of India. Founded in 1941 by Sayyid Abul A'la Maududi (d. 1979), one of the most prolific writers and systematic thinkers of the twentieth century Islam, the Jama'at propounded a program of action which clustered around four major points: (1) to elucidate the teachings of Islam with reference to the contemporary social, economic and political situation; (2) to create an organization of highly dedicated, disciplined, and righteous people to form an inner core of Islamic revival; (3) to initiate, at the level of civil society, changes that are conducive to the transformation of human society and (4) to establish an Islamic state which would implement the *Shariah* (Islamic law) and would direct and manage all affairs of the society in accordance with the Islamic scheme of things (Ahmad and Ansari 1979).

When the Jama'at became formally organized into two separate entities at the time of partition in 1947, the Pakistani Jama'at took the establishment of an Islamic state as the most important means for creating the order envisaged by Islam while the Indian Jama'at, finding itself in a secular constitutional framework, expunged all references to the goal of establishing an Islamic state from its program of action. According to the Jama'at-i-Islami of Pakistan, Islam does not admit any division between religious and public affairs. Hence, the Islamic state is not a matter of choice but a fundamental obligation of Islamic way of life. This state which is based on the political and legal sovereignty of God is to be governed by people of clear Islamic vision, commitment, and character (*ibidem*). The Jama'at-i-Islami of India, in contrast, had no choice but to abandon the idea of an Islamic state. It was, however, able to find a convenient justification for its revisionist ideology in the original critique of its founder, Sayyid Maududi, against the creation of Pakistan, i.e., the geographical delimitation of Islamic *umma* in the territorial confines of Pakistan would delay the growth and spread of Islam as a universal message. The Indian Jama'at has thus successfully avoided the question of establishing an Islamic state as it was articulated in its original constitution of 1941 by emphasizing the concept of the worldwide Islamic *umma* and the Indian Muslims being an integral part of it. According to the Two Nation theory of the Muslim League, the Muslims who chose to remain in India should be considered as members of the same Muslim nation which had established a separate homeland for itself, namely Pakistan. The Jama'at-i-Islami of India has sought to resolve this anomaly by disassociating the notion of the Muslim nation from the state of Pakistan and, instead, relating it to the concept of universal *ummah Islamiya*. This is not only a politically safe conceptualization but is also intended to provide the Indian Muslims with an enormous psychological sense of security and strength in their immediate environment of numerical and political weakness. What is most interesting to note is that while the Jama'at in Pakistan denounces secularism as "an evil force" and "the greatest threat to Islam" (*Asia*, October 1983), the Jama'at of India is equally vigorous in defending secularism as "a blessing" and as "a guarantee for a safe future for Islam" in India.

The only area where the Islamic revival in India has taken a radical political stance and where the slogans of the Islamic state have been publicly raised is Kashmir (Khayal 1985). This Muslim majority state exhibits an increasing convergence of political forces representing the old-style Islamic fundamentalists of the Jama'at-i-Islami, Islamic radicalists "following the line of Imam Khomeini," and secessionists of the People's League, Jammu and Kashmir Liberation Front, Mahaz-i-Azadi, and Liberation League (*Srinagar Times,* 5 May 1984). Both the Jama'at-i-Islami and Al-Jihad movement, a clandestine organization influenced by the ideology of the Iranian revolution, have used Islamic revivalist idioms to proclaim their rejections of the political status quo in Kashmir and to demand the right of self-determination for the Kashmiri Muslims (*Kasheer,* 26 November–2 December 1985, p. 5). While the Al-Jihad movement talks about the "Islamic revolution" in Kashmir as the "primary objective" of the organization and "the only way to liberate" Jammu and Kashmir (*Al-Jihad,* No. 34, 1985, p. 1), the Jama'at-i-Islami and its student wing believe that Islamically-inspired political mobilization of Kashmiri Muslims would culminate in the establishment of an Islamic state in Kashmir (*Aaeena,* Srinagar 15 August 1984, p. 6 and *Aftab,* Srinagar 4 December 1984, p. 7). The March 1987 election alliance between the National Conference and the Congress (I) in Kashmir was prompted, in part, by what Prime Minister Rajiv Gandhi described as "the dangers posed by the dark forces of religious fundamentalism" in the state (*Kasheer,* 2 March 1987, p. 6).

In the case of Bangladesh, Islamic revival can be studied within the context of the conflict between the religious and ethnic identities of Bengali Muslims. While Bangladesh was created on the basis of modern secular nationalist thought and a deep sense of a separate Bengali identity, it was nevertheless dependent upon the religious experience of the Bengalis (Ihtesham 1981). With the creation of Bangladesh, ethnicity apparently triumphed but not necessarily at the cost of a permanent damage to Islam. A brief look at the major trends in the political loyalties of the Bengali Muslims in the recent past indicates that the focal points of their collective identity have been in a state of constant tension. During the 1930s and 1940s, the Bengali Muslims identified themselves as "Muslims" and participated in the creation of a separate Muslim homeland along with the rest of the Indian Muslim community. During the 1950s and 1960s, the tension between their Islamic–Pakistani identity on the one hand and their Bengali identity on the other, expressed itself in controversies associated with the ideological character of the Pakistani state, federal-provincial relations, national language, and distribution of national resources. But even during the 1960s, the Bengali Muslims of East Pakistan did not see any inherent contradiction between their being good Muslims and their demand for cultural and linguistic autonomy. It was the West Pakistani elite who formulated the entire "East-West" issue in terms of necessary relationship between Islam, Urdu, and a strong center in Islamabad. Yet even through the late 1960s, Bengali Muslims were ambivalent and did not seem to be prepared to resolve the tension one way or the other. By the early 1970s, however, the ideals of Islamic solidarity as reflected in the Pakistani state had given way to Bengali nationalism. So, while Pakistan caused Islam to accommodate the notion of Muslim nationalism when it was conceptualized on the basis of the Two Nation theory, the emergence of Bangladesh caused Islam to accommodate ethnic nationalism as an equally Islamically legitimate political identity.

7

Buddhist Revivalism, Nationalism, and Politics in Modern Sri Lanka

K.M. DE SILVA

INTRODUCTION

In recent years the world has experienced the amazing resilience and forbidding tenacity of religious revivalism. Iran, the Islamic world in general, the Punjab, and the United States, all in turn have borne witness to the powerful political ferment of religious reassertion, a ferment so strong that the term used most often to describe it is fundamentalism. Yet fundamentalism is an ambiguous term. Since such clarity as it now has stems largely from its association with Islamic revivalism in all its varieties, its applicability to Buddhism and Sri Lanka poses formidable difficulties.

There are indeed some common features in all forms of modern religious revival, whether fundamentalist or merely resurgent. The first is the striking potential for politicization—socialist, radical, conservative, and reactionary. Indeed some scholars (Voll 1982: 282–291) see in Islamic fundamentalism a natural division into radical and traditional forms, a division which is a central element in the politicization and political impact of Buddhist revivalism in Sri Lanka. Secondly, most forms of revivalism spring from the grassroots of society, quite often from the mass of citizens, and are led by the alienated and frustrated, in brief, by those with a grievance against the powers that be in the political system. Thirdly, most forms of fundamentalism and religious revivalism are:

(N)ot religion as contemplation or a private experience of divinity; but religion as the essence of a culture, the binding brotherhood transcending material need. . . .

Thus speaks V.S. Naipaul (1984:12), turning his sceptical eye on the political face of religious fundamentalism in its current manifestation in the United States. He captures the essence of the problem with elegant lucidity.

The Buddhist commentarial tradition and its works of classification and analysis are similar to many of the scholastic traditions of other major world religions. To that extent, there is a "fundamentalist" strand in Buddhism. All religions have basic scriptures which preserve the message of the founder or founders of that religion. Buddhists generally consider the *Sutta Pitaka* to be the original message of the Buddha. Thus we may speak of the importance of the "word of the Buddha" and its special place in early Buddhist tradition. But the strand of fundamentalism in Buddhism was never a prominent one. Indeed, through a kind of "internal criticism," the Buddha's teachings on their own present a corrective against fundamentalism as found in its Islamic and Christian forms. The *Kalama Sutta*, for instance, urges the would-be Buddhist not to accept anything merely because it is found in the scriptures or sacred books, because it is a traditional belief, because it is the opinion shared by large numbers of people, or because of the prestige the teacher enjoys.

The Buddha refers to three kinds of thinkers: traditionalists who depended on scriptural tradition; rationalists who relied on logic and reason; and the experientialists whose strength lay in personal knowledge and meditative experience. He identified himself with the third group. This view provides a corrective to fundamentalism in religion, as does the strong pragmatist strand in Buddhism.

Fundamentalism in Islam and Christianity has at its core a "back to the inspired word of God" ideology in which the Koran and the Bible supply the all-sufficient guide for every condition and circumstance of life. The Buddhist tradition shifts the focus of attention from the *book* to the individual's *own* verification of the truth. The ultimate judge in these matters is thus the contemplative individual and his search for the truth in which the word of the Buddha and its inner meaning are but guides or, to change the metaphor, merely signposts on the path to wisdom.

Buddhist fundamentalism, then, is a contradiction in terms.

The more appropriate term is Buddhist revivalism, and that is what we use in this chapter.

The German Indologist, Heinz Bechert, observed (1972:130) that the Buddhist societies of South and Southeast Asia are "historically conscious" societies. The reference was to Sri Lanka, Burma, and Thailand, all of them old societies with long and troubled histories. Sri Lanka's is the oldest Buddhist society in the world, and the country carries a huge burden of historical memories that have powerfully affected the link between religion, nationalism, and politics in modern times.

Sri Lanka and Burma have had periods of subjection to Western rule while Thailand was spared that experience and its resulting humiliation. Burma's experience of Western rule and domination was substantially shorter than Sri Lanka's. Indeed, there are very few parts of Asia with a longer record of Western influence and control than Sri Lanka's coastal regions.

The legacy of that colonial experience common to both Sri Lanka and Burma is the confrontation between Buddhism and the intrusive Western culture, civilization, and Christian religion. In Sri Lanka that intrusion and its inevitable tensions with indigenous religions began in the middle of the sixteenth century with Portuguese influence and, later, Portuguese rule in the littoral. Portuguese colonialism was very much the child of the counter-reformation. If its emphasis on the principle of *cujus regio illius religio* perpetuated a central feature of the Sri Lankan political system—since the local link between state and religion had originated as long ago as the third century BC—the zealotry and harsh intolerance which characterized the imposition of Roman Catholicism on Sri Lanka were something new and unfamiliar. Sri Lankan society and civilization had seldom confused the obligation to encourage adherence to the national religion with the suppression of other faiths.

Sri Lanka provides one of the most striking illustrations of the truth of Anthony Low's comment (1973: 114) that "Empire was as much a religious as a political or economic or ideological problem." Christianity, Roman Catholic and Protestant, came to the island with the three Western powers—Portugal, Holland, and Great Britain—which from the mid-sixteenth century controlled parts of Sri Lanka (Portugal and Holland) or the whole of it (the British). As successive official religions, Roman Catholicism,

Calvinism, and Anglicanism each had a special relationship with the ruling power which provided it with prestige and authority. Converts to the prevailing orthodox version of Christianity—especially under the Portuguese and the Dutch—came to be treated as a privileged group. Severe restrictions and, often, penalties were imposed on the practice of the traditional religions—Buddhism, Hinduism, and Islam. These were severest under the Portuguese; the Dutch widened the scope of these restrictions to include Roman Catholicism as well (Arasaratnam 1958; Boxer 1958, 1960). Forced conversions increased the numbers of adherents of the official religion. Once again, these were more frequent and the pressure most persistent under the Portuguese.

The colonial state under Portuguese rule in Sri Lanka, the *Estado*, was a Roman Catholic one. The role of religion in the state system was no less significant under the Dutch, despite the fact that the maritime regions conquered by them from the Portuguese were administered by a commercial company, *Vereenidge Oost-Indische Compagnie* (V.O.C.) or the Dutch East India Company, as it was known. At the time of the conquest of the Dutch possessions in the island by the English in 1795–6, the majority of the citizens of these territories were classified as Protestant Christians. With the more relaxed outlook of the English, the superficiality of conversions to the Dutch Reformed Church was amply demonstrated when most people returned to their traditional faiths. Once the legal restrictions on the Roman Catholics were removed between 1806 and 1829, they emerged as the largest of the Christian groups in the island, a position they retain today. Conversions to Roman Catholicism under the Portuguese thus stood the rigorous test of persecution under the Dutch and the disdain and indifference of British officialdom.

The link between state and Christianity continued in the early years of British rule in the maritime regions of Sri Lanka, although the attitude to the Anglican Church—theoretically the established Church—was ambiguous at best. The problem of church–state relations became infinitely more complicated once the British gained control over the whole island between 1815 and 1818 with the conquest of the Kandyan kingdom, the last of the independent Sinhalese kingdoms.

With the absorption of the Kandyan kingdom, the British confronted one of the most perplexing and intricate problems they were called upon to handle in Sri Lanka: the definition of the state's relations with Buddhism (de Silva 1965:64–137). The undertaking given by the British in 1815, through the Kandyan Convention about the status of Buddhism was unambiguous: "The Religion of Boodhoo [sic] professed by the Chiefs and inhabitants of these Provinces is declared inviolable, and its Rites, Ministers, and Places of Worship are to be maintained and protected." When he sent a copy of the Convention to the Colonial Office, Governor Sir Robert Brownrigg explained to his superiors in Whitehall that he had been obliged to consent to "an article of guarantee couched in the most unqualified terms" because it was vitally important to quiet the apprehensions of the Kandyans about their religion. Only by making it clear that the fifth clause of the Convention would be scrupulously observed could the British gain the adherence of the *bhikkhus* (members of the Buddhist order, the *sangha*) and chiefs. These guarantees were softened considerably through a Proclamation of 11 November 1818 after the suppression of the Kandyan rebellion of 1817–18, but even so they were by no means repudiated. The fact is that these guarantees recognized the strength of the notion—which had become "an essential part of political thinking in Theravada Buddhist countries . . . "—"that the state has a responsibility for the religious institutions . . . ." (Bechert 1972:131).

From the outset, the attitude of the British rulers towards Buddhism was an ambiguous one, veering towards reluctant adherence to the letter of the treaty rather than to its spirit, and the requirement of positive support. As we shall presently see the link between Buddhism and the state was severed in the 1840s under Evangelical pressure. The historical significance of this could scarcely be exaggerated, for it marked the severance of the traditional bond between the state and the national religion that had lasted for over 2,000 years almost without interruption from the earliest days of the ancient Sinhalese kingdom. The withdrawal of the traditional patronage accorded to Buddhism, and the consequent loss of precedence and prestige, deeply disturbed and often excited the indignation of Sri Lanka's Buddhists.

The disestablishment of Buddhism was part of the common colonial heritage in Sri Lanka and Burma, even though the strength and durability of Christianity set Sri Lanka apart from Burma where Christianity was a minority religion in every sense of the word. Thailand, in contrast, escaped colonialism's grasp during the nineteenth century and the *sangha* there, far from being disestablished, was brought closer to the government. By the early twentieth century, the links between the monarchy, state, and Buddhism in Thailand had mobilized the

concept of nation and the older symbols of kingship and religion . . . as a safeguard against colonialism (Suksamran 1982:2).

King Wachirawut (1910–25), one of the principal monarchical ideologues of this traditional Theravada notion of a link between state and religion, sought to reaffirm and revitalize

the traditional Thai religio-political belief that the prosperity and progress of the nation is closely related to the prosperity of Buddhism, and that the religion and the king constitute the moral foundations of the nation—they are inseparable (*ibidem*).

Representatives of Buddhist interests in Sri Lanka refused to acquiesce in the unilateral decision to sever the link between the colonial state and Buddhism. Even if they were reconciled to the impossibility of the restoration of that link in its original form, they continued to insist that some institutional and legislative mechanism be devised to protect the property of Buddhist institutions from adverse consequences after the precipitate severance of the link in 1847. An assurance had been given in the 1840s and 1850s that some such institutional machinery and legislative mechanism would be established (de Silva 1965:64–137). It took nearly fifty years before this promise was met so pressure for its fulfillment was a principal Buddhist demand during the second half of the nineteenth century.

The British, for their part, would not go back to the *status quo ante* 1840 by restoring the formal link between the colonial state and Buddhism. But by the 1870s they began to see advantages to themselves in an accommodation with Buddhism that would be mutually beneficial. This pragmatic concession to political realities eventually resulted in a formula which provided for a special concern, if not a distinctive position for Buddhism in the colonial polity. This notable example of British pragmatism at work had unusually significant long-term effects. When pressure for the restoration of the link between Buddhism and the state continued after Sri Lanka achieved independence in 1948, Sri Lankan politicians adapted and elaborated upon this formula. It was embodied in the constitutions of 1972 and 1978 as a substitute for the elevation of Buddhism to the position of the state religion (de Silva 1981, 1986a, 1986b).

The second theme to be emphasized in this introductory section is the size of the Christian community and its powerful influence under British rule. Although Roman Catholics and Protestants in Sri Lanka together never numbered more than one-tenth of the population during the period of British rule and in the early years of independence, that proportion was significantly greater than in British India where Christians numbered only about two percent of the population. More important, the Sri Lankan Christians—nine-tenths of whom were Roman Catholics—were also, quite unlike their Indian counterparts, a privileged group with a larger number of persons of elite status than any other religious group in the country. Not surprisingly, therefore, the privileged position of the Christian minority became one of the most divisive issues in Sri Lankan politics in the years before independence and for over two decades thereafter.

The extent to which Sri Lanka's Buddhist movements were affected by their perception of Christian dominance is seldom considered in analyses of the nature of Buddhist revivalism in Sri Lanka, but it affected them in a number of ways: in the high priority given to eliminating sources of Christian privilege, especially in education; in the conscious and unconscious imitation of the techniques and mechanisms adopted and used by Christians to popularize their faith: and above all in the passionate quest for a redress of grievances accumulated over the many centuries of Christian domination, a quest which often served to distort perceptions and to heighten a sense of historic deprivation.

The peculiar demographic configuration resulting from the overwhelming numerical dominance of the Roman Catholics within the Christian community had a distorting effect on the relationship between the Christian minority and the rest of the Sri Lankan society. For much of the first half of the nineteenth century, the Roman Catholics had little influence on official policies and attitudes. The pace was set by the Protestants in general, and not necessarily the elite Anglican group. But over time the Roman Catholics asserted themselves and, with numbers very much on their side, the interaction between Christianity and the indigenous society was often very complex.

BUDDHISM IN SRI LANKA, 1870–1920:
RECOVERY, RESISTANCE, AND REHABILITATION

The fifty years after 1870 marked a period of religious ferment in the island, especially in its littoral regions. The revival of Buddhism, Hinduism, and Islam was contemporaneous with the vigorous recovery of Roman Catholicism. Unlike the recovery of Roman Catholicism in Sri Lanka and South Asia, the Buddhist revival and its impact on the country are now very familiar territory to scholars and students of Sri Lankan affairs (de Silva 1972, 1981; Malalgoda 1976; and Wickremeratne 1985). There are three significant aspects of the Buddhist revival in Sri Lanka: the recovery of self-confidence; the resistance to missionary enterprise; and the rehabilitation of the surviving institutional structures of Buddhism. The first and third of these followed upon the second, the successful challenge to a powerful but divided missionary movement which by the middle of the nineteenth century seemed poised to obliterate the traditional religions as comprehensively through peaceful means as the Dutch had done through repressive legislation and the social and economic pressure directed to that end by the governing commercial company and its officials.

The period reviewed here had two distinct phases with the governorship of Sir Arthur Gordon (1883–1890) forming a convenient dividing line. One sees a distinct duality in the processes of Buddhist recovery, between those who sought to and were indeed encouraged to operate within a non-political framework which accepted the preeminence of British rule, and the more radical forces which sought to politicize the movement and to assert the primacy of Buddhism within the Sri Lanka polity.

In the first phase the issues seemed more clearly focused than in the second, but that clarity came from a reluctance to be drawn into political activity. The emphasis was on resisting missionary activity and the use for this purpose of techniques and instruments of propaganda popularized by the missionaries themselves: public debates, tracts, pamphlets, newspapers, and of course the educational process through schools established and controlled by the Buddhists themselves (de Silva 1973; Malalgoda 1973, 1976). Pressure for restoring a link between Buddhist institutions and the state was a hardy perennial in the "politics" of Buddhist revival. There was pressure to restore at least part of the Buddhist heritage, whether the recognition of Vesak (the annual celebration of the birth and death dates of the Buddha) as a national holiday, or the protection of the archaeological treasures at Anuradhapura and Polonnaruwa from encroachment by non-Buddhists and by state institutions. The problem of education and the complications it posed to the state and to Buddhists illustrates the increasingly politicized revivalism. In the last quarter of the nineteenth century, the state's responsibility for the provision of educational facilities was clearly if somewhat narrowly defined; the state was to concentrate its energies on vernacular education. The major role in education was conceded to the Christian missions. Protestant missions initially reaped the benefits of this decision because of the superior organization of their educational programs. One of the most striking developments of this period was the phenomenal increase in the number of state-aided missionary schools, of which very soon a substantial number were Roman Catholic. There was correspondingly a steady reduction in the proportion of schools run by the government relative to the total number of Buddhist schools.

The challenge to the superiority of the Protestant missions in the field of education came first from the Roman Catholics, then from Buddhists, Hindus, and Muslims. The credit for the recovery of Roman Catholic self-respect and self-esteem in Sri Lanka was due, in large measure, to the efforts of the redoubtable apostolic delegate, Msgr. C. A. Bonjean, especially in the sphere of education. From 1860 on Bonjean conducted a purposeful campaign for a denominational system of education with a conscience-clause safeguarding the religious scruples of those who did not belong to the religious denomination which ran the school; a system of state grants in support of schools controlled by the various religious groups; and for the neutrality of the state in religious affairs. Bonjean believed that state neutrality would ensure a large measure of equality among the several (competing) Christian missions in their educational activities, as well as among the Buddhists and Hindus whose cause he chose to champion.

Indeed, the revival of the indigenous religions was inextricably bound up with the expansion of the Roman Catholics' own educational activities. Without quite ceasing to be the battleground of rival Christian groups—largely Protestant versus Roman Catholic, education became the focus of growing "nationalist" opposition to the Christian missions. The Roman Catholics came to control a stake in education which overshadowed that of the Protestants,

but by the 1880s the very effectiveness of their success brought
them into constant conflict with the increasingly militant Buddhists.
This confrontation between Roman Catholics and Buddhists
broke out into sporadic acts of violence. The first such episode
was in 1883 (de Silva 1981:345) in a suburb of Colombo. On that
occasion the aggressors were Roman Catholic and the victims
Buddhist. There were subsequent clashes in and around Colombo
where a resurgent Buddhist revival clashed with a well-entrenched
Roman Catholic minority. Unlike the clash in 1883, none of these
clashes resulted in loss of life but they spread to other parts of the
littoral. In the first decade of the twentieth century sectarian conflict
occurred in the town of Anuradhapura. In 1903 vigorous Buddhist
protests against encroachment by government institutions, non-
Buddhist traders, and religious organizations into the ruins of the
ancient city led to violence which included the destruction of a
recently established Catholic church.

The Buddhist revival of the last quarter of the nineteenth century
posed awkward difficulties for the colonial government in the
sensitive area of relations between state and religion. Opinions
expressed by the more articulate Buddhist activists of this period
ranged from a nostalgic adherence to the traditional position of
Buddhism in the Sri Lankan polity, to a realistic demand for some
institutional mechanism for supervising the properties of Buddhist
institutions, to the more controversial views of men like the
Anagarika Dharmapala (1864–1931) described as "visual[izing]
the restoration in modern Sri Lanka of an ideological state in
which the rulers.... would be totally identified with Buddhism"
(Wickremeratne 1985:218).

Because the Buddhist movement did not present demands for
constitutional or administrative reform—which constituted the
two main points of interest in the incipient formal political activity
of the day—Governors like Sir William Gregory (1872–77) and Sir
Arthur Gordon (1883–90) were inclined to regard it with sympathy
and sought an accommodation with it. Whatever the motive
behind this attitude there was no mistaking the advantage to the
Buddhist movement. A breakthrough came first over establishing
the crucial principle of the state's neutrality in religion. It came
with studied deliberation, and moved from one precedent to another.
Gordon went beyond this principle to accept that the state had a
special obligation towards Buddhism, a judicious patronage of
Buddhism which could easily be transformed into a special

responsibility towards that religion. With this acceptance the Buddhist breakthrough was consolidated (de Silva 1981).

The state's neutrality in religious affairs was asserted so often in the mid-1850s and thereafter was demonstrated in a manner at once open and vigorous by the disestablishment of the Anglican Church in 1881. With that the separation of church and state was very nearly complete. It soon became clear, however, that a total separation could not be made if for no more pressing reason than the burgeoning revival of Buddhism which brought with it a persistent demand for state assistance in the maintenance and supervision of Buddhist temporalities.

Gordon, reviving an initiative attempted by Gregory, broke through the barriers of bureaucratic inertia and missionary opposition to give the Buddhists some satisfaction over this long-standing grievance. This he did in 1888 through proposing an ordinance of considerable complexity. There was opposition to this bill both within and outside the Legislative Council, but Gordon steered it through to Colonial Office approval in 1889, though not without some concessions to his critics (*ibidem*: 347–49; Kemper 1984). The ordinance of 1889 was important because of its principles rather than for its impact on the problems it was devised to remedy. It proved to be too complicated and cumbersome, and it did not eliminate or even significantly reduce corruption and peculation among the trustees of these temporalities. The Buddhist movement regarded this state of affairs as an intolerable scandal, a blot on the reputation of Buddhism, and continued to agitate for stronger measures to eradicate it. In response to this pressure and in recognition of the validity of the charges levelled by Buddhist activists the colonial government in the early years of the twentieth century decided on fresh legislation to prevent, more effectively than in the past, misappropriation of trust property.

By this time, the Buddhist movement was pitching its demands higher. It wanted the state to assume direct responsibility for the administration of Buddhist temporalities and urged that there be, more positively, a formal link between the state and Buddhism. There were also more vigorous expressions of growing impatience with the Roman Catholic presence in places regarded as historic sites of Buddhism whether on the coast, or more passionately at Anuradhapura which—along with Polonnaruwa, the other ruined capital of ancient Sri Lanka—was now a prominent place of Buddhist pilgrimage. There was dissatisfaction over the establishment of government buildings in such locations. This bitterness triggered the Anuradhapura riots of 1903. The leader of the agitation at Anuradhapura was Harischandra Walisingha, an associate of Anagarika Dharmapala and a man who shared his views on the restoration of Buddhism to a place of primacy in the Sri Lankan polity.

The frequency of Buddhist-Roman Catholic clashes—in which the Buddhists became the more aggressive party—diminished in the early years of the twentieth century. But religious conflicts arising from attempts to restrict Buddhist processions continued to cause trouble, not so much from the Roman Catholics as from the Muslims. Attempts to reassert the traditional rights of Buddhists in this regard precipitated the Sinhalese-Muslim riots of 1915 (de Silva 1973:390–393; 1981:381–385).

By the turn of the century the Buddhist movement had gained great self-confidence. Its leaders turned their attention to what was regarded as one of the great social evils of the day, and one associated with the processes of westernization: intemperance. They confronted several contradictions. For one thing the manufacture and distribution of liquor—largely arrack—were controlled by Sinhalese capitalists, many if not most of whom were *karava* Christians (Roberts 1982). Secondly, there were also Buddhists of the same and other castes who had large investments in the liquor industry. Thirdly, to the British government, excise duties were a legitimate source of state revenue. While there was an increasing awareness of the evils attendant on excessive alcohol consumption, there was too a reluctance to endanger a valuable source of revenue by the wholehearted pursuit of temperance objectives. The Buddhist movement had no such inhibitions. By the turn of the century temperance activity was a vitally important facet of the religious revival. Some of the money that went into the support of temperance agitation came from wealth amassed in the liquor trade, conscience-money from Buddhists who thus repudiated a lucrative source of income. There were many prominent Buddhists in this category and it was often the case that they had inherited fortunes wholly or partly based on the arrack trade.

By the first decade of the twentieth century, the Buddhist temperance agitation had spread far and wide, especially in the Sinhalese areas of the Western and Southern Provinces. The response evoked was such that there were hopes that it would develop into a political movement. On occasion, temperance agitators indulged in criticism of the government by associating it with the evils of intemperance. Diatribes against foreign vices and Christian values were cleverly scaled down into more restrained and subtle criticisms of a "Christian" govenment. Although the temperance agitation gave added momentum to the Buddhist movement, it afforded only a tentative and astutely restrained introduction to formal political activity. The politicization of the movement seemed the logical and inevitable next step, but this was never taken. Equally significant, the mass grassroots support which the temperance agitation achieved came without the assistance or involvement of such political organizations as existed.

The colonial authorities in the island either ignored these political organizations or treated them with studied contempt, although many British administrators in Sri Lanka were perturbed by temperance agitation. Recognizing that the Buddhist revival in its newest manifestation through temperance agitation could, potentially, disturb the hitherto placid political life of the island, they viewed the proliferation of temperance societies with the utmost suspicion. In this mood of deep suspicion and fearing the worst they reacted to the Sinhalese-Muslim riots of 1915 with an unwarranted ferocity. They mistook these riots as the precursor of a more formidable political movement of opposition to the British.

Despite its persistently vehement anti-Christian tone, one of the most interesting features of the Buddhist revival of the late nineteenth and early twentieth centuries was the extent to which its organizational apparatus came to be modeled on that of the Protestant missionary societies. The Buddhist movement had absorbed Victorian Protestant ethical ideas, the missionaries' rules of sexual morality as regards the conduct they prescribed for the laity, their ideas on monogamous marriage and on divorce. These were woven into the framework of ethics which came to constitute part of the popular Buddhist culture. The result was that the Buddhist movement in the hands of men like the Anagarika Dharmapala was almost the mirror image of Protestant Christianity.

As regards Dharmapala himself, despite a pronounced antipathy to the Christian missions, his early education in the mission schools appears to have left its mark on him. His techniques of propaganda were modeled, consciously or unconsciously, on those used by the missionaries against the Buddhists, to the point where one might claim without much exaggeration that the new Buddhist revivalist was old missionary writ large. He was an unabashed advocate of a Sinhalese Buddhist domination of the island, and his propaganda bore a remarkable similarity to that of the great champion of Hindu resurgence in western India, Bal Gangadhar Tilak. Dharmapala lacked the political acumen and organizational skills of Tilak, and as a result his political program remained inchoate. His religious campaigns had a more compelling attraction for the rank and file of the Buddhist movement, though these too might have left a more indelible mark, had they not been the irregular forays which, in retrospect, they appeared to be. Nevertheless, his religious programs were never without political overtones.

One point needs special emphasis. Dharmapala grasped, as few of his contemporaries in Sri Lanka did, the significance of the emerging force of the reawakening of national consciousness in Asia. In his career as a Buddhist activist he never lost sight of the need to set the Buddhist revival in Sri Lanka within this wider framework. That he did not altogether succeed in the attempt is less important than the fact that the effort was regularly made. Part of this re-awakening process involved, almost inevitably, the downgrading of Christian missions in order to demonstrate that their work was not so much

the sharing of an inestimable treasure, but an unwarranted imposition from without, inseparably associated with the program of the Colonial powers .. (Neill 1964:250).

In this blend of religious fervor and national pride, of a sophisticated internationalism with a coarse insularity, Dharmapala served as a model for the Buddhist activists of post-independence Sri Lanka.

THE INTERWAR YEARS: THE BUDDHIST MOVEMENT AND THE SEARCH FOR THE CENTER

Buddhist activists of the interwar years either could not or chose not to direct the groundswell of religious enthusiasm generated through the temperance movement into an overtly political program. After the riots of 1915, Dharmapala's brand of Buddhist militancy receded to the background for over two decades. The reasons lie in the field of politics rather than in any decline of interest in Buddhism. Indeed in this same period a firmer institutional structure and a more complex organizational network was devised for the Buddhist movement.

The Buddhist Theosophical Society (BTS), which played a decisive role in the Buddhist revival of the last quarter of the nineteenth century, provided the nucleus of the Buddhist movement. Its main emphasis was on the organization and administration of Buddhist schools so new organizational machinery was required for social work and consciousness-raising. The model chosen for emulation was the Young Men's Christian Associations (YMCAs). As in contemporary Burma, Young Men's Buddhist Associations (YMBAs) were established, the first YMBA having been established in 1898. The YMBA units in the island were brought together in 1918 to form the All Ceylon Congress of Buddhist Associations which in 1940 changed its name to the All-Ceylon Buddhist Congress. By this time it was the most prominent, as well as the most articulate, of Buddhist pressure groups.

With the exponents of Buddhist "radicalism" unable to make much headway either as lay leaders or more directly in the political sphere, the leadership went by default to more conservative men. These reflected a new mood of caution and restraint. A crucial feature of this period was that the principal Sinhalese political leaders were also lay leaders of the Buddhist movement. F.R. Senanayake (1882–1925) and D.B. Jayatilaka (1868–1944), the two most prominent of these leaders, kept as tight a rein on their religious institutions as on the newly established Ceylon National Congress. They set the tone in Buddhist activism from about 1918 when, together with C.A. Hewavitharana, a brother of the Anagarika Dharmapala, they helped form the All Ceylon Congress of Buddhist Associations. F.R. Senanayake was dominant till his untimely death in the last week of December 1925. Thereafter Jayatilaka assumed that role until his own retirement in 1943. As a result of this change in both national mood and leadership of the Buddhist movement, the Christian minority and the Christian missions found themselves under less pressure for a reduction of their privileges and a diminution of their customary prominence in Sri Lanka's public life. Yet they themselves were more indecisive than they had been in the past. This noticeable lack of self-confidence ended their expansionist phase. Instead they adopted a policy of contraction and occasional retrenchment of their activities. In retrospect the interwar period was the most decisive phase in the reconciliation of the Christian minority—or at least its influential

Protestant sects—to a diminished role in public affairs, if not yet to a ready acceptance of Buddhist dominance in the Sri Lanka polity (de Silva 1986:63–83).

The Christian missions could no longer afford to dissipate their energies in sectarian disputes. Most of them recognized the need to close ranks in the face of a resurgent, if temporarily quiescent, Buddhism. The coordination of activity which characterized the Christian missions in this period did not, in general, encompass the Roman Catholics. The latter stood aloof from other Christian groups and resisted every attempt to promote Buddhist interests at the expense of the Christians. They became the strongest defenders of the *status quo*, especially in education, which brought them into regular conflict with the Buddhist movement.

The interwar years, especially after 1931, saw a rapid transformation in the country's constitutional status. Three successive increases in the size of the national legislature occurred in 1920, 1923–4, and, most significantly, in 1931 when universal suffrage was introduced for the first time in a British crown colony. The implementation of many recommendations of the 1928 Donoughmore Commission marks a crucial watershed in the country's political evolution towards self-government.

Politicians of the first (1931–1935) and second (1936–1947) State Councils, unlike their predecessors of the reformed Legislative Council of the 1920s became subject to the pressures of a democratic electorate. Buddhist pressure groups could now work through the electoral process to influence the election of supporters to the national legislature and this they proceeded to do. No Buddhist had been elected to the Legislative Council in the 1921 general election (when the electorate was around four percent of the population; all elected representatives of the Sinhalese were Christian. In the elections of 1924 the cry of "Buddhism in danger" was raised in a number of constituencies in which Buddhist candidates faced Christian opponents. It had the desired effect of ensuring the election of a large number of Buddhists. The situation changed dramatically with the introduction of universal suffrage. At the general election of 1931, the first under universal suffrage, 38 Sinhalese were returned to the national legislature of 50 elected members. Of these, 28 were Buddhists or claimed to be, since it was now politically advantageous to be a Buddhist. Thus the Buddhists had a clear majority in the legislature for the first time.

Sinhalese Buddhists were awakening to a new political awareness. The very nature of democratic "parliamentary" politics produced political groups which sought to build a political program emphasizing the traditional cultural and religious patterns associated with Buddhism. The most notable of these groups was S. W. R. D. Bandaranaike's Sinhala Maha Sabha. There are few doubts now about the viability of religio-cultural nationalism as a major political force or more importantly of its appeal to a democratic electorate. But in the 1930s its potentially divisive effect on a plural society such as Sri Lanka deterred the moderate leadership in the Board of Ministers—the duumvirate of D.B. Jayatilaka and D. S. Senanayake—from enthusiastically supporting such a program.

The Sinhala Maha Sabha had no such restraints. They urged a Sri Lankan polity essentially Buddhist *and* Sinhalese in orientation. In the late 1930s it took issue with the premier political organization of the nationalist elite, the Ceylon National Congress, on the latter's concept of a "Ceylonese" national entity wherein ethnic and religious minorities retained their distinctive identities while conceding to the Sinhalese Buddhist majority a primacy in the Sri Lankan polity. The Sinhala Maha Sabha would not accept this formulation and insisted on an assertion of Sinhalese-Buddhist preeminence in the most unmistakable terms.

The duumvirate drew a distinction between a government in which the Buddhists were a predominant influence and a Buddhist government. The former they preferred and were indeed committed to it because, quite unlike the latter, it was compatible with the requirements of their negotiations on the transfer of power as well as their personal inclinations. The latter they strongly opposed because of its political implications. In doing so they successfully postponed what now appears to have been an inevitable confrontation between the more militant sections of the Buddhist movement and those who were committed to the maintenance of a secular state, to a careful demarcation of the boundaries between state power and religion, and to a scrupulous observance of those boundaries. The moderating influence of D. B. Jayatilaka, the most prominent Buddhist leader of this period, is most significant in this regard because of his dual role as elder statesman in both political and religious affairs. D. S. Senanayake lacked his scholarship and was seen—and preferred to be seen—as a political leader rather than as a lay leader of the Buddhists. But his commitment to the principle of Sri Lanka as a secular state was even firmer than Jayatilaka's.

What the moderate leadership in the national legislature sought to do, and did successfully for a while, was to embark on a policy of redressing Buddhist grievances on a piecemeal basis through *ad hoc* measures. They sought a central position between the die-hard defenders of the *status quo* (who could rely on the support of the British administrators) and the proponents of a speedy implementation of a comprehensive program of change. Significantly the issue of Buddhist temporalities was settled very early. Ordinance 19 of 1931 conceded the demand which Buddhist opinion had made for several decades for state intervention in and supervision of the management of the properties of Buddhist institutions by trustees both lay and "clerical." Then again there was the ordinance approved by the State Council in 1942 for the preservation of the sacred city of Anuradhapura. It was based on sober necessity but it was also the culmination of a half century's pressure and agitation to protect the holy places of Buddhism from any further encroachment by state institutions, by public and commercial establishments, and by places of worship belonging to persons of other faiths, especially the Christians.

These, however, were relatively simple, straightforward issues which did not need complex legislation nor lengthy negotiations with parties likely to be adversely affected by the change. There were, in fact, no such parties. It was easier, therefore, to give Buddhist activists satisfaction over these long-standing grievances of theirs than it was to be over education policy. The educational issues involved were both complex and complicated by conflicting interests. There was also another significant difference: on education policy powerful vested interests put up a dogged defence of the *status quo*. The most striking feature of the schools system was precisely the one to which the Buddhists took strongest objection, namely the dominance of the Christian schools. That dominance was no longer as overwhelming as it had been in the last quarter of the nineteenth century, but the schools system had long been feared as a means of religious conversion.

These fears persisted and tended to divert attention away from the more constructive achievements of the missionaries in education. If the mission schools were seldom designed for purposes unrelated to evangelization, their students nevertheless did find new vistas of secular knowledge and their intellectual horizons were widened, quite often well beyond the scope intended for them by those who organised their education.

If the Buddhists opposed the existing schools system because of its dominance by the Christian minority, others opposed it for quite different reasons. To these latter the most objectionable feature of the educational system was its elitism. These emerging radical forces, joined after the mid–1930s by Marxist groups, combined with the Buddhist movement in seeking a reconstruction of the education system. They sought to make its benefits more accessible to all and to bring it under greater state supervision. The Buddhists, of course, were not as committed as were the radicals and Marxists, to a secularization of education, but this issue did not divide them from the forces of radicalism in their common struggle against the defenders of the *status quo* in education.

This alliance between Buddhists and radicals was an uneasy one, but it was strengthened by the emergence of a new force in Sri Lankan Buddhism. The political *bhikkhus* (Buddhist monks) began to play a conspicuous and very effective role in this struggle against Christian dominance over education. This phenomenon of politicized *bhikkhus* appeared for the first time in Sri Lanka in the 1930s nearly twenty years after its appearance in Burma (Sarkisyanz 1965; Smith 1965) and thirty years before its appearance in Thailand (Suskamran 1977, 1982). The theme of political *bhikkhus* and their impact on Sri Lanka's politics will be discussed later, but their intervention during the struggle over education reform helped to clarify some issues, such as the need for expanding educational opportunities, but caused confusion over others, such as the emerging link between radicalism and secularism. It also raised new issues such as the form and nature of the connection between state and religion in a multi-ethnic society. For all their radicalism these political *bhikkhus* were just as insistent as the traditional *bhikkhus* on the elevation of Buddhism to the status of the most visible symbol of Sri Lankan nationalism.

The debate over educational policy during the interwar years has been reviewed in several recent books (Sumathipala 1968:I &II; de Silva 1973, 1981, 1986). Three particular features are germane to the issue of religion and politics. First, the most far-reaching and controversial change was the proposal for a system of "free" (i.e., "free" of tuition fees) education at all levels: primary, secondary, and tertiary. Had "free" education been confined to the state schools there would have been little opposition from the denominational interests. But the state was anxious to extend the benefits of the new scheme to students in denominational schools. For this purpose the system of financial assistance provided to the latter schools by the state—its grants-in-aid—was to be revised. The state would continue to afford a maintenance grant and pay the salaries of teachers in the denominational schools, provided that they made "free" tuition available to their pupils. The Christian missions regarded these new financial arrangements as a potent threat to their interests. Only the elite mission schools could survive without grants-in-aid from the state. Absorption into the new scheme of "free" education posed the dangers of increased state interference and bureaucratic control.

Second, the determination of the Minister of Education, C. W. W. Kannangara, to carry through this policy of far-reaching reforms was resisted not merely by the Christians and the "denominational" interests, but also by influential colleagues in the Board of Ministers itself, the most notable of whom was D. S. Senanayake. The peculiar constitutional structure introduced in 1931 gave individual Ministers (or for that matter backbench legislators) much greater influence over the determination of policy and the introduction of legislation than under a cabinet system. Therefore Senanayake could warn his colleagues in the national legislature about the financial implications of these reforms and about the danger of precipitate changes damaging the existing education system rather than improving it. He also pointed out the potential damage to the whole fabric of relations among the country's various ethnic and religious groups. But he could not prevent the adoption of this legislation. Indeed while he opposed it in many ways, he did not vote against it. However, he softened its impact on the existing system by setting a time table for implementation of the reforms which was considerably longer than the advocates of these reforms had wanted. As a result, education remained an area of controversy.

Third, the opposition to the "free" education scheme came mainly from the Roman Catholics. It is ironic that the bitterness of the Buddhists against the injuries and neglect suffered at the hands of Christians during the period of western rule should be directed against the Roman Catholics rather than against the Protestants who, for the preceding two centuries, had enjoyed special favors from the imperial powers. That bitterness remained a factor in Sri Lankan politics until the early 1970s.

POLITICAL *BHIKKHUS* AND POLITICIZED BUDDHISM

Had the Sri Lankan political establishment been aware of developments in contemporary Burma they would have been better prepared to understand and cope with the phenomenon of political *bhikkhus* when it first appeared in Sri Lanka. But they were not. To be fair, not many in the Buddhist movement itself knew much about the links between nationalism and Buddhism in Burma where, to a greater extent than in Sri Lanka, the defence of Buddhism became a powerful form of nationalist expression. Among the leaders of Burmese Buddhism were nationalist *bhikkhus*, the earliest and most famous of whom was U. Ottama

who provided modernistic elitist aspirations for independence with roots in traditional folk Buddhism (Sarkisyanz 1978:92).

Inspired by Gandhi and his non-violent movement for India's independence, Ottama had returned from India in 1921 and sought to introduce these ideas to Burma. He was soon arrested by the British for his advocacy of independence for Burma and spent several years in jail for his nationalist agitation. Another political monk was U. Wisara who died in a Rangoon jail in 1929 after a hunger strike. Burmese Buddhist monks were involved in and indeed led the anti-Indian strikes of the 1930s. Saya San, an ex-monk and nationalist leader who led a revolt against the British, failed in this enterprise, and paid for his failure with his life.

Burma, as Sarkisyanz (*ibidem*: 87) points out was thus the

only Theravada Buddhist country to reach independence through a revolutionary mass movement during an acute crisis of traditional culture. Among her striking acculturation phenomena is Buddhist-Marxist syncretism.

Indeed, Buddhist philosophical terminology was used to explain Marxist terminology, but as in so many things there was a sharp contrast between the Burmese Marxists of the 1930s and their Sri Lankan counterparts who gloried in their overt secularism and inconoclastic attitudes. The latter generally kept aloof from the Buddhist movement.

The so-called *"political bhikkhus"* first appeared on the Sri Lankan scene in the late 1930s when a group of young radicalized *bhikkhus* from the Vidyalankara *pirivena* (educational institute attached to a temple) in Kelaniya near Colombo led an attack on Christian privileges in the educational system. They enthusiastically supported the reforms initiated by C. W. W. Kannangara. Such support also provided an opportunity to discredit the opponents of these educational reforms within the Board of Ministers and the national legislature, the most prominent of whom was D. S. Senanayake himself.

One of the radical *bhikkhus'* main contributions to this campaign was their consistent effort to enlarge the area of battle. They sought to displace the Sri Lanka political elite itself and not merely the Christian religious elite. While the lay leaders of the Buddhist movement were not inclined to reject their support in this latter battle, they were quite often greatly embarrassed at the attempt to widen the range of the conflict to include the Sri Lankan political elite, the emerging establishment led by D. S. Senanayake. Most of the leaders of the Vidyalankara pressure group had studied in India, often in Bengal, when they had been drawn into the political struggles of the subcontinent. Many had gone to India at the invitation of the Anagarika Dharmapala in order to aid his ultimately futile campaign to win a secure position for Buddhism in India. Thus these political *bhikkhus* were products of Dharmapala, the Buddhist nationalist *par excellence*.

Of the *bhikkhus* who went to India in the 1930s and 1940s five are of very substantial importance. They are: Udakandawala Saranankara (1902–1966), Naravila Dhammaratana (1900–1973), Hedipannala Pannaloka (1903–1953), Walpola Rahula (1907–), and Bambaranda Siri Sivali (1908–1985). All of them were associated with the Vidyalankara *pirivena*, and all of them imbibed in Bengal the current orthodoxies of Indian nationalism as well as Marxism. On their return they turned to political activity with the newly established Marxist party, the Lanka Sama Samaja Party, and other radical forces. All of them became prolific pamphleteers intent on introducing to a Sinhalese readership the radical and Marxist notions then current in India. Three of them became committed Marxists who saw no contradiction between their calling as *bhikkhus* and the advocacy of Marxist solutions to the country's problems: Udakandawela Saranankara, a founder-member of the Ceylon Communist Party; Naravila Dhammaratana; and, Hedipannala Pannaloka who became Vice-Principal of Vidyalankara in 1945.

The Vidyalankara *bhikkhus* won their political spurs in the notable success they achieved in their first real political struggle: the campaign to have the education proposals of the 1940s accepted by the State Council, the national legislature, in 1943–47. From its outset their campaign provoked considerable opposition from the more orthodox Buddhists, lay and clerical, even from those who otherwise welcomed their support in the struggle to reform the education system (Sumatipala 1968a, 1968b).

At issue was the role of the *bhikkhu*. Was he to renounce the world or seek to reform it? There was no doubt where the sympathies of the Vidyalankara *bhikkhus* lay on this issue. They would reform the world, not renounce it. Among their most prominent critics was D.S. Senanayake himself and J.R. Jayewardene, the present President of Sri Lanka, who was then a backbench member of the State Council for Kelaniya in which constituency the *pirivena* was located. They expressed deep concern at the political involvement of the *bhikkhus*, who breached what were regarded as age-old rules and practices governing the behavior of *bhikkhus*.

In response to mounting pressure from this quarter the *bhikkhus* compiled a statement clarifying their position. This document entitled "Bhikkhus and Politics" was approved unanimously by the teaching staff of their institution and released to the public on 13 February 1946. It was a defiant restatement of their position. The Vidyalankara declaration asserted that it was,

nothing but fitting for the *bhikkhus* to identify themselves with activities conducive to the welfare of the people—whether these activities were labelled politics or not—as long as this activity did not impede the religious life of the *bhikkhu*.

It went on to state,

... today *bhikkhus* by being engaged actively in education, rural re-construction, anti-crime campaigns, relief work, temperance work, social work and such other activities are taking part in politics. Such activity they noted was approved of by the society at large. It was only when certain vested interests were threatened that the cry '*bhikkhu* politics' was being raised.

The declaration added that,

It is incumbent on the *bhikkhu* not only to further the efforts directed towards the welfare of the country, but also to oppose such measures detrimental to the common good. For example, if any effort is made to obstruct the system of free education, the great boon which has been recently conferred on our people, it is the paramount duty of the *bhikkhu* not only to oppose all such efforts but also to endeavour to make it a permanent blessing.

They took their campaign to the country by launching a newspaper which first appeared on 14 March 1946 and came out thereafter at irregular intervals. They published books and pamphlets on a variety of themes congenial to their cause, both to propagate their views as well as to raise funds for their campaigns. The most significant publication to emerge from Vidyalankara at this juncture was a polemical work by Walpola Rahula written to demonstrate that the *bhikkhus* had always played an active role in the educational, cultural, social, and political life of the community. In support of this theme Rahula selected material from Buddhist scriptures and from the long history of Buddhism in Sri Lanka and India. The point was made that the *bhikkhu's* role had never been a narrowly defined personal quest for salvation, but rather a life of service to the community. That service assumed a variety of forms, including political, when circumstances warranted it. The modern *bhikkhu* who is aware of that heritage and aware too of the contemporary decline in national and religious affairs would regard it as his duty to arrest that decline. It was a powerful restatement in the Sri Lankan context of arguments that Burmese counterparts of Rahula had popularized in Burma. Significantly Rahula's book written in Sinhalese bore the title *Bhiksuvagē Urumaya* or the *Heritage of the Bhikkhu*. This latter was its title when it appeared nearly thirty years later in an expanded English version (Rahula 1974) by which time Rahula enjoyed an international reputation as a Buddhist scholar and as the author of an excellent introductory work on Buddhism (Rahula 1959).

What impact did the political *bhikkhus* of Vidyalankara have on the rapidly changing political scene of Sri Lanka at the transfer of power? Following their triumphant intervention in the "Free Education Bill" campaign they launched a political movement in earnest. They followed the Marxist parties in their opposition to the policies on the transfer of power adopted by the Board of Ministers under the leadership of D. S. Senanayake and in particular the acceptance of the status of a Dominion within the British Commonwealth for Sri Lanka. On 6 January 1947 at a meeting held in the Kelaniya temple a statement of policy which came to be called "The Kelaniya Declaration of Independence" was adopted. It affirmed (Rahula 1974:134) that,

We, the *Sangha* of Sri Lanka . . . do hereby declare and publish on behalf of the people that Sri Lanka claims its right to be a Free and Independent Sovereign State, that it has resolved to absolve itself from all allegiance to any other power, State or Crown, and that all political connection between it and any other state is hereby dissolved. . . .

During the election campaign of 1947 the radical *bhikkhu* stalwarts such as Walpola Rahula, Kalalalle Ananda Sagara, and Kotahene Pannakitti were prominent speakers at the meetings organized by the Marxist parties against the newly formed United National Party (UNP)—the successor to the Ceylon National Congress— led by D. S. Senanayake. Two seats in which they were most active were Kelaniya and Mirigama. The UNP candidates in these two seats, J. R. Jayewardene and D. S. Senanayke, had expressed very strong opposition to *bhikkhus* involving themselves in political activity. Both of them won their seats, the latter more easily than the former. The *bhikkhu* activists went on to claim that the sub- stantial increase in Marxist representation in the new Parliament owed much to their own campaigns. In so doing they greatly exaggerated the importance of their role in the election campaign. Unlike their Burmese counterparts Sri Lanka's Marxist-oriented political *bhikkhus* were a minority group. For all their eloquence and political vitality they were neither the spearhead of a nationalist movement nor of Sri Lankan radicalism. In campaigns to change social policies their pressure had been more effective, but their coordination of activity with the more orthodox groups in the Buddhist movement provided the really decisive factor.

The Vidyalankara *bhikkhus* provoked strong opposition from large sections of Buddhist activists, lay and clerical, because they gave every impression of becoming the nucleus of an alternative religious elite. For that reason they were regarded as a potential threat to the orthodox Buddhist establishment. The more orthodox Buddhist activists were acutely troubled by this.

A prominent and influential *bhikkhu*, Yagirala Pannanda, argued in 1947 in the Vesak number of the *Sinhala Baudhaya*, the foremost Sinhalese-Buddhist journal of the day, that Buddhism must be protected against the destructive forces represented by the political *bhikkhus*. He said,

In the past so many attempts had been made by impious *bhikkhus* to destroy the *sasana*. Their attempts, however, came to nought. Even those *bhikkhus* never considered the Buddha as an equal. They never stated that *nirvana* was unnecessary.

He accused them of seeking the destruction of Buddhism in order "to foster the religion of Karl Marx."

The All Ceylon Buddhist Congress, the leading lay Buddhist organization in the country, expressed some concern about *bhikkhu* participation in politics. Yet its criticisms were more circumspect than some of the orthodox *bhikkhus*. Thus at the 26th Annual Session of the Congress its President, Professor G. P. Malalasekera, expressed his disapprobation (reproduced in Sumathipala 1969: 68–69) with considerable restraint and in measured tones,

Some *bhikkhus* today maintain that they have entered the political field in order to eradicate social inequalities. . . . Some among them even state that in effecting such a revolution even the abrogation of certain precepts of *bhikkhus'* discipline is permissible. . . but these *bhikkhus* must realize that when they received ordination they took a vow pledging to maintain those precepts.

There was, unmistakably, a sting in this last sentence. Malalasekera was by now the leading lay Buddhist leader. A highly regarded Buddhist scholar, and one of the leading campaigners for education reform, his exposition and defence of the orthodox attitude on the role of the *bhikkhu* in society could not be as easily brushed aside as were the effusions of less erudite defenders of orthodoxy.

All this dovetailed neatly into the campaign waged by the political establishment of the day against the Marxists and the radical political *bhikkhus*. It also enabled D. S. Senanayake to divert attention away from the wider issue of a closer association of the new state with the Buddhist religion and the restoration of its traditional patronage along with the precedence and prestige that would accompany such patronage. He thwarted all efforts to abandon the concept of a secular state and the principle of the state's religious neutrality. He succeeded to the extent that in 1948, despite some Buddhist displeasure over the continued prestige and influence enjoyed by the Christians, there was little evidence of the religious turmoil and linguistic conflict which were to burst to the surface after 1956.

For nearly a decade after 1947 the issues which the Buddhist activists of the 1940s and the Vidyalankara *bhikkhus* had raised lay dormant, but not extinct. The confrontation between the advocates of a secular state and those who sought to underline the primacy of Buddhism and the Sinhalese in Sri Lanka—and sought also to redress the grievances of the Buddhists about the slights, injuries, harassment, justice denied, unfair treatment, and curtailment of historic privileges inflicted on them during three centuries of

western rule—was renewed in the mid-1950s. For beneath the
placid surface of the late 1940s and early 1950s religio-ethnic sentiments were gathering momentum and developing into a force
too powerful for the existing social and political institutions to
accommodate or absorb.

The radical and reformist zeal which one saw among the Vidyalankara *bhikkhus* in the 1940s appeared to have lost some of its
spirit in the years after independence. Some of the more active
and articulate *bhikkhus* who led the campaigns of the 1940s were
now absorbed in other ventures including the tedium of administration and teaching in *pirivenas* and other religious establishments.
Others had abandoned their robes. And yet others—most notably
Walpola Rahula—had left the island. Nevertheless, it would be
fair to say that the lamps that they had lit in their day were not
entirely extinguished. When the time came and the fuel of religious
enthusiasm was added once more, the flames roared back into
fervent life.

The year 1951 is crucial in this regard. It saw the establishment,
by S. W. R. D. Bandaranaike, of a new political party, the Sri Lanka
Freedom Party (SLFP), which vowed to espouse the Sinhalese-
Buddhist cause. Bandaranaike resigned his Cabinet position in
the first post-independence government and crossed over to the
opposition. The second event is less well known but just as significant. This was the publication in April that year of the resolutions
adopted at the 32nd annual sessions of the All Ceylon Buddhist
Congress under the Presidency of Professor G. P. Malalasekera.
The resolutions were published along with a memorandum, as a
pamphlet entitled *Buddhism and the State* and addressed to D. S.
Senanayake as Prime Minister of Sri Lanka.

The memorandum stressed the

... disappointment, almost resentment, growing among the Buddhists
with regard to the present position of Buddhism in [Sri Lanka] ... the
present Government ... is legally and morally bound to protect and
maintain Buddhism and Buddhist Institutions. The Buddhists feel,
however, that our present rulers have shown a marked reluctance to
acknowledge this fact ....

Although politicians were not

slow to exploit the unique position which [Sri Lanka] enjoys among the
nations of the world, by reason of her proud heritage of Buddhism and
Buddhist culture ... [they] have shown no earnest desire to rescue
Buddhism from the great state of neglect to which it has been deliberately

reduced by foreign rulers of this country nor to secure for the Buddhists the paramount position which should be theirs in the life of the nation.

This theme of restoring Buddhism to "the paramount position of prestige which rightfully belongs to it" was repeatedly emphasized in this document, and along with it the demand that the Buddhists "be given all-out assistance to rehabilitate themselves and to resuscitate their Institutions . . . ." The document asserted that "it is incumbent upon the present government of Free Lanka to protect and maintain Buddhism . . . ." and added that the "definite steps to be taken by Government to discharge this duty and obligation is a matter for decision after thorough investigation by a competent Commission."

The final paragraph of the memorandum made a specific request: that "measures be taken at once" to provide the Buddhist religion with an "autonomous constitution." "For this purpose," the memorandum went on

[the Buddhists] ask for the immediate enactment of an Act on lines similar to the Buddha Sasana Act 1312 B E (1950) of Burma, relevant extracts from which are given as an Appendix to this [document]. To secure the enactment and implementation of such an Act, they ask that a Buddha Sasana Department be forthwith established under a suitable Ministry by the Government of [Sri Lanka].

These demands were to be repeated with greater frequency but not with any greater clarity over the next few years. While the government in power tended to ignore them, they attracted wider and stronger support from the Buddhist public with each passing year.

In the first years after independence one of the major preoccupations of the government was the need to establish a sense of a Sri Lankan nationalism on territorial lines. D. S. Senanayake's government was intent on subordinating ethnic differences to the common goal of strengthening the foundations of nationhood through the establishment of a stable equilibrium of ethnic forces within Sri Lanka's polyethnic polity. He would give no satisfaction to the All Ceylon Buddhist Congress and, indeed, rejected its demands. He did not concede even the need for a Commission of Inquiry to report on the state of Buddhism. But politicized Buddhism was already a powerful force which would upset the equilibrium of forces he had set up. When Bandaranaike moved out of the government he was essentially seeking to exploit this new force and to give the Sinhalese-Buddhist majority, long dormant, a political institution for the fulfillment of their aspirations. This was the role of the SLFP.

From the outset the new party offered a home to those who rejected the concepts of a polyethnic polity, of a Sri Lankan nationalism, and of a secular state. It welcomed to its ranks *bhikkhu* activists, and some of them held positions of influence in its executive committee. Among them were Mapitigama Buddharakkhita, the *Viharadhipathi* (the chief *bhikkhu*) of the Kelaniya temple and an alumnus of the Vidyalankara *pirivena*, and *bhikkhu* Talpavila Silavamsa, who had a solid base of support in the city of Colombo.

There were other centers of support for the SLFP among the *bhikkhu* activists. There was, for instance, the Sri Lanka Vidyalaya located in Maradana in the heart of the city of Colombo. Its head, *bhikkhu* Baddegama Wimalawamsa, had great influence among and strong support from the Sinhalese traders and the people of the area. Wimalawamsa was one of the most effective activists for the Sinhalese Buddhist cause. As pamphleteer and propagandist there were few to equal him in the zeal with which he conducted his campaign against the Christian minority and its influence in public life, especially education. Equally important was the support he received from Buddhist activists in government departments who saw the Buddhist movement as a means of reducing if not undermining the continuing dominance of religious and ethnic minorities in the bureaucracy. Among his strongest supporters were *bhikkhu* Henpitagedera Piyananda, his vice-principal at the Sri Lanka Vidyalaya, and *bhikkhu* Davamottāvē Amarawamsa soon to earn a reputation for his platform oratory and highly emotive speeches.

These were by no means the traditional, conventional *bhikkhus* who would renounce the world, but men who were just as intent on reform as the Vidyalankara *bhikkhus*, although their inspiration was not Marxist or even socialist. Their political ideology was at best a vague populism, mixed with a deep and abiding nationalist fervor. They were themselves avowedly political *bhikkhus*, but their activity was less vulnerable to the criticisms directed at the Marxist *bhikkhus* because it was rooted securely within the conventional tradition of twentieth century Buddhist activity in Sri Lanka. They worked in tandem with the lay Buddhist leadership. They also cooperated with the Vidyalankara *bhikkhus*.

The mid-1950s marked a critically important watershed in the recent history of the island. Against the background of the 1956 *Buddha Jayanthi*, the worldwide celebration of the 2500th anniversary of the death of the Buddha, an intense religious fervor became the catalyst of a populist nationalism whose explosive effect was derived from its interconnection with language. Language became the basis of nationalism, and this metamorphosis of nationalism affected both the Sinhalese and Tamil populations (de Silva 1986). Buddhism and Sinhala were so closely intertwined that it was impossible to treat either in isolation.

The crucial significance of the renewed link between language and religion was that Buddhist activism, which had been directed so far against the privileged position enjoyed by Christianity and Christians in Sri Lanka, shifted its attention to the Tamil minority as well. Buddhist activists and the Sinhalese-educated intelligentsia had seldom, in the recent past, exerted influence on a national scale. They felt that they had been unjustly excluded by the English-educated elite from a share of power commensurate with their numbers, and that rewarding careers were closed to them by the pervasive dominance of English as the language of administration. Concentrating their attention on the superior educational advantages enjoyed by the Tamil minority, they set their sights on the demolition of the language settlement arrived at in 1943–44 wherein both Sinhalese and Tamil should eventually replace English as the national languages. They insisted instead on its replacement by Sinhalese alone, or "Sinhala only." the slogan which became the main plank of the coalition of parties set up by Bandaranaike in anticipation of the general election of 1956. (Bandaranaike himself had strongly endorsed the language settlement of 1943/44.) The "Sinhala only" campaign brought together a formidable array of forces which had hitherto been unable to unite in support of a common program: the Sinhalese school teachers, *Ayurvedic* physicians (practitioners of traditional herbal medicine), Sinhalese writers, and above all the *bhikkhus*.

The *Buddha Jayanthi* offered Buddhist activists the opportunity to appeal over the heads of the government and the political establishment of the day directly to the people for a restoration of the traditional convergence of nation, religion, and ethnicity—Sri Lanka, Buddhist, and Sinhalese. However, the government and its critics were both confronted with the political implications of a situation in which the advantages of this convergence in sustaining a national identity and self-confidence were negated by the vocal dissent of minority groups who rejected this facile identification of sectional—albeit majoritarian—with national interests.

The crux of the problem was that while the political system had accommodated itself since 1931 to the fact of Buddhist-Sinhalese predominance, other areas of public life lagged far behind in adjusting to that demographic reality. In the mid-1950s a concern for the enhancement of the status of Buddhism became, in the millenarian atmosphere of the *Buddha Jayanthi*, the prime determinant of a process of change whose main thrust was the extension of the predominance established by Sinhalese Buddhists in the political sphere into all other areas of activity.

The religious confrontation that erupted was between the Buddhists and the Christian minority, in particular the Roman Catholics. Because of linkage between the linguistic nationalism of the Sinhalese and the religious resurgence associated with *Buddha Jayanthi*, it was inevitable that there would be intensified pressure for a closer association of the state with Buddhism and even for the declaration of Buddhism to be the state religion. It was inevitable, too, that the Christian minority would come under attack because of Buddhist displeasure at the continued prestigious and influential position enjoyed by the Christians, the most conspicuous evidence of which lay in the impressive network of mission schools.

Buddhism and Buddhist interests had suffered and, in the perception of Buddhist activists, still suffered from the decline in status and prestige that had occurred under colonial rule. The drive by the Buddhist leadership—a coalition of laymen and *bhikkhus*—to restore their influence in national life commensurate with the historic position of Buddhism in the Sri Lankan polity gathered momentum in the mid-1950s. The position of Buddhism and Buddhists had improved quite substantially at independence and in the first decade after independence, but these advances only served to emphasize the narrowing gap between aspiration and achievement and give it an exaggerated salience.

Thus, despite the education reforms introduced in the 1940s, Christian schools still retained much of the prestige and influence they had enjoyed in the days of British rule. The preponderance of Christians and other minorities, especially in the higher bureaucracy, in the professions and in public life, remained intact although under increasing pressure. While the balance was shifting in favor of the Sinhalese Buddhists, this process was inevitably slow and seemed to be in measured stages. As a result, Buddhist activists were not only thoroughly dissatisfied with the pace at which the balance was shifting, but they also attributed the survival of the privileged position of the Christian and other minorities to the existing rules of the political game. These were presumed to bear a heavy and unfair bias against the Sinhalese Buddhists.

There was at this time a common belief in all Buddhist countries that this anniversary [would] initiate a great revival of Buddhism throughout the world when the Buddhist way of life and thus universal peace [would] prevail (Smith 1965:158).

Buddhism was being hailed as a new political force. The Sri Lankan Buddhist leadership found, to their great disappointment, that U Nu's Burma had emerged as the pre-eminent Theravada Buddhist country. The Buddha Sasana Council and the Ministry of Religious Affairs established by U Nu in 1950 were regarded by the All Ceylon Buddhist Congress as appropriate models for Sri Lanka. In 1951 U Nu had decided on a more ambitious project which would emphasize the international aspects of the Buddhist revival: the decision to convene the Sixth Great Buddhist Council. Convened in 1954 and lasting for two years, the council established Rangoon as the center of international Buddhism by attracting Buddhists from all over the world as well as from the five main Theravada Buddhist nations: Burma, Thailand, Sri Lanka, Laos, and Cambodia. It completed its work in May 1956, by which time Buddhism appeared to have established itself as the new global political force U Nu had envisaged:

The significance of the Sixth Great Buddhist Council had many dimensions, national and international, religious and political, its implications for government, Sangha, and laity were profound. The council's greatest significance was symbolic; it dramatized in unforgettable fashion the government's commitment to the promotion of Buddhism, which was regarded as an essential component of the Burmese national identity.... The council, while it had special meaning for the Burmese, was also a demonstration of the solidarity of all Theravada Buddhists and, in a more limited way, of all Buddhists. In one sense it was an expression of resurgent Buddhist Asia in the post-colonial era, pointing to the spiritual bankruptcy of the Christian West in failing to achieve world peace and reasserting the validity, vitality, and relevance of the message of the Buddha.... (*ibidem*: 165).

In Sri Lanka, S. W. R. D. Bandaranaike successfully channelled the religious discontent of the Buddhists into an election campaign which swept the UNP out of office in April 1956. His decisive victory was a significant turning point in Sri Lanka's history, for it represented the rejection of a Sri Lankan nationalism based on an acceptance of pluralism as an essential feature of the democratic system which D. S. Senanayake had striven to nurture. Instead the SLFP victory introduced a more populist nationalism which was at the same time fundamentally divisive in its impact on the country because it was unmistakably Sinhalese and Buddhist in content.

In this emphasis on the presumed unifying influence of the religion, culture, and language of the majority, there was a remarkable similarity in objective, methods, and even political styles between Sri Lanka under Bandaranaike (and later on under his wife and successor Sirimavo Bandaranaike) and Burma under U Nu. The latter desperately sought to use Burmese culture and the Buddhist religion to give the fragile post-colonial Burmese state a sense of national unity. On a long term basis this program was not unviable, but the time span required had to be measured in decades, not years. For example, Thailand had taken a century or more to work out a similar policy of national unification of Tai states and the hill peoples within a Thai-Buddhist polity. There these policies achieved remarkable success, although some resistance has come from Thailand's minute Malay-Muslim minority. In Burma the resistance to these policies was wider, stronger, and seemingly more effective in thwarting them. Thus U Nu's program failed to create national unity. In Sri Lanka a metamorphosis of nationalism through its link with language brought the Sinhalese majority into conflict with the indigenous Tamils of Sri Lanka. Thus an existing unity was weakened if not effectively undermined.

A second point is equally significant: the essence of this program in Burma and Thailand is an assimilationist policy. In Sri Lanka, on the other hand, none of the governments since independence has deliberately or consistently followed assimilationist policies. The attitude to the minorities has been embodied in a mixture of policies, sometimes emphasizing national integration, and sometimes recognizing the advantages of a pluralist approach. Above all, there has been no conscious attempt to assimilate the diverse minority groups in the country to the dominant Sinhalese-Buddhist culture.

The minorities, needless to say, did not see things in this light.

While they did enjoy an advantageous, if no longer a privileged, position in public life, this was threatened by the pervasive influence of a politicized Buddhism. For the achievement-oriented Tamil minority, the implications of the change in language policy forced upon them in 1956 seemed starkly clear. The Tamils were disproportionately represented in public sector employment as clerks, teachers, and technicians, and in the professional services as doctors and engineers as well. Their advantageous position in government employment had been a point of contention and division in politics since the 1930s. Tamils saw the change in language policy as heralding the beginnings of hard times ahead in the competition for such employment. The rules of the game had been changed to their disadvantage. More importantly, once language became the determinant of ethnic identity, as it did with the tranformation of nationalism to a linguistic form, there were fears that the new dominance conferred on the Sinhalese language would lead to an erosion of the Tamils' ethnic identity through a policy of assimilation. While these fears were exaggerated, when not imaginary, the fact remains that the Tamils were extremely vulnerable and exceptionally sensitive to changes in language policy.

The language conflict in Sri Lanka was generated by the campaign to elevate Sinhalese to the status of the national language. The "Sinhala only" campaign brought together a formidable array of forces which had hitherto been unable to unite in support of a common program: the Sinhalese school teachers, *ayurvedic* physicians, Sinhalese writers, and the *bhikkhus*. On 4 September 1954, a meeting convened by the Sinhalese teachers' association, the Lanka Jatika Guru Sangamaya, brought these groups together in a federation of five associations (including representatives of peasants) which came to be called the Pancha Maha Bala Mandalaya. Significantly the chairmanship was offered to and taken by *bhikkhu* Kiriwattuduwe Pragnasara, then principal of the Vidyalankara *pirivena*.

The Pancha Maha Bala Mandalaya was formed to intensify pressure on the government, but the full force of its fury first fell on the two Marxist parties, the Trotskyist Lanka Sama Samaja Party and the Communist Party. Both at that time were firm supporters of a policy of parity of status for Sinhalese and Tamil as national languages. These two parties had introduced a motion in Parliament calling for a declaration on these lines. To explain their stand to the public they organized two public meetings at the Colombo Town

Hall, on 12 October 1955 by the Communist Party and on 16 October 1955 by the Lanka Sama Samaja Party. Both meetings were broken up by "Sinhala only" activists led by *bhikkhus*. In a bid to mobilize even wider support for the cause of Sinhalese as the sole national language, the Pancha Maha Bala Mandalaya organized an oath-taking ceremony at Anuradhapura on 29 October 1955. The symbolism of choosing Anuradhapura as a site for this ceremony was unmistakable. A motorcade that left from Colombo proved to be triumphal procession and the ceremony, presided over by *bhikkhu* Kiriwattuduve Prajnasara, attracted an enormous crowd.

In the meantime a committee of inquiry appointed by the All Ceylon Buddhist Congress—since the government had refused to accede to its appeal for an official Commission of Inquiry—was preparing a major report on the state of Buddhism in the country. Its membership was composed of prominent laymen, including Professors G. P. Malalasekera and L. H. Mettananada, and a number of eminent *bhikkhus*. The committee visited 37 urban centres on the island and was greeted everywhere with processions and large public meetings at which the presumed parlous plight of the Buddhist religion was the main theme of speakers from the area and of the spokesmen of the committee.

The committee issued a pathbreaking report on 4 February 1956. It contained a detailed exposition of the disadvantageous position of Buddhism in the mid-twentieth century and blamed this on the cumulative effect of several centuries of foreign rule and on the neglect of post-independence governments of Sri Lanka. The demands it made on behalf of the Buddhists were an expansion of those which were presented for the consideration of D. S. Senanayake's government in 1951 through the previously mentioned memorandum entitled "Buddhism and the State." The report made it abundantly clear that the redress of Buddhist grievances was a matter of the utmost urgency and that this could only be achieved through the political process. The fact that the report was presented to the "People of Lanka" and not to the government signified that in the committee's view the solutions lay with the former. The English version of the report carried the title: *The Betrayal of Buddhism*.

How the two major parties, the UNP and the SLFP, both hurriedly changed their language policy to one endorsing "Sinhalese only" has been dealt with in detail in many monographs (Wriggins 1960; Smith 1966; Kearney 1967). The SLFP's change of policy came at its annual conference held on the 17 December 1955 at Nittambuva in S. W. R. D. Bandaranaike's own electorate. The resolution calling for the change was moved by *bhikkhu* Mapitigama Buddharakkita. The UNP's *volte-face* on language, which was less principled than that of its main rival, came at its annual conference on 18 February 1956. Parliament was dissolved almost immediately thereafter.

To fight the elections the SLFP had formed a coalition with a number of smaller political groups. This coalition, the Mahajana Eksath Peramuna (MEP) or the People's United Front, issued its election manifesto on 7 March 1956. It pledged to make Sinhalese the sole official language of the country, to accept the recommendations of the Buddhist Committee of Inquiry, to foster *ayurveda*, and to reorganize the system of education in accordance with national culture.

The MEP coalition scored a decisive victory but found the implementation of its policies a matter of the utmost difficulty. This was especially so with regard to language. The government sought to reconcile its commitment to make Sinhalese the sole national language with the political and indeed practical necessity to make some concession to the Tamils about use of their language. Extremists on both sides made this reconciliation almost impossible to achieve. Every concession to the Tamils was fought bitterly by forces within the SLFP, led by *bhikkhus*, as well as by opponents of the government such as the UNP. Thus the years 1956 to 1958 were years of turmoil and violence, of race riots, and of long periods of rule under emergency regulations as the armed services and police sought to restore law and order.

Much of the agitation against compromise on language policy and against concessions to the Tamils was organized and led by *bhikkhus*. The most notable of such instances occurred on 9 April 1958 when a group of *bhikkhus* led by *bhikkhu* Baddegama Wimalawamsa organized a sit-in on the lawn of the Prime Minister's private residence in Colombo. They compelled Bandaranaike to tear up an agreement he had reached on language policy and related matters with S. J. V. Chelvanayakam, the leader of the principal Tamil political organization, the Federal party.

Two major concessions were made to the Buddhist activists at this time. First there was the creation of a Ministry of Cultural Affairs in 1956 with N. Q. Dias, a senior civil servant as its first Director. His background of militant Buddhist activism set the tone of this new administrative unit. Amid attempts to promote indigenous literature and the traditional arts and crafts its major concern was the promotion of Buddhist activities.

Second, there was the elevation of the two principal seats of Buddhist learning, Vidyodaya and Vidyalankara, to university status in 1958. This decision was an *ad hoc* one, in the nature of a quick, if not desperate, remedy for an impossible situation; it was a classic instance of how not to establish universities. The two new universities began as non-residential arts colleges teaching in Sinhalese. This format was devised to accommodate the large number of students taught in Sinhalese who found the doors of the University of Ceylon closed to them. More to the point, the government's original intention had been to confer university status only on the Vidyalankara *pirivena* in recognition and appreciation of its long record of service in the cause of establishing a socialist government. But the government yielded to pressure from the sister institution, Vidyodaya, founded two years earlier (1873) than Vidyalankara, when it appealed for similar status.

By this time the triumph of linguistic nationalism had made pressure for stronger links between Buddhism and the state, and for a corresponding reduction if not eradication of Christian influence in the Sri Lankan polity, almost irresistible. There was pressure for the elevation of Buddhism to the status of the state religion. In 1951 the All Ceylon Buddhist Congress had gone on record as saying that:

A great deal of deliberate confusion has been caused by the cry that the Buddhists want their religion made the State Religion in Free Lanka. The Buddhists have made no such demand. But the Buddhists do want legislative enactments enabling them to manage their own affairs efficiently, by means of an autonomous constitution with legal sanctions. This concession is made by them because they recognize the undesirability of the Government, as at present constituted, controlling the internal affairs of any religion.

There were no such inhibitions in 1956–57 about the elevation of Buddhism to the status of the state religion. But the new government was entangled in the coils of the language crisis of 1956–58 and preferred to delay consideration of this controversial issue. The means adopted for this delay was the appointment of the Commission on Buddhist Affairs that the All Ceylon Buddhist Congress had asked for 1951. The publication of the report of the Committee of Inquiry appointed by that Congress in 1955–56 and which report the government was pledged, through its election manifesto, to adopt and implement complicated the issue. Was not this new Commission superfluous?

When in February 1957, Bandaranaike proceeded to appoint the Buddha Sasana Commission, its terms of reference were seen to be much wider than that of its non-official predecessor of 1955–56. The term *sasana* itself was one of infinite flexibility, encompassing as it did the institutions, property, including monastic lands, and the rights, obligations, duties, and privileges of the *bhikkhus*. The term generally covered doctrine as well, but that seemed less relevant on this occasion. It had something to satisfy everybody. Advocates of institutional reform could regard it as a mandate for modernization; adherents of the *status quo* were encouraged to believe that there was no inherent incompatibility between their interests and those of the reformers.

The task before this Commission of *bhikkhus* and prominent Buddhist laymen was the unenviable one of reconciling these obviously conflicting interests. Looked at in historical perspective, it was an attempt by Buddhist activists to identify the issues and set out the solutions to the problems that emerged from the severance of the historic link between the state and the Buddhist religion which had occurred in 1840. British Governors of the colony and Sri Lankan politicians alike had come up against the impossibility of returning to the *status quo ante* 1840. For all of them the religious neutrality of the state was a major premise of their thinking; and for many of them— including men like Gregory and Gordon, D. B. Jayatilaka and D. S. Senanayake—the only adjustment possible to the reality of the burdens of past history and perceptions of national destiny seen as an unfolding of Buddhism's inextricable links with the state was a pragmatic recognition of a special status for Buddhism. To recognize this officially was worrisome enough in the context of those times; to spell out a policy of action based on this was as problematic in the years 1948–56 as it had been under British rule.

The terms of reference of the Buddha Sasana Commission included an examination of the implications of the general but vague principle of "according Buddhism its rightful place in the country," to which the government was publicly committed. The commission was also asked to make recommendations for a reform of the *sangha*, one of the crucially important aspects of the ruler's, and the state's, traditional responsibility in regard to the maintenance and protection of Buddhism as the national religion, and one which had been in abeyance since the fall of the Kandyan kingdom in 1815.

Bandaranaike was all too aware of the legal and constitutional difficulties to be overcome if Buddhism were to be declared the state religion. Above all there was the formidable hurdle of section 29(2)(c) of the Soulbury constitution which laid down that no law enacted by Parliament shall: " . . . confer on persons of any community or religion any privilege or advantage which is not conferred on persons of other communities or religions." It was not at all certain that the legislature would provide the special majority required for the purpose of overcoming this constitutional obstacle (de Silva 1986:196–206).

There was a greater chance of success with regard to the quest for increasing state control over the schools, in brief, for a completion of the work begun in the 1940s. There was strong support for this reform from Marxists and other left-wing groups. But the Minister of Education, W. Dahanayake, was adamantly opposed to a takeover of the schools run by the Christian missions and other religious organizations. And he had the support of the Prime Minister. It would appear that the government was not at all eager to get embroiled in another contentious issue while coping with the political fallout from the language crisis.

The report of the Buddha Sasana Commission was submitted to the Prime Minister in mid-1959, and was scheduled for publication in November 1959. There was the prospect that with its publication the government would turn, at last, to the intricacies of defining and implementing a policy on the "rightful place" of Buddhism, and to grasp the nettles of Buddhist institutional reform.

Meanwhile, the coalition of forces that had done so much to ensure the success of Bandaranaike's own political career was crumbling in the face of the turmoil that had characterized the last two years (1958–59) of his administration. *Bhikkhu* activists were divided on a number of issues, and some of the most prominent among them—most notably the *viharadhipathi* of the Kelaniya temple, Mapitigama Buddharakkhita—had become controversial because of their involvement in the ugly factionalism within the Sri Lanka Freedom Party (SLFP), of which they were such visible members. Many of them were also prominent opponents of some of the key social and economic reforms initiated by the left-wing members of Bandaranaike's cabinet. Among the most noteworthy of these acts of opposition was the agitation against the *Paddy Lands Acts of 1958*. The *bhikkhu* opposition came principally from the two powerful and wealthy chapters of Malwatta and Asgiriya, the principal representatives of monastic landlordism.

The Buddhist public was now becoming increasingly soured by the spectacle of *bhikkhus* engaging in political infighting, and using pressure for financial gain—for kinsfolk if not for themselves—through influence-peddling and the manipulation of bids for contracts. Their disgust turned into deep consternation and shock when the Prime Minister was assassinated on 26 September 1959. The chief figure in the conspiracy to murder Bandaranaike was Mapitigama Buddharakkhita, and the actual shooting was done by another *bhikkhu*, a close associate of the principal conspirator (Weeramantry 1960). The assassination of Bandaranaike, with its powerful mix of political and sordid commercial motives, not to mention other even more distressing factors, underlined as nothing else did so sharply before or after, the perils involved in *bhikkhus* engaging in partisan politics. Never again did *bhikkhus* wield the same influence in political affairs as they did in the years from 1943 to 1959.

The assassination of Bandaranaike provided reformist groups among Buddhist activists the opportunity they so desparately needed to initiate moves for far-reaching institutional reforms in the *sangha*. But the political confusion that followed on his death prevented any such initiatives. There was nobody to provide the leadership in converting the upsurge of revulsion against the excesses of the political *bhikkhus* into a constructive program of reform of the *sangha*. In the meantime, political energies were devoted to coping with the shattering impact of Bandaranaike's death, and with the two general elections of March and July 1960. The first was indecisive; the second brought to power Bandaranaike's widow at the head of a revived SLFP which, having excluded or expelled all those in any way linked to the political forces within that party associated with Mapitigama Buddharakkhita, had regrouped under her leadership.

THE TRIUMPH OF ORTHODOXY, 1960–1986

At the time of Mrs. Bandaranaike's accession to power, the process of elite displacement, Christian by Buddhist, had stopped well short of the objectives set by Buddhist activists in the mid-1950s. That considerable progress had been made towards the achievement of these objectives during this period only rendered the survival of Christian privilege all the less palatable to them. The struggle for supremacy was now resumed. Her husband, despite his anxiety to restore to Buddhism the traditional patronage accorded to it in precolonial times, had not been able to do much in this sphere. Furthermore, he was unwilling to endorse the demand that Buddhism be raised to the status of the state religion. As the new leader of the SLFP, Sirimavo Bandaranaike pressed ahead in seeking to satisfy some of the demands of Buddhist activists. She was intent on continuing the language policy initiated by her husband, and on doing so with as few concessions to the Tamil minority as possible. She displayed greater rigidity on principles underlying this policy than he may have showed had he been alive. Even more important, although the times seemed hardly propitious to enlarge the area of conflict from language to religion and education as well, she embarked on this two-pronged attack on behalf of Sinhalese-Buddhist interests. At that stage, she was not interested in the complicated question of the status of Buddhism in the Sri Lankan polity. It was education reform and the completion of the changes initiated in the 1940s that absorbed her attention.

When the recommendations of the Buddha Sasana Commission were published late in 1959 they proved to be immediately controversial. Among their principal recommendations was the creation of an incorporated body with wide powers over the *sangha*, empowered to regulate entry into it, the education and residence of *bhikkhus*; it would also regulate their engagement in social and political activities, and in paid employment outside of their temples. That body was also empowered to adjudicate disputes between *bhikkhus*, especially on matters relating to succession as heads of temples, issues on which *bhikkhus* generally sought legal remedies in the civil courts. Among the other areas of activity which would come under its purview were: the collection of funds for temples and Buddhist activity, the building of temples, and publications relating to Buddhism.

There were immediate objections by the two chapters of the prestigious Siyam *nikaya* (sect). (The political *bhikkhus* were too discredited to voice any opposition to these recommendations.) There was considerable irony in this opposition because historically the Siyam *nikaya* has had close links with secular authorities since its inception in the eighteenth century. It generally has sought centralized control over the order of *bhikkhus*—which was more or less what the Buddha Sasana Commission report recommended—while the other *nikayas* had emerged into autonomous existence partly because there was no central authority to regulate the affairs of the *sangha* in colonial times (Malalgoda 1976).

Despite the opposition from the more orthodox *bhikkhus*, the new government could well have embarked on an implementation of a program of Buddhist institutional reform. Mrs. Bandaranaike's government had other priorities, and it turned to these. Thus, a historic opportunity was missed for lack of the political will to seize it and exploit its potential for a purification of the *sangha*. Had these recommendations of Buddhist institutional reform been implemented, Sri Lanka may well have today resembled Burma and Thailand as regards the status of Buddhism in relation to the state.

To move into educational reform was certain to engender conflict with the Roman Catholics in Sri Lanka. But Mrs. Bandaranaike calculated on support from the Marxist and other left-wing groups in Parliament and outside it which may not have shown the same enthusiasm for moves to make Buddhism the state religion. For them state control over education was a desirable end in itself. The Buddhists, however, saw it as nothing less than the restoration of a balance that had been tilted far too much in favor of Christians. Indeed, they looked upon the existing education system as the fountainhead of Christian privilege in Sri Lanka. The fact that the vast bulk of the mission schools were almost totally dependent on governmental finances, while in all but a handful of them the great majority of students were Buddhists, made it nearly impossible to meet the arguments of the advocates of state control. There was also a more practical consideration, namely that once the schools came under greater state control, Buddhist influence on the education process at the grassroots level would be greatly increased.

Once again the Roman Catholics led the resistance and bore the brunt of the attack. Though all the religious groups—including the Hindus and Muslims, not to mention the Buddhists themselves—were affected by the decision to bring the state-aided secondary schools directly under state control, the Roman Catholics were the biggest losers. Most of the state-aided denominational schools accepted the painful decision to be absorbed by the state.

A few big schools, mostly Roman Catholic institutions in the urban areas, decided to retain their independence by becoming private institutions without the benefit of state aid. Deprived by law of the right to levy fees from their students, they maintained their precarious existence under very severe financial handicaps. The long drawn-out Buddhist agitation for state control over education had, at last, achieved its goal.

The constitution afforded no protection to the minorities against these changes in language and education policy, though they were adversely affected by both. The constitutional obstacle of Section 29(2)(b) would not operate as long as legislation was so framed that there might be a restriction in fact but not in legal form, and the restriction was made applicable to all sections of the community and not to a specific group. (When S. W. R. D. Bandaranaike's *Official Language Act*—the "Sinhala only" Act, as it came to be called—was introduced in the House of Representatives in 1956, the Speaker ruled that it was not a constitutional amendment and therefore required only a simple majority.) Nevertheless, the proven ineffectiveness of Section 29(2)(b) as a check on encroachments on the interests of the minorities did not make that clause any more palatable to Buddhist activists. They continued to view it as an ostentatious concession to minority influence, and persisted in an agitation for its elimination. Indeed, one of the reasons given, in 1972, for the adoption of an autochthonous constitution rather than a revision of the Soulbury constitution was the need to eliminate this clause (de Silva 1986).

An abortive *coup d'état* in 1962, in which the leaders were Roman Catholic and Protestant officers of the army, navy, and police, further strained relations between Roman Catholics and the government (Horowitz 1980). It had the double effect of reviving the sagging popularity of the government and, more important, of providing justification for the government to support Buddhist activists in their campaigns against the Roman Catholics and their influence in public life—in the bureaucracy, in the armed services and police, and the national press.

In the course of Mrs. Bandaranaike's first (1960–64) term of office, the primacy of Buddhism and Buddhists in Sri Lanka's political system and public life had become a reality. Significantly, this achievement was won by the lay Buddhist leadership within the government and governing party, and outside it, and not by the *bhikkhus* whose contribution was by now very limited. This is not surprising considering that the *sangha* in general had suffered a grievous loss of prestige after the assassination of S. W. R. D. Bandaranaike and had not sufficiently recovered to return to their pre-1959 level of political activism and influence. The absence of *bhikkhus* on political platforms in the election campaigns of March and July 1960 was notable. With the abortive *coup d'état* of 1962, *bhikkhu* involvement in politics resumed, but the scale of this involvement was limited and its nature was different in that the *bhikkhus* were no longer almost entirely on the side of the SLFP and its allies. The *bhikkhus* themselves were sharply divided with some of the most prominent political *bhikkhus* of the mid-1950s having switched their political loyalties to the UNP. Thus during the election campaign of 1965 many erstwhile supporters of the SLFP appeared on UNP platforms, *bhikkhus* Talpavila Silavamsa and Devamottāwē Amarawamsa being the most notable among them.

The issues in dispute in this realignment of political forces demonstrate the ambiguities inherent in the uneasy and shifting relationship between Buddhist activists and the new government. In the response to the recommendations of the Buddha Sasana Commission there were contradictory impulses between the lay and *bhikkhu* leadership of Buddhist revivalism. On the whole the lay leaders responded more positively to these proposals but, bereft of a strong political leadership committed to their implementation, they lacked the nerve to campaign for them in the face of almost unanimous opposition from the *bhikkhus*. As Kemper (1984:423) points out

Even the prospect of making Buddhism once again the state religion in the cases of Sri Lanka and Burma has met with unlikely opposition.

He quotes Tambiah's well-known work on Thai Buddhism (Tambiah 1976:527) which observes that

The allied problem faced by Sri Lanka and Burma is that restoration of religion by the state implies also the attempted regulation of the *sangha* by the state, a proposition that is antithetical to those monastic interests that have come to cherish the decentralized autonomy resulting from [the] British dis-establishment of religion.

Opposition to these recommendations was by no means limited to the *bhikkhus* of the Siyam *nikaya*. The main recommendations of the report were those that concerned them, and there was no attempt to consider implementation of these important ones. But an attempt was made to introduce some minor changes which would have affected the *bhikkhus'* opportunities of employment and conditions of service in the state sector. These provoked so hostile a response from *bhikkhus* readily identified as political *bhikkhus* that they were immediately withdrawn, thus demonstrating that the political *bhikkhus* had not entirely lost their influence in secular affairs. Some of the more vocal were permanently alienated from the SLFP as a political party.

As for governments and political leaders within governments and the major national parties alike, the interaction with Buddhist activists, both lay and *bhikkhu*, called for great delicacy in practice because all parties were subject to conflicting pressures. Thus the SLFP's coalition with the Trotskyist LSSP negotiated in 1964 provoked determined opposition from many of the political *bhikkhus*. Some of the latter were quite prepared to tolerate the association as long as the gains of the immediate past were not threatened, and the new Marxist allies of the SLFP scrupulously refrained from providing evidence of any such threats like advocating generally a secular state. However, not all their critics were won over or even mollified by this seemingly accommodative attitude. The coalition government's attempts to bring the national press under state control led to a renewal of fears that Marxist influence within the government was inherently erosive of Buddhist values. The SLFP sought to break the press monopoly held by Lake House which was politically associated with the UNP. Buddhist activists found common cause with the SLFP because they perceived that institution to be a stronghold, perhaps an impregnable stronghold, of Christian influence on public life. The LSSP shared the SLFP's attitude to Lake House, and enthusiastically joined forces in a bid to bring it under state control. But this combination provoked the opposition of a section of the political *bhikkhus*. The opposition to this assault on the freedom of the press was led by the UNP. Their campaign attracted wide support from Buddhist activists increasingly disillusioned with the SLFP for its drift to the left and its association with the Marxists.

The ambiguities in the relationship between Buddhist activism and the government were revealed afresh with the return of the UNP to power in 1965 at the head of a coalition. In opposition the UNP had opposed the educational reforms of 1960–61; in office there was no relaxation of the restrictive measures against which they had voted nor any concessions to the Roman Catholics despite the pledge given to them in 1967. In a bid to prove its *bona fides* on Buddhism the government introduced the *poya* holiday scheme under which the weekly holiday was based on the phases of the moon while the traditional Christian sabbath holiday was abandoned. Once more U Nu's Burma was the model emulated, with total disregard of the impact this variable weekend scheme would have on Sri Lanka's trade links with the rest of the world. Despite the acquiescence of the church hierarchy, the *poya* holiday also caused some discontent among the Roman Catholics—without any compensating support from the Buddhists for the UNP.

Bhikkhus in politics and political agitation was a constant factor during this period. A young *bhikkhu* was killed when the police opened fire on a mob demonstrating against the government's proposals to introduce regulations to give effect to the *Tamil Language (Special Provisions) Act* which Bandaranaike had piloted through Parliament in 1958. The SLFP under his wife's leadership now opposed these regulations when the new government introduced them in January 1966. Buddhist activists were divided politically, but a large section of them opposed the regulations and demonstrated against them in their customary role of articulators of the people's aspirations. But even if this particular form of involvement in politics received approbation from a large section of the Buddhist public, other instances of political *bhikkhus*' patent disregard of the tolerable limits of partisanship served to revive public memories of the excesses committed by the political *bhikkhus* during S. W. R. D. Bandaranaike's government. In April 1966 a leading political *bhikkhu* linked with the SLFP, *bhikkhu* Henpitagedera Gnanasiha, was closely associated on charges of complicity in an attempted *coup d'état*. He was indeed one of the prime suspects, and was kept in remand for three years until, after a lengthy trial, he was found not guilty of the charges laid against him by the state prosecution.

The government sought to construct a new policy for interacting with the Buddhists. Its central feature was an attempt to emphasize the role of what may be termed the "establishment" in the *sangha* since the two *Mahanayakes* (chief *bhikkhus*) of the Malvatta and Asgiriya chapters of the prestigious Siyam *nikaya* were acknowledged as the principal articulators of Buddhist opinion and as the most authentic representatives of Buddhist interests. In doing so the government took a calculated risk, but there was the undoubted advantage that the Buddhist public widely accepted these *bhikkhus*

in this role. Because of their political non-partisanship this acceptability rose in inverse proportion to the perceptible decline in the
prestige of the politically active *bhikkhus*. Their leadership also
had a formal and institutional aspect to which the political *bhikkhus*
could never aspire. The two *Mahanayakes* were traditionally the
highest dignitaries of the *sangha*, and the government's new policy
buttressed their status with some tangible and some intangible
forms of official recognition. The tangible forms included two
official residences for them in Colombo. The intangible but very
conspicuous form included the practice for all appointees to
important official positions in government and public life to
make ceremonial courtesy calls on the two *Mahanayakes* in
Kandy.

Also in 1966–67 in a gesture symbolic of a decline in status, the
two *pirivena* universities of Vidyalankara and Vidyodaya were
converted into secular institutions and the *bhikkhus* who headed
these two universities lost much of their patronage and influence.
Beneath this avowed design to secularise these institutions there
was also much irony and individual ambivalence in the choice of
the first Vice-Chancellor of Vidyodaya under the new dispensation:
it was none other than Walpola Rahula himself. His appointment
had nothing to do with his former connection with the Vidyalankara
pirivena but rather recognized his established reputation as an
internationally known Buddhist scholar.

The official recognition and buttressing of the orthodox *bhikkhus*
did not inhibit their interventions on political issues whenever an
occasion demanded. Throughout the last two decades *bhikkhus*,
including the two *Mahanayakes* of Malwatta and Asgiriya, have
generally taken a strong stand on issues involving relations between
the Sinhalese majority and the Tamil minority, a stand which
reflected an instinctive ethnic nationalism. There was general
opposition to the concessions on language made to the Tamils in
January 1966, but on this occasion the *bhikkhus* played a subsidiary
role in a campaign led by politicians and laymen. The opposition
was stronger among the political *bhikkhus* of old than among the
more orthodox *bhikkhus*. The latter's opposition to the District
Councils scheme envisaged by the government in 1967–68, however, was more vocal because it coincided with concessions made
at about the same time to the Indian residents in Sri Lanka about
their citizenship rights (de Silva 1986a, 1986b).

The defeat of the UNP in 1970 and the return to power of Mrs.

Bandaranaike at the head of the center-left United Front coalition saw the final phase of the process of redressing Buddhist grievances and establishing Buddhist ascendency in the Sri Lanka polity. This phase was all the more significant because it marked support from the principal Marxist parties of the country which had hitherto taken pride in their commitment to the concept of a secular state. Chapter II of the new Republican Constitution of 1972 read as follows:

The Republic of Sri Lanka shall give to Buddhism the foremost place and accordingly it shall be the duty of the state to protect and foster Buddhism while assuring to all religions the rights guaranteed by section 18(1)(d).

When this proposal was originally made in the Constituent Assembly, its supporters included the UNP. This time there was no opposition from the Christians in general or the Roman Catholics in particular. When the 1972 constitution was replaced by a new one in 1978 under a UNP regime this same principle was incorporated in the second republic's constitutional structure. The innovation introduced in 1972 came at a time when the Roman Catholics had themselves embarked on a change of policy in their attitude to other religions. Their increasing acceptance of religious pluralism followed the Vatican Council of 1963–65. All this occurred without any attempt by the SLFP to change its education policy. The government, nevertheless, had become much more conciliatory to the Roman Catholics. Equally significant, when the UNP government which came to power in 1977 adopted the second Republican Constitution in 1978, the status—the "foremost place"—accorded to Buddhism in the previous constitution remained unchanged.

In both instances the governments concerned were operating within the limits of the formula adopted in the late nineteenth century by the British governors Gregory and Gordon. The formula proved to be elastic enough to cope with the pressures of Buddhist activists for a special status for Buddhism within the Sri Lankan polity, without making it the state religion on the Burmese model. However, in 1978 the All Ceylon Buddhist Congress urged that Buddhism be declared "the State Religion." Other less prestigious, if not less vocal, Buddhist organizations proposed that the constitution should require that the President, the Executive Head of State, be a Buddhist. Nonetheless the UNP government remained content with sustaining the primacy of Buddhism in the Sri Lankan polity at the level established in 1972, a primacy which fell distinctly short of declaring Buddhism to be the state religion.

Even so the position accorded to Buddhism was much too elevated for some non-Buddhists who complained that the constitution "does not prohibit the state from providing munificent financial assistance to Buddhism or from placing restrictions on the efforts of other religious organizations to propagate their faith" (cited in Wilson 1980:103). The opposition to this special status for Buddhism no longer came from the Roman Catholics on religious grounds, but from spokesmen for the Tamil minority on political grounds.

By the late 1970s Buddhist activism was but a shadow of the vibrant force it had been in the previous seventy years. Partly this was because many of the issues about which Buddhist activists had agitated had been settled very much in their favor. But there is no mistaking the fact that the euphoria and the idealism of the early post-independence era had worn thin over the years. This is as true of Sri Lanka as it is of Ne Win's Burma.

While most of the gains of the mid-1950s and early 1960s were securely established, others were lost. The most conspicuous example of the latter was the abandonment of the *poya* holiday scheme in July 1971. Almost all political parties supportd this move, including the UNP itself which had originally introduced it. Significantly, the SLFP-led coalition took the initiative in a matter in which a section of the *sangha* and some lay Buddhist activists adamantly opposed the abandonment of a change for which they had had long agitated. Again the concessions on the levying of fees which had been promised the Roman Catholics by the then UNP-led coalition in 1967 came at last in 1978. With them, too, came wider government financial assistance to schools run by religious minorities, largely Christian, but also Hindu and Islamic, all of which lay outside the national schools structure. This bold initiative aroused surprisingly little opposition from Buddhist activists. The apparent equanimity with which Buddhist activists accepted this decision is evidence of changed priorities in their demands and their perception of the potential harm to the interests of Buddhists and Sinhalese. The Roman Catholics, it would appear, have ceased to be regarded as a threat to Buddhist interests—perhaps because the former have accepted the political reality of Buddhist dominance in Sri Lanka.

Despite all the contradictory impulses set off by Buddhist activists, they have seldom engaged in any direct pressure for assimilating minorities into the Sinhalese-Buddhist culture. In this Sri Lanka provides a contrast to the other major Theravada Buddhist states of Burma and Thailand. Buddhist activism in Sri Lanka has been directed mainly at the redress of historic grievances, at the restoration of a status and prestige lost in the years of imperial rule, and at the purposeful elimination of the privileges of a powerful Christian minority, rather than at any efforts at assimilation of minorities. Unlike Burma or Thailand, there has been very little Buddhist missionary activity in Sri Lanka among minority groups. Even where a minority is eminently vulnerable to such proselytization, as for example the depressed caste Tamil plantation workers, Roman Catholics rather than the more powerful Buddhist *sangha* have been resourceful in converting them. For a time efforts were made by Buddhist groups to convert some of the depressed caste Tamils in the northern province to Buddhism, but such efforts were neither consistent nor persistent. Nor did they yield any substantial results by way of large numbers of converts.

Marxist and radical critics of Buddhist activism often question the latter's lack of interest in social issues, in particular the condition of the urban poor. Buddhist activism is charged with a lack of social conscience. There is some justice in this criticism, but again this lack of interest in social issues is more apparent than real. Buddhist pressure groups working through successive governments have been among the most powerful influences in the establishment and consolidation of a welfare state in Sri Lanka. A pragmatic improvisation of a Buddhist state ethos preserved in the Buddhist historical tradition and in Buddhist folklore with its compassionate concern for the poor has accomplished this task even though the linkage between Buddhist activist thought and socialist doctrine in all its forms was never as strong in Sri Lanka as it was in Burma.

Buddhist activism in Sri Lanka is currently concentrating its energies on Sri Lanka's ethnic tensions. This has had the effect of reviving the importance of the two Mahanayakes of Malwatta and Asgiriya both as officially accepted representatives of Buddhist opinion and as legitimate guardians of Sinhalese interests. But they were only the most prominent among other representatives of the *sangha* invited to participate at an All Party Conference in January 1984 to devise measures for a resolution of the island's ethnic problems. The other *bhikkhu* representatives included the heads of the Amarapura and Ramanna *nikaya* (sects) and of small splinter groups of the Siyam *nikaya* itself—the Kotte and Kalyani factions.

Two other Buddhist *bhikkhu* leaders attended as well. The first was *bhikkhu* Madihe Pannasiha, of the Amarapura *nikaya*, who enjoys national recognition as a politically independent but pugnacious upholder of Sinhalese interests. The other special invitee was none other than Walpola Rahula who now lives mostly in Europe but still enjoys a national status. Because of his position as an internationally renowned scholar, he has been Chancellor of Kelaniya University since 1979. In the aftermath of the ethnic disturbances of July 1983 and at the All Party Conference, he became at once the principal spokesman for Buddhist interests as well as an eloquent voice for moderation and pragmatism. In one of the rich ironies that characterize Sri Lankan politics, his presence and prominence owe much to the persuasive skills of President Jayewardene, his erstwhile opponent of the 1940s when Rahula was the most articulate of political *bhikkhus* while Jayewardene was a rising star of the post-independence political establishment.

The All Party Conference had other significant participants representing all the major religious groups in the country. Hindus, Muslims, and above all the Christians were invited to send delegates, and did so. It was indicative of how far Sri Lanka had travelled since the religious controversies of the past generation. The Buddhists were secure enough in their position of primacy in the Sri Lankan polity to have Roman Catholic and Protestant Christian representatives engaged in an essentially political process of developing a national consensus on the current ethnic crisis.

Significantly no representatives of religious groups were invited to join the second of the major national conferences on Sri Lanka's ethnic conflicts. Held in Colombo in 1986 it was deliberately restricted to political parties and was called the Political Parties' Conference. It provides a telling demonstration of the point that the country's political leadership often disregards the wishes of the *bhikkhus* when the national interest, as that leadership perceives it, or political expediency, demands. The *bhikkhus* enjoy considerable influence among the people as representatives of Sinhalese Buddhist opinion and, where a threat to the gains of the post-independence period is perceived, they become, in all but name, a permanent second chamber in Sri Lankan politics. The *bhikkhus* wield a significant if not always decisive influence over national policy.

Radicalized political *bhikkhus* are no longer the revitalizing force they were in the 1930s and 1940s. Each passing decade brought a few into prominence but they have tended to be individuals working in isolation rather members of a cohesive group. The lay leaders of the Buddhist movement demonstrate this same loss of vitality. A number of overlapping explanatory reasons have manifested themselves since the 1960s but the most significant of these is the success they, and their predecessors, achieved in securing the adoption by successive governments of the causes they espoused. The institutional framework built over the last century has survived but it, too, seems bereft of much sense of purpose and idealism. The only purpose it now serves is to defend Sinhalese Buddhist interests against the threat posed—as they see it—by Tamil forces within and outside the country.

8

Rural Violence in South Asia: Straws in the Wind

Kuldeep Mathur

A salient feature of recent political developments in South Asia is the frequent occurrence of incidents of collective violence. These incidents result from conflicts between religious groups, ethnic communities, or caste agglomerations and threaten the existence and cohesion of a country. Though most of the sources of conflict are embedded in the historical development of each society, these conflicts have sharpened in the recent past after the state began to intervene more actively to initiate social and economic changes. Concealed within the manifested forms of conflict are factors that emanate from the consequences of state development policy and initiatives for change.

In most countries of the region benefits of development are distributed unevenly. For various reasons, sharp inequalities among individuals and communities have emerged and regions within the country are also marked by widening disparities. Unbalanced development has politicized civil relations and led to violence in the form of interregional conflicts and ethnic rivalries.

Thus, while it is important to examine the outward manifestations of violence and investigate religious revivalism or social and cultural divisions among ethnic communities, it is equally important to recognize that development strategies that foster unequal social and economic relationships in turn become breeding grounds for communal, ethnic, or religious rivalries. One such development strategy that holds the key to rural peace and stability is the one connected with the green revolution. This chapter examines the occurrence of rural violence as a consequence of the rural transformation taking place in India. It is assumed that sharpening conflicts in the countryside will have far-reaching consequences on the kinds of policies which any state can pursue for development. The pattern of such policies in turn will influence social and economic relationships among groups and individuals.

In recent years, Bihar has come to represent one of the most backward areas of India. It has achieved notoriety as the graveyard of development projects and as the site of scandalous "feudal" barbarities (Timberg 1982:450). Widespread violence in the rural areas in the last decade is taken as a sign of increasing frustration of the people and it is asserted that Bihar is on the verge of a revolutionary uprising. Whether revolution is around the corner or not, the picture of Bihar that dominates the minds of observers is that of poverty and violence.

Bihar is the second most populous state in the country and has ten percent of India's population but only five percent of its area. Between 1971 and 1981 the density of population rose from 324 to 402 persons per square kilometer. Around 90 percent of its population lives in rural areas as compared to 80 percent in the rest of the country. Life expectancy at birth is below the national average, standing at 44.4 years for men and 43.1 years for women. Similarly, the literacy rate is 26 percent, well below the national average of 36 percent. Rural literacy is 20 percent.

Despite several attempts at land reform during the years after independence, severe inequality in landholdings persists in Bihar. Between 1970–71 and 1976–77 the average size of landholdings decreased from 1.5 to 1.1 hectares. Significantly, the number of landholdings in the size category below 1 hectare rose by 48 percent during the same period. The total area of operation of these small plots increased by 40 percent. As a proportion of the total number of operational holdings in the state, holdings in this category increased from 69 to 73 percent. In 1977 the area occupied by holdings above 4 hectares (6 percent of the total) was 40 percent of the total operational area. In contrast, the area occupied by holdings below 1 hectare was 23 percent of the total.

A consequence of this pattern of land distribution has been that the proportion of people living below the poverty line increased from 52 percent in 1969–70 to 57 percent in 1977–78. The per capita income in Bihar was Rs. 435.24 at constant prices in 1978–79 while that of India was Rs. 727.60 (Bihar 1982). Bihar is poor and its economy lacks dynamism and is falling further. The output of foodgrains increased only by 1 percent per annum during the period 1961–62 to 1976–77 (Singh *et al.* 1981) and net per capita availability of foodgrains declined (Nayyar 1977; Das 1978).

The backwardness of Bihar stands out prominently amidst the state's rich endowment of mineral resources. The state contributes about 45 percent of the national production of coal, 16 percent of iron ore, 35 percent of bauxite, and 54 percent of mica. The large industrial units that have been created are isolated units within a largely agrarian society. Processes of industrialization have remained stunted and the expected ancillary sector has not emerged. Bihar has industries without industrialization.

Bihar is characterized by widespread violence in rural areas. Newspapers have reported village caste wars in which women and children have been burnt in their huts and inhabited areas of specific communities or occupational groups have been razed. It is alleged that the state's official machinery has collaborated with groups in perpetrating these barbarities and in striking terror. Naxalism, a name for armed struggle in the rural areas, has encouraged violent attacks on groups and members of communities leading to killings and murders. Naxalites became special targets for counter-violence by the state (Sinha 1977; Dhar & Mukherjee 1978; Mukherjee 1979).

Even before violence became a focus of attention in Bihar, scholarly interest in peasant movements and rural unrest had led to analyses and descriptions of particular uprisings. Many of the studies have been "case histories;" some are autobiographical accounts of participants in the movements; and a few are omnibus accounts of the major peasant movements (Das 1982:5). The roles of individuals and organizations in spearheading peasant struggles have also been studied (Das 1983; Gupta 1983).

Thus, while numerous writings are available on the backwardness of Bihar and the emergence of rural unrest, little systematic work has been done in analyzing the context in which violence is taking place. The purpose of this study is to fill this gap and to investigate the relationship between the characteristics of socio-economic development and the incidence and nature of rural violence across districts in Bihar. The questions are: What are the specific social and economic features of districts that are undergoing violent rural unrest? What kind of social and economic changes are associated with persistence and intensity of violence?

These questions are embedded in a debate centered around the concern whether the green revolution is turning into a red one. This debate, begun in India in the early 1970s, stemmed from the discussion of the impact of capital inputs on agriculture and the transformation of traditional into capitalistic agriculture. Even though the government had been constructing new irrigation facilities and promoting new technologies since independence, the sudden impact of the new inputs was only felt when they were applied on a massive scale in selected areas and after the technological breakthrough of high yielding varieties of seeds. While there was an impressive increase in agricultural output, there were differential benefits to regions and farmers. Disparities among regions and farmers were sharpened and the rising inequalities in the countryside began to be accepted as the inevitable consequence of the strategy of agricultural development. During the 1970s considerable attention was focused on delineating the nature of the capitalist transformation of Indian agriculture, class formation in the countryside, and the sources of class conflicts.

In a review of this debate, Thorner (1982) points out that while it is accepted that capitalist farming dominates Indian agriculture, one should not lose sight of contradictory practices in the transformation that has occurred. Relatively mobile wage labor has replaced servile, debt bonded, and traditionally tied labor but master–servant behavior contained within extra-economic relationships has by no means disappeared.

There is little agreement on the set of rural classes that has emerged as a consequence of the capitalist transformation. There is wide regional variation but Prasad (1979) writing of Bihar identifies three broad classes: the top peasantry, the middle and poor peasantry, and agricultural laborers. He points to the respective dominance of the upper castes, middle castes, and scheduled castes and tribes in the three classes. For him, it is this intermeshing of class and caste that has fostered antagonistic relationships in the rural areas.

While the debate continues on the above two issues, it was broadly agreed that conflicts in the rural areas were going to get sharper and wider as the application of capital inputs in agriculture spreads. It has been hypothesised that these areas will be more conflict prone than others (Sharma 1973).

During the last decade caste conflicts have surfaced prominently. Some have argued that class analysis needs to be tempered by caste considerations because "while atrocities against Harijans are occurring throughout India, it is precisely in the more capitalistically developed areas that they are taking the most widespread forms" (Omvedt 1981:A146). The reasons are not hard to find. The lower caste groups are predominantly landless peasants or agricultural laborers or poor artisans. Even though there is no perfect correlation, very few lower caste persons rise to higher class groups and so they remain depressed both socially and economically.

To the extent that caste reinforces class in the rural areas, "class conflict is that much more sharp and explosive" (Hayami 1981:710). But caste also tends to divide the homogeneity and solidarity of class groups. Casteism cuts across class lines and many groups are based on caste loyalties. Whether the class conflicts have sharpened through castes or not, caste based conflicts have intensified because the rich peasantry has used casteism to foment violence in many villages (Prasad 1979). The argument is that more often than not such conflicts surface where there is greater capitalist development of agriculture. This is because the genesis of violence lies in wage disputes or land disputes. Those who are in conflict belong to opposing caste groups and each group has in common not only caste affinities but also economic interests.

In essence, the hypothesis that these studies present is that rural violence is an outcome of the adoption of a new agricultural strategy that has led to a green revolution. The hypothesis can be extended by suggesting that the incidence of violence will vary with the differential adoption of this strategy. Thus, as all areas are not equal in experiencing the impact of a green revolution, they should also be unequal in experiencing violence.

In light of these explanations, Bihar presents a paradox. It is not in the forefront of the green revolution and does not exhibit a rapid rate of economic change. Yet there is violence in the countryside and its intensity has retarded development.

For purposes of this study I confine my attention to violence, not the broader categories of conflict or unrest. There is little agreement about what constitutes a violent event and hence any definition of violence is somewhat arbitrary. I will use the "brute harm" concept of violence and accept that violence is any "observable interaction in the course of which persons or objects are seized or physically damaged over resistance" (Tilly 1975:513). This definition excludes psychological or economic violence and concentrates on physical harm. It also includes both violence by the state and by its citizens. Further, I consider only those violent incidents that arise from collective acts outside the normal institutional framework of the society and involve participants who share some sense of identity. Thus, only those events are considered that are collective and have an element of confrontation. This confrontation can be between the various rural occupational, social, or caste groups or between one or more of these groups and agencies of the state. In addition confrontation results when the collective action is either illegal or not sanctioned by societal institutions. An event is a collective action when there is evidence of group action or if there are 10 or more persons involved in the incident. It is a group action if the group shares some identity, such as being scheduled caste persons or agricultural laborers. Rape has been included as a violent act but rape committed by an individual is excluded. Gang rape is a collective action perpetrated by a group attempting to demonstrate its power over another group or to terrorize it.

The source of my data are two newspapers: the *Hindustan Times* (Delhi) and *The Hindu* (Madras). Each of them commands a large readership in North and South India, respectively. The daily circulation of the *Hindustan Times* was 267,020 in 1979 and that of *The Hindu* 134,794. Each newspaper of the period 1970 to 1980 was read and violent events were recorded. These events were classified and later coded for analysis.

What is the nature of violence in Bihar? To answer this question I have used principal component analysis. This technique reduces the complexity of a multivariate problem. In social research it is often the case that variations in a phenomenon can only be explained in terms of large sets of variables that are closely correlated with one another. Principal component analysis uses the correlation matrix to produce components which are uncorrelated with one another. In delineating independent components, this analysis groups variables together. Another advantage of principal component analysis is that it produces factors in descending order of their ability to explain variance in the data. Finally, the principal components can be used to rank the cases on the basis of the general characteristics of the variable set. Thus, when a component represents violence, it can be used to rank districts on the basis of their scores on this principal factor (Rummel 1970).

The varimax factor solution presented in the Table 1 identifies three principal components that accounted for 80 percent of the variation in the original matrix. The first factor brings out sharply the nature of violence occurring in rural Bihar. The groups perpetrating violence are both the police as well as armed gangs. Their target is the scheduled castes and rural poor as well as those who have been labelled Naxalites. There is clear collaboration between the police units and the armed gangs. The number of people killed also loads highly on this factor. This factor reveals violence by armed groups against the weaker sections of society with the connivance of state machinery. It is now well documented that in the name of stamping out rural insurgency, landlords supported by the state government machinery have cruelly assaulted the rural poor, killing them and destroying their property (Mukherjee and Yadav 1982). This factor resembles the internal war dimension delineated by Paige (1975) in his study of agrarian movements.

The second factor centers on riots. The characteristics that load highly on this factor include irregular groups as the actors, absence of any formal method of violence, and general villagers as target. The overall pattern suggests diffused crowd violence with varied objectives.

The third factor represents sexual oppression. The object of violence is women and the form of violence is general assault or rape. In sexual violence upper caste domination is pronounced. Some observers have commented that *izzat ki larai* (struggle for dignity) is inextricably linked with upper class domination (Das 1980:233; Mukherjee 1979:1536).

The first two factors highlight a significant feature of collective violence in Bihar. In the first dimension, where there is heavy involvement of the agents of state in perpetrating violence, many people are killed. The second dimension connects rioting to damage of lower caste property. Thus, killings occur when organized groups attack and property is destroyed when riots take place. Tilly (1975:515) suggests "there is a sort of division of labor: repressive forces do the largest part of killing and wounding whereas the groups they are seeking to control do most of the damage to the property."

In which districts are the incidents of violence most common? Using factor scores on the first dimension, the districts fall into three categories. Table 2 lists High Violence and Low Violence districts.

TABLE 1: ROTATED FACTOR MATRIX

	F1	F2	F3
1. Acting Groups			
Armed bands	.860	.174	.238
Irregular groups	.168	.928	.041
Police units	.880	.029	.111
2. Provocation for Violence			
Police action	.961	.009	.158
Forced harvesting	.041	.804	−.289
Old enmity	.264	.861	.371
Caste conflict	.557	.415	.235
3. Nature of Violence			
Murder	.568	.462	.451
Rape	.394	.396	.733
Arson	.500	.224	.366
Assault on women	.425	.034	.851
4. Target of Violence			
Scheduled castes	.628	.397	.179
Women	−.167	.470	.876
Naxalites/extremists	.952	−.071	.122
Unidentified	−.013	.961	.168
5. Intensity of Violence			
Number killed	.812	.340	.198
Damage to property	.353	.501	−.252
Casualties not known	−.439	.700	.022

TABLE 2

High Violence Districts	Low Violence Districts
Shahbad	Bhagalpur
Patna	Singhbhum
Monghyr	Dhanbad
Purnea	Saharsa
Champaran	Ranchi
	Santhal Pargana

As a map of Bihar would reveal, Shahbad, Patna and Monghyr lie in the fertile tract through which the Ganges river flows. Purnea and Champaran are in North Bihar and are not contiguous with these three districts. Excepting Saharsa and Bhagalpur, the low violence districts are part of the Chhotanagpur plateau which is a hilly and forested region. This area is less suitable for agriculture but occupies an important position on the mining and industrial map of India.

Having classified the districts in this way, we may investigate whether the two groups have distinct social and economic characteristics. Are the high violence districts also those that have experienced the greatest impact of the green revolution? Table 3 lists district-wise data on nine variables and their group means. The ratios between the latter indicate significant differences between the two groups of districts.

High violence districts are characterized by greater penetration of new agricultural technology and by greater inequality in the distribution of landholdings. They have higher average cropping intensities with more abundant irrigation facilities that allow land to be used for more than one crop. The low violence districts have fewer tractors per 1000 hectares of net area sown. The increasing use of mechanical technology in agricultural production may displace labor and thus increase the pressure on unemployment. The consumption of fertilizer also differs between the two groups of districts and the high violence districts have a higher proportion of electrified villages. Use of electricity is a characteristic of development and a requirement for further growth. Thus, the two groups of districts differ in several characteristics of development. Their group averages show that high violence districts are more developed.

The high violence districts also have greater proportions of scheduled castes in their populations, a situation that may threaten the upper castes. Finally, there is inequality in the distribution of landholdings. The average size of holdings, the proportion of the number of holdings below one hectare, and the proportion of area in plots under one hectare highlight significant differences between the two groups.

From this preliminary analysis, it is difficult to establish a simple causal relationship between agricultural development and rural violence. Data show that the sources of violence may be in agricultural development and in population characteristics and pressures. The painful process of capitalist transformation of agriculture is accentuated where there is more population pressure. This may be happening in Bihar even if some green revolution areas in India are not as violence prone. The feudal characteristics of Bihar need to be examined further, since the feudal traditions have not broken down completely. The green revolution has been superimposed on economic relationships which are not entirely commercialized. What may occur is that green revolution areas show increased violence when characterized by population pressures, a greater proportion of scheduled castes among the

TABLE 3: DIFFERENTIATING SOCIO-ECONOMIC CHARACTERISTICS

	Proportion of Scheduled Castes to rural population	Average Cropping Intensity	Average Proportion of wheat area	Tractors per 10,000 ha of net area sown	Average Fertilizer consumption kg per ha	Average Proportion of electrified villages	Average size of land holdings	Proportion of land holdings under one hectare	Proportion of area under one hectare holdings or less
DATES OF DATA	1981	1970–80	1972–80	1977	1974–81	1972–80	1977	1977	1977
Champaran	14.32	1.39	39.71	2.92	15.45	22.21	1.00	76.73	28.78
Monghyr	16.00	1.35	25.19	1.39	16.03	36.12	.90	77.35	25.02
Patna	19.22	1.47	18.30	2.81	29.13	74.28	.80	77.12	37.33
Purnea	11.43	1.41	10.97	1.73	6.36	7.27	1.15	70.18	22.41
Shahbad	17.44	1.46	27.79	2.71	25.35	41.52	1.25	65.29	18.78
MEAN (High Violence Districts)	15.58	1.42	24.38	2.31	18.46	36.28	1.02	73.33	28.46
Bhagalpur	11.40	1.33	14.38	1.16	15.32	19.88	1.00	75.78	27.38
Dhanbad	17.36	1.05	4.63	.11	4.17	19.25	1.40	67.90	20.74
Ranchi	5.28	1.08	2.68	.11	5.49	8.28	2.50	47.23	7.23
Saharsa	1.63	1.45	15.62	1.28	6.21	17.06	1.40	66.22	19.61
Santhal Pargana	8.33	1.12	3.38	.05	4.92	5.98	2.00	54.84	9.92
Singhbhum	4.45	1.14	0.93	.02	2.64	3.43	1.50	62.96	15.87
MEAN (Low Violence Districts)	8.07	1.18	6.93	.45	6.46	12.31	1.63	62.49	16.79
RATIO HIGH:LOW MEANS	1.93	1.20	3.52	5.13	2.86	2.95	0.63	1.17	1.70

rural population, an unequal distribution of landholdings, and persistence of feudal economic relations.

Are conditions ripe for a revolution in Bihar? This is a difficult question to answer. Incidents of violence do not make a revolution. In fact, intermittent violence allows the landowning elites to demand from the state an intensification of the use of coercive power. A major dimension of violence of Bihar is the collusion of landowning elites with the state machinery to exercise coercive power. Such repression serves to teach a lesson more than to punish the disobedient. It aims to carve the pain of brutality into the memory of the recalcitrant poor. In such a situation the risks of organized revolutionary action are exorbitantly high and discouraging. Otherwise wherever exploitation occurred, there would have been violence leading to revolution.

The assertion that Bihar is on the threshold of revolution simplifies the role of the state and does not take into account the predominant type of violence occurring there. At present, the richer classes are on the offensive against the poor. In this effort, the state machinery provides support to the rich and there is little evidence to show that this support has weakened over the years.

The data presented in this chapter indicate that violent consequences may emerge from the agricultural transformation in India. Antagonism among groups is becoming a common feature of the Indian rural scene. Farmers who have commercialized their agriculture are now in the forefront of farmers' agitations demanding higher prices for their crops. They are attempting to mobilize the entire peasantry against the urban sources of power which they feel are not allowing them a fair share of the national cake. This same group is also turning against the rural poor when the latter demand higher wages, better social conditions, or economic facilities. As recent incidents in Maharashtra and Andhra Pradesh have shown, these conflicts often manifest themselves as atrocities against Harijans. The rural poor are not united and are organizationally weak. Consequently they are unable to fight back effectively and have to bear the fierce onslaught of rich farmers. The dominating theme of rural violence is repression of the rural poor rather than the successful expression of their revolutionary potential.

9

The Political Uses of Religious Identity in South Asia

SURJIT MANSINGH

Intricate relationships exist between religious identity and political purpose in South Asia. These relationships are neither uniform over time nor predictable by situation. Religious differences translate into political strife under some conditions and not others. In other words, religious identity is only one variable of political culture in South Asia, along with ethnic, regional, linguistic, economic, and ideological identities. Some of the political uses to which religion has been put in South Asia are surveyed in this chapter.

Perhaps the most remarkable feature of South Asia is the persistence of multi-racial and multi-religious societies over many thousands of years. Excavations at sites of the Harappan Culture (*c.*3000–1500 BC) reveal the remains of distinct racial types living side by side. The myths, legends, laws, and epigraphic records of ancient times testify to the multiplicity of faiths and religious practices in any given area of the Indian subcontinent. Throughout recorded history no single group became all-engulfing in number, or uniformly dominant in power, either across South Asia or in its constituent units. In this respect India presents a striking contrast to China, comparable in size, antiquity, and attractiveness to new settlers, but overwhelmingly Han in population. Without wishing to over-romanticize diversity in Indian civilization—or to underestimate its existence in China—it seems reasonable to inquire why and how diversity survived. Had violent conflict been the sole, or even a frequent, response of discrete groups to their physical juxtaposition, the configurations of faiths and peoples in South Asia surely would be less of a *compôte* today.

Indeed, it is impossible to conceive of a completely homogeneous state anywhere in South Asia, no matter how narrow the criteria of its creation or how small its size. If we wish to conserve this diversity and prevent forced migrations or mass killings from imposing a new uniformity on the inhabitants of various parts of South Asia, pointers must be found in past and present norms of legitimacy as well as social and political structures.

Contemporary South Asia has adopted as legitimate certain modern concepts which are in striking contrast to those of its past traditions. One is the concept of equality, which stimulates competition for scarce resources and aggravates discontent with obvious disparities. Another is the concept of democracy, or participation in political decisionmaking by the masses. Democracy places a premium on techniques of mass mobilization and the numerical count of political groupings. A third is the concept of economic development which both implies and demands disruption in traditional divisions of labor. Equality, democracy, and economic development have been widely accepted as legitimate goals throughout South Asia, even in countries ruled at present by monarchs or military regimes. Thus, what Milton Gordon calls the "liberal expectation" (Glazer and Moynihan 1975:84–110) is widespread: the significance of ascriptive qualities for public life is expected to decline, and individual merit irrespective of caste, creed, or sex will gain wider recognition.

The practice of democracy varies widely and is imperfect, even in India and Sri Lanka whose laws, constitutions, and political structures are explicitly based on the norms of equality, democracy, and development. Contemporary political practices in South Asia belong to the realm of trial and error. Many concepts and goals—including those based on religious identity—compete for popular legitimization. In these circumstances, some political leaders have chosen to use religious symbols and religious groupings for a variety of purposes: to mobilize followers, to bolster group demands, to resist change, and to generate nationalism. The potent mix of religion and politics has frequently disrupted order, civility, and diversity in South Asian societies.

Before examining present day causes and patterns in the political uses of religious identity, a brief look at South Asian history is in order. What concepts and structures enabled the Hindu, Buddhist, Islamic, and Sikh empires of the past to preserve ethnic and religious diversity within their borders?

The earliest legends on the origins of kingship in Hindu literature highlight both divinity and social contract. The *Aitareya Brahmana*, a later Vedic text, narrates how the gods appointed Indra as their *raja* to lead them in battle, endowing all subsequent kings with his attributes. The *Arthasastra* of Kautilya (fourth century BC) repeats a story then current in Hindu, Buddhist, and Jain texts of mankind choosing the first king to preserve order at a time of cosmic decay. The functions of a king were conceived almost entirely in terms of protection. A king protected his subjects not only from external invasion but also from moral confusion and social disorder. It was the duty of the king and the martial class, *ksatriya*, to preserve custom and an ordered society, the *varnasrama-dharma*. In return for providing protection, they received the blessings and cooperation of the priestly intelligentsia, the brahmans. Thus, political, military, and religious leadership were interdependent. Society was ascriptive and hierarchical. Every social and economic function enjoyed a recognized status and remuneration; every individual had a prescribed place and form of employment. This system evolved over thousands of years. Over time, it allowed for the accommodation and sanskritization of numerous groups of newcomers without apparent disruption. It achieved a remarkably high degree of stability, prosperity, and legitimacy and permitted both cultural excellence and physical expansion through the subcontinent.

The *varnasrama-dharma* system worked as well as it did under conditions which do not and cannot prevail today. (Nor can we be sure that it worked as well in the past as Brahmanic literature would have us believe.) First, it was premised on inequality and the non-competitiveness of different social groups. Allocations of power and resources were fixed by custom or altered by force. There was no provision for participation in political decision-making by the masses. Secondly, by assuming the superiority of the status quo and a continuous disaggregation of skill into hereditary occupational groups, the system militated against social change and economic development (Raychaudhuri 1982:278). Thirdly, it flowered at a time when land was abundant in relation to population, allowing for much mobility and dynamism. And fourthly, it rested on the wholesale exploitation of peoples deemed to be outside the *varnasrama-dharma* system: the untouchables. Moreover, while violent conflict between groups *within* a given polity was low, there was constant fighting among the numerous kingdoms occupying the Indian subcontinent. Then,

as now, violence directed outwards was legitimized by the rules
of war but was nonetheless destructive. Neither the norms of
legitimacy that prevailed in ancient Hindu kingdoms, nor their
social structures, are appropriate for the demands of our times in
South Asia.

Much more worthy of emulation today is the remarkable tolerance of heterodoxy summed up in the Vedic phrase: "Reality is
One; sages speak of it in different ways." This philosophical
approach, which is notable in all religions originating in the
Indian subcontinent, can provide a firm basis for the operation of
a modern secular state. As explained by Smith (1963), the underlying philosophies of both Hinduism and Buddhism are conducive
to religious freedom for individuals and groups, separation of the
political functions of the state from patronage of any one particular
religion, and respect for different faiths—including those professed
by minorities or aliens. It is not necessary here to recapitulate
Smith's analysis of the doctrinal and administrative aspects of
South Asian religions. Rather, two points are noted. First, the
belief that there are many paths to spiritual liberation enables
people of different faiths to live together harmoniously despite
proselytizing activities around them. In other words, religious
tolerance does not imply the absence of religious activity. Secondly,
wise rulers in South Asia harnessed the energies and abilities
of different groups and individuals, for the greater peace and
prosperity of the state, by reinforcing this belief in many roads to
salvation.

The outstanding example of a wise ruler is the Mauryan
Emperor Asoka (reigned 268–231 BC). Asoka came to power in a
vast empire embracing peoples of many ethnic stocks, cultural
traditions, and religious beliefs. The time was one of profound
economic, technological, and social change. Pastoral or nomadic
ways of life had been supplanted by settled agriculture, commerce,
and urbanization; village and tribal self-governing institutions
had given way to a centralized bureaucracy; the intellectual ferment
of centuries had produced several heterodox sects as well as increased
rigidity in the orthodox Brahmanic code, all competing for royal
favor. Asoka was an ambitious ruler and a moral man. His response
to the challenges he faced was both practical and imaginative; it
was the policy of *Dharma* whose ramifications Thapar (1963) has
explored. Politically and administratively, *Dharma* served to
reconcile diverse elements through inclusiveness other than ex-

clusiveness, through self-control rather than confrontation. Asoka's twelfth Major Rock Edict illustrates this point:

. . . progress of the essential doctrine (of all sects) takes many forms, but its basis is the control of one's speech, so as not to extoll one's own sect or disparage another's on unsuitable occasions, or at least to do so only mildly on certain occasions. On each occasion one should honor another man's sect, for by doing so one increases the influence of one's own sect and benefits that of the other man; while by doing otherwise one diminishes the influence of one's own sect and harms the other man's. Again, whosoever honors his own sect or disparages that of another man, wholly out of devotion to his own, with a view to showing it in a favorable light, harms his own sect even more seriously. Therefore, concord is to be commended, so that men hear one another's principles and obey them.

Asoka's abjuring of excessive force as an instrument of state policy, and his recognition of non-violence, non-confrontation, and benevolence as elements with the greater power to cement society, remain highly relevant to contemporary South Asia. Asoka's principles of governance were not only moral, they made practical good sense in all times for lands of diversity. This fact was recognized, perhaps subconsciously, by many later rulers in South Asia—Buddhist and Hindu, Muslim, and Sikh.

Sri Lanka, an island mosaic of groups, was one recipient of Asoka's messages. The multi-ethnic kingdom of Anuradhapura subsequently thrived on the intricate irrigation system it perfected, which called for a high degree of cooperation among its inhabitants. Though the kingdom was subjected to many strains, including particularistic demands and military pressures from South India, it survived until the thirteenth century. Royal protection of the Buddhist monastic order, the *Sangha*, did not preclude respect for other faiths nor gifts to other temples. Indeed, Sri Lanka retained its multi-ethnic, multi-religious character throughout the colonial era (de Silva 1981). During the nationalist movements of the nineteenth and twentieth centuries, however, some found a combination of religious and ethnic identity to be a convenient instrument of confrontationist politics. During the 1950s the Buddhist religion became explosively entwined with the Sinhalese language and *sangha* involvement in politics. The new "emphasis on the sense of uniqueness of the Sinhalese past . . . in which Buddhism stood forth in all its pristine purity, carried an emotional appeal compared with which the concept of a multi-racial polity was a meaningless abstraction" (de Silva 1984:33). Neither ethnic composition nor residential patterns had changed much in the island, but attitudes towards right and wrong behavior, that is, political legitimacy, had altered. The consequences are seen today in the horrific statistics of violence perpetuated both by and against Tamils.

Generalizations about the political concepts and structures of India during the period commonly described as Islamic (thirteenth to eighteenth centuries) are more difficult. On the one hand, official chronicles of most Muslim courts, especially the Delhi Sultanate, stressed the ruler's obligation to stamp out idolatory and heresy, to uphold and extend Islam, if necessary by the sword. On the other hand, many Muslim rulers including the renowned Mughal Emperor Akbar, recognized the practical necessity of choosing their advisors and generals on the basis of individual ability rather than religious identity and of coming to workable terms with the majority of their subjects, who were non-Muslim. Moreover, the subcontinent was not one unified state but a congeries of Muslim and Hindu kingdoms. In the many conflicts that raged across the land between the raids of Muhammad of Ghur at the end of the twelfth century and the defeat of the Mughal–Maratha armies by Ahmad Shah Abdali in 1761, neither allies nor enemies were drawn along religious lines. Political and military expediency, not religious identity, determined choice of allegiance. The fact is easily documented by any detailed history book, notwithstanding propagandistic efforts in India from time to time to portray the contrary impression of continuous strife between "native Hindu" and "foreign Muslim."

It is no easy task to distil the criteria of legitimacy operating in medieval India. The concept of an elected head of the Islamic faithful, ruling in the name of the Caliph on the basis of the Shariah, with the assistance of the Ulama, was uneasily grafted on to the more ancient concept of hereditary emperor, father and mother to all his subjects, upholding their customary law and established social order. Similarly, Brahminic fulminations against the *mlechcha* did not prevent numbers of high caste Hindus from having intimate working and social relations with Muslims nor large numbers of low caste Hindus from converting to Islam. Structurally speaking, all the kingdoms of the period came to resemble each other. Drastic changes in the upper levels of the social ladder were not accompanied by a revolutionizing of society at the lower levels. Divisions among groups along lines of kinship and occupation continued to operate among both Hindus and Muslims, though the followers of some Sufi and *Bhakti* saints, such as Kabir and Nanak, denounced caste differentiations and preached the universality of God.

The period between the thirteenth and the eighteenth centuries conditions political realities in present day South Asia partly because religion was used for as many political purposes then as now, and partly because the political and religious debates of nineteenth and twentieth century South Asia have been permeated by historical half-truths and questions arising from that period.

Among the many political uses of religious identity in pre-modern India are the following. Those who wrested political power by force sought and received legitimization from recognized religious leaders. Firuz Shah Tughlaq in the fourteenth century styled himself "deputy of the Caliph" and ruled with the encouragement of the Ulema. In 1674 the Maratha rebel hero Shivaji assumed the title of Chhatrapati at a formal investiture ceremony attended by a full panoply of brahmans. Sometimes religious leaders tried to act as the conscience of the king. Thus, Nizamuddin Auliya reproached Alauddin Khalji, and Nanak reproached Babur, for their excessive killings. Religion was often used as a rallying call to the flag, as when Babur appealed to his men to swear allegiance on the Koran before the crucial battle of Khanua in 1527. Alternately, religion could motivate peasants to organize and resist oppressive landowners and rulers, as did the Sikh peasantry led by Guru Gobind Singh. Religion was invoked to acquire more territory—as when Akbar marched against the Shia kingdoms of the Deccan—or to raise more revenue—as when Aurangzeb reimposed the *jiziya* tax on non-Muslims. Then, as now, sectarian differences played their role in the factional squabbles of courts; notably in the fratricidal struggle between Dara Shikoh and Alamgir.

The private faith of a ruler did not necessarily determine his public policy toward followers of his own or other religions. Maharaja Ranjit Singh was a devout Sikh who struck coins in the name of Guru Nanak and called his govenment the *Sarkar Khalsa* of the people. He ruled a sovereign state of the Punjab (and well beyond) between 1801 and 1839 in a way that convinced his people that "he did not intend to set up a Sikh kingdom but a Punjabi state in which Muslims, Hindus, and Sikhs would be equal before the law and have the same rights and duties" (Singh 1963:203).

These few examples indicate no inevitable correlation between religious identity and political behavior in pre-modern South Asia. In an age of fluctuating fortunes and low institutionalization of political procedures, ambitious men made use of such instruments as they found available to further their ends; religion was one of them. Today, another instrument has been added, historical memory.

Historical memories of the British Raj are more recent and much better documented than those of earlier periods, but nonetheless controversial. The colonial era in South Asia has obviously shaped present day politics in more ways than can be assessed here, but some aspects need to be stressed.

First, the concepts of political legitimacy were not derived from religion. The British gained power mainly by force, manipulation of local factors, and superior organizational ability. They remained in power because they were better able to keep order than their competitors and, perhaps more importantly, because they convinced themselves and a substantial number of their subjects that they were the only possible rulers *because* they were outsiders, above and beyond the historical group conflicts of the subcontinent. As Britain gradually democratized itself, however, its political ideals and institutions seeped through the Empire as well. In the end, the concept of legitimacy derived from popular will challenged the concept and reality of the Crown, and won.

Secondly, British rule, combined with the impact of an international trading system and some industrialization, shook the traditional order in South Asia. Birth in an ascribed status, occupational, or religious group become less relevant to worldly advancement than familiarity with the new commerce and English education. A class of Westernized men became the new influentials in South Asia—but remained always subordinate to the British. From that point, it was but a short step for them to embrace the concept of racial equality.

Thirdly, British rule shattered the pride of the elite all over South Asia. They looked for, and found, explanations for their defeat, and for what they came to believe was their "backwardness," in traditional religious practices. Thus began in the nineteenth century a process of self-searching among South Asians which resulted in a substantial reform of social customs and beliefs among various groups. As Heimsath (1964) has described the process taking place among caste Hindus, reforms (especially relating to women) were undertaken both by those wishing to emulate the new rulers (who were Christian) and by those seeking to revive Vedic values. Whether "reformist" or "revivalist," a succession of able social and religious leaders aimed at restoring the self-esteem of Hindus by shedding the worst abuses that had crept into their social system and by asserting their claims to participate fully in the public life of their own country. Similar sequences of self-examination, reform, revivalism, and assertion took place at different times in India among Muslims, as illustrated by the career of Sayyid Ahmad Khan, among Sikhs through the Singh Sabha movement and the Shiromani Akali Dal, and among Ceylon Buddhists, as de Silva (1981) has shown. One type of South Asian response to political subjugation by the British was redefinition of religious identity.

Fourthly, the British Raj itself followed a policy of "religious neutrality" (Smith 1963:66–84) both in India and in Ceylon. That is to say, though the Church of England was "established," the government did not encourage Christian missionaries, occasionally acted as patron and protector of native religions, and permitted freedom of worship to all. At the same time, religious identity formed an important consideration in the employment and military recruitment practices of the Raj. Favor was shown to those who demonstrated loyalty to the Crown, as did the Sikhs, and a tacit quota system was in operation reserving certain occupations for particular groups, such as the Christians. Post-independence efforts in India and Sri Lanka to alter substantially the quotas established by the Raj have met with criticism and resistance, as seen in Sikh complaints about their reduced percentage in the Indian armed forces and in Tamil grievances about fewer seats in Sri Lankan colleges.

Fifthly, one of the most controversial actions of the British Raj was to introduce a system of separate electorates for Muslims in India. Not coincidentally but deliberately, this was done just when the Morley-Minto Reforms of 1909 raised the number of elected members in the provincial and central legislative councils and enlarged their functions. The communal principle was extended more widely in the Montague-Chelmstord Reforms of

1919. A quota of Muslim constituencies, in which all Muslim electors of a given area were included, was allocated to the center and each province. In addition, Sikhs were given their separate constituencies in the Punjab and Christians theirs in Madras. Other special constituencies were established. At the next major step of reform taken in 1935, "Communal representation ran right through the constitution, both in the legislatures and in the public services. There were separate constituencies for Muslims and other major communities; there were reserved seats for the untouchables or "Scheduled Castes," and for other special interests. Finally safeguards, including reserve powers for governors, often thought of as a reactionary feature of the Montford era, were extended" (Spear 1961:387). In short, the British introduced representative institutions on the Indian subcontinent in a manner which hardened vertical divisions along lines of religious identity.

By projecting themselves as upholders of order against a rising tide of democracy and nationalism which threatened the existing regime, the British retained to the end their role as arbiter of competing groups in India. Until the Second World War sapped military power and political will, the British were motivated by a desire to retain power over the subcontinent which, they believed, only they could hold together. Considerable doubt exists, however, about the impartiality of British arbitration between groups and the impact of the institutional structures they initiated to protect minorities. Questions of minority rights were debated as frequently in the twilight of the Raj as the inexorable demands of Indians for self government were resisted. Communal electorates and communal parties are to be viewed against that background.

Communal electorates increased the saliency of religious identity to electoral politics. They militated against the building of horizontal political coalitions around those shared economic interests which cut across vertical or communal divisions in society. By elevating the religious element at the expense of other elements of political identity, communal electorates perpetuated unchangeable and ascriptive political divisions. Thus two major premises of electoral democracy were negated (Taylor and Yapp 1979:255–265). One premise is that political identity is part of a total cultural identity and not derivative from only one element, whether linguistic, economic, or religious. Another is that access to political power remains open to all political parties because the voting patterns of individuals and groups can change. The contrary premises of communal electorates led to a political game in which each religious community vied with others to create or claim numerical strength and political importance for itself in order to gain increased representation and power without the necessity of accommodating others.

A disasterous cycle of the numbers game was played out before independence and partition on the subcontinent. The Muslim League, which claimed to speak on behalf of the largest all-India religious minority, escalated its demands for reservation of seats in proportion to the numbers of Muslims in a given province, to weightage in proportion to their historical and political importance, to parity with the majority Hindu community, and ultimately in 1940 to a demand for a separate homeland in which Muslims would form a majority. More or less simultaneously, a section of the Hindu elite fanned fears that the all-India numerical superiority of Hindus would be negated by separate electorates and weighted representation for minorities, and that Hindus living in Muslim majority areas would be especially vulnerable as they would enjoy neither the protection and privileges offered Muslims, Sikhs, or Christians as minority communities, nor the security of belonging to a political majority.

These attitudes are reflected in a letter to the *Tribune* of August 1909 quoted by Prabha Dixit in her account of the genesis and growth of Hindu communalism. "Following the example of the Muslims, we must make it a point that whatever we do, we do for the exclusive benefit of the Hindu and need not bother for other communities who can well take care of themselves without our help" (Dixit 1974:147). The assertiveness palpable in this letter was strongest in the Punjab, where Hindus formed a large minority of the population, where the Arya Samaj was active, and where few Muslims supported the Muslim League until the 1946 elections.

A third important community in the Punjab was the Sikhs. They struggled to regain control of their religious shrines from hereditary *mahants* who were either Hindu or non-keshdhari Sikhs (that is, lacking the outward symbols of the Khalsa). The Sikhs succeeded under the leadership of the Akali Dal, and a law of 1924 gave the Sikh panth or community full control of the Gurdwaras. As in the case of other Indians, Sikhs too sought a voice in the political future of their province and country with inclinations which ranged over the spectrum from anti-British revolutionary activity to cooperative participation in the institutions of the Raj. Recruitment to those institutions, especially to the military services, added material incentives to preservation of the Khalsa. Any substantial ambitions harbored by Sikhs in the 1940s, however, were shattered when the Punjab was partitioned without regard for Sikh opinion, property holdings or residential patterns. Their numbers, it was said, were not statistically significant in an all-India context.

Communal electorates and the tactics adopted by the ruling power served to legitimize political use of religious identity and attitudes of mind which, in turn, contradicted those of the nationalist movement led by the Indian National Congress. Congress claimed to represent all Indians, irrespective of religion or class, and demanded democratization of the political process. Communal parties denied this claim and sought alliances with the Indian Princes and the British Indian government to stem the tide of democracy and frustrate the ambitions of Congress leaders. Congress leaders such as Jawaharlal Nehru looked to economic and educational modernization as the hope of the Indian masses in the future. The leaders of communal parties evoked social and religious values of the past to resist Westernization and to protect the privileges of their own higher ranks. Congress spoke in the name of Indian nationalism, defining India by territory alone.

Communal parties denied the territorial concept of nationhood by asserting the claims of culture, language, and religion. They tried to strengthen ties within their own fragmented communities by such tactics as *tabligh* (propaganda), *tanzim* (organization), and spreading Urdu among Muslims, and *Shuddhi* (purification), *sangatham* (reabsorption), and exclusive use of Hindi among north Indian Hindus. Thereafter, it was but a short step for the Muslim League to describe Indian Muslims—residing throughout the subcontinent—as a separate nation in their own right deserving a homeland, and for the leader of the Hindu Mahasabha to say that "mere geographical independence of a bit of earth called India should not be confused with real "Swarajya."" To the Hindu, the independence of Hindustan could only be worth having if it ensured their *Hindutva*—their religious, racial and cultural identity" (Savarkar, quoted in Dixit 1940:170). The partition of India in 1947 satisfied neither the Muslim nor the Hindu communalists, and sacrificed the Sikhs. What Mohammed Ali Jinnah called a "moth eaten and truncated Pakistan" did not include within its borders the over 40 million Muslims who continued to reside in India. Independent India adopted secular and democratic institutions, so that although the majority of the population were Hindus, India was not a Hindu country. Yet a pernicious doctrine of treating religious minorities of one state as hostage to good behavior towards minorities in the other state gained some currency. Equally important, the relationship of religion to the political life of the newly independent states was left undefined.

As is well known, Congress was by no means free of communalism and did not hesitate to use appeals of religious, cultural, or linguistic identity in building up grassroots support for the nationalist struggle. Mahatma Gandhi himself excelled at evoking religious symbols for political goals. His public prayer meetings provided unique opportunities for mass communication and mass organization. He is often accused, with good reason, of allying himself with those who stood for social conservatism and economic privilege. His attitudes towards modernization, and Westernization, were at best equivocal. Moreover, some historians have blamed Gandhi for unwittingly stimulating Muslim separatism by trading Congress endorsement of a sectarian issue in the Khilafit Movement for mass Muslim participation in the Noncooperation Movement of 1921–22, for dwelling on the "Ramrajya" of the future, and for taunting Jinnah at the defeat of the Muslim League in the 1937 elections. According to Wolpert (1984), Jinnah was provoked into using "Islam in danger" as a slogan to mobilize the Muslim masses behind him, at the expense of his earlier commitment to Hindu-Muslim unity. The creation of Pakistan was commonly regarded as a vindication of religion as the determinant of nationality and a gain for the Muslims of the subcontinent. Yet according to Jalal (1985:2), "the most striking fact about Pakistan is how it failed to satisfy the interests of the very Muslims who are supposed to have demanded its creation." She shows how Jinnah's bid to be recognized as the sole spokesman of Indian Muslims on the all-India stage led him to use the communal factor as a political tactic without giving precise definition to the demand for Pakistan. On the basis of detailed archival research, Jalal questions whether Jinnah's actual aims were achieved by partition or not.

In Gandhi's case, the man transcended appeals to particularistic religion and revived awareness of the universal ethical and moral content of political action. Ashoka had done the same. Gandhi's contributions lay not in the avoidance of conflict or pretence at social harmony, but rather in his attitude towards those subjects. Crucial tenets in Gandhi's theory of conflict resolution were that the cause for struggle must be a just one (*satyagraha*), that one must be unselfish and that those who take up the struggle employ no violence towards the adversary in thought, word or deed, but be willing to bear any suffering themselves (*ahimsa*). He de-legitimized the age-old custom of violent self-aggrandizement under the cloak of religious and patriotic fervor. Gandhi's thoughts on social harmony in a land of scarce resources and competing groups need not be outlined here except to point out his emphasis on both self-reliance and trusteeship. As Gandhi saw the world, it had sufficient resources for everyone's need, but not enough for anyone's greed. Therefore, he taught that those seeking material improvement must couch their demands in minimal terms while those resisting must offer maximum concessions. Gandhi's eclecticism in the choice of religious texts and hymns is famous, as alsos are his practice and advocacy of understanding religions different from one's own. By highlighting the role of individual conscience and the imperative of non-violence, Gandhi sought to infuse politics with norms of high ethical principles. Such principles are not always valued by high organizations or religious groupings in South Asia, but remain present in the consciousness of people beneath the surface of all religions. They are discernible in what Morris-Jones (1963) has called the "saintly idiom" in post-independence Indian politics, and they form touchstones of legitimacy, not practice.

In the post-independence period, governments, groups and individuals in the countries of South Asia have used religious identity for as many and varied political purposes as did their historical predecessors. The phenomena are most visible in Pakistan, because the need to protect the religion and culture of Islam through control of the political system was the given reason for separation from India. They are present elsewhere as well.

The ideology of Islam—with some variations of interpretation—was used to strengthen a congenitally weak state in Pakistan and marshall support for successive regimes. General Zia ul-Huq has used Islamic revivalism to equate his military rule with Pakistan and with Islam; political opposition can thus be treated as religious heresy and treason against the state. In addition, Islamic identity has provided for Pakistan diplomatic prominence and external economic assistance through a network of international relationships with other Islamic states. Within Pakistan, the concept of religious identity as the basis of citizenship rights has been used to exclude non-Muslim groups from power sharing. Recent legislation prohibiting the Qadianis (or Ahmadiyyas) further narrows participation in the higher ranks of the political system. At the same time, Zia's "Islamization" program has ushered in economic reforms and social legislation which apparently appeal to a broader stratum of society than the Westernized upper middle class so powerful in the 1960s.

Some similarities in the use of Islam have become visible in Bangladesh since the late 1970s, albeit less explicitly. With 98 percent of the population Bengali, and only 83 percent classified as Muslim, language and culture have given a wider base for nationalism than religion; this was evident in the liberation struggle of 1971. Subsequent outmigration of Hindus (as well as tribals, Christians, and Muslims) is due as much to economic factors as religious ones.

Religious ceremonies are important facets of monarchical governments in Nepal and Bhutan, but we omit these kingdoms from our discussion. More complex and compelling are the cases of Sri Lanka and India where commendable records of maintaining multi-ethnic and multi-religious societies in secular and democratic political systems have been badly tarnished by rising curves of communal violence, separatist terrorism, and discriminatory state repression. Some causes and consequences are noted below.

The 1972 and 1978 constitutions of Sri Lanka "give to Buddhism the foremost place" and say "it shall be the duty of the state to protect and foster Buddhism" while assuring to followers of all religions the rights of freedom of worship and equal citizenship. This fell far short of making Buddhism an established state religion, but permitted higher visibility and a more active political role to the *bhikkus*. As de Silva argues, the positions of individuals and groups on such key questions as elite competition, governmental policies on language and on education, as well as mobilization of votes by political parties and the building of political coalitions, all came to be influenced by considerations of religious and ethnic identity. Furthermore, a breakdown in national consensus in the 1970s combined with increasing arbitrariness in Mrs. Bandaranaike's government to discredit the political system. Subsequently, the grievances of a displaced literate elite were fused with the fears of an ethnic, religious, and linguistic minority concentrated in the northern part of the island, to produce a full throated and often violent Tamil separatist movement. The ineffective, and yet repressive, measures taken by President Jayewardene's government to meet the crisis further worsened the situation. The problem of restoring confidence among all citizens in the religious and ethnic impartiality of government remains unsolved, so that the legitimacy of the political system is itself threatened.

In India, the secular provisions of the constitution are explicit but bear repeating. Article 14 gives equal protection of the law to all citizens, and Article 15 forbids the state to discriminate against any citizen on grounds of religion, race, caste, sex, or place of birth in employment or any other matter. Article 25 guarantees freedom of conscience to all, and equal rights to profess, practice, and propagate religion, subject only to public order, health, and morality. Article 26 gives each religious denomination the right to establish and maintain institutions, to own and acquire property, and to administer its affairs itself in accordance with law. Articles 27 and 28 prohibit the state from levying taxes in support of religion or making religious instruction compulsory in state schools. Article 30 gives all religious and linguistic minorities the right to establish and administer educational institutions which may qualify for grants from the state without discrimination. These constitutional provisions are part of the chapter on fundamental rights and therefore justifiable. Equally important, political participation is possible for all citizens. Adult suffrage is the basis of elections, unqualified by separate electorates, proportional representation, religious or caste identity, or property. No legal or constitutional connection exists between the state in India and any particular religion.

The Indian constitution emphasized *individual* rights—social or religious identity was not legally permitted to impede or advance individuals. The modernizing and developmental policies adopted by the central government also offered greater economic opportunities for able and hardworking individuals. An all-India economic and political system, in which freedom of movement, residence, acquisition of property, and employment were constitutionally assured to all individuals, argued well for an erosion of vertical group barriers among Indians. One spectacular illustration of benefits flowing from the new system was the rapid and successful resettlement of Sikh refugees from West Punjab in different parts of India additional to adjacent East Punjab. Other illustrations abound in the lives of individual former untouchables. During the 1960s, when earlier hopes of rapid economic growth faded, when regional economic disparities became vivid, and when the number of births, entrants to the labor force, and educated unemployed leaped far above the estimates of national planners, competition among individuals increased unbearably. Pressures on a democratic secular system increased.

Competition for middle class jobs meant that individual competence needed reinforcement from group identity and political patronage. Groups competing for economic and political goals mobilized again on the basis of kinship, caste, language, or religion. Their success depended in part upon internal organization, and in part upon the external environment represented by the government. Two contrasting examples illustrate the point.

Notwithstanding a relatively low rate of mobility among the total population of India, nativist or "sons of the soil" movements sprang up to resist perceived dominance of "outsiders" in middle class occupations. In Bombay, a tightly organized Hindu chauvinist party, the Shiv Sena, emerged under the leadership of Bal Thackeray as champion of the Maharashtrians. Katzenstein (1979) shows how the responses of state and central governments were generally supportive, despite concerns that national objectives of inter-ethnic unity, economic efficiency, and individual meritocracy were being compromised. The Shiv Sena's attitude towards religious minorities is, perhaps, best expressed by Bal Thackeray's remarks after communal riots in which many Muslims had been killed in June 1984: "Why should Hindus in their own country seek permission for celebrating Shivaji's birthday only because the Muslims object to it?" (*Far Eastern Economic Review*, 14 June 1984).

In contrast, the central government opposed demands in the Punjab for continuation of traditional patterns of recruitment to the armed forces (which had favored Sikhs). New Delhi also opposed, ignored, or failed to implement other economic demands made by the Punjab in the late 1970s and early 1980s where the land-owning Sikh farmers formed a dominant section of the population, though not a majority. Other, less tangible, causes of discontent were exacerbated among the Sikh youth newly experiencing prosperity, leisure, education, and unemployment, in quick succession. Some turned to religious fundamentalism and political activism in much the same way as some had turned to the Ghadr, or to Marxism, in earlier decades. Correspondingly, there was a renewal of Sikh orthodoxy to battle "modernizing" forces, bitter intra-Sikh doctrinal disputes as with the Nirankaris, and startling rise to prominence of a village preacher, Jarnail Singh Bhindranwale. Factionalism within the Akali Dal, the major political party representing rural Sikhs, as well as among Sikh members of the Congress(I), reduced Sikh political efficacy while increasing the militancy of dissident elements.

Economics does not provide the whole explanation for the politicization of religious identity. Ambiguities within the Indian constitution, the behavior of various political leaders, and short term exigencies of electoral politics have often intertwined to dilute the practice of secularism in India. The examples are many.

The Indian constitution does not completely separate religion from the state. It gives government the right to regulate the finances, administration, and secular functions of religious establishments, some of which enjoy very considerable income. A functional connection between civil and religious administrators of funds provides opportunities for political bargaining at local and state levels, as is quite evident at religious centers such as Tirupati. The constitution also gives the state a reformist role in continuation of the social reform movement which merged into the nationalist struggle. By legislating reform, or refraining from doing so, that state touches on a realm preserved by tradition to familial, caste, and community institutions. Whether the response to reform is positive or negative, it takes a political as well as a private shape—as can be seen in the women's struggle against dowry abuses.

Article 17 of the Indian constitution "abolished" the concept of untouchability and "its practice in any form." It also provided for preferential treatment of the "backward" castes and tribes enumerated in its Schedules by reserving seats for them in educational institutions and governmental services. Notwithstanding changes in the legal framework, the overall situation of the scheduled castes and tribes in independent India remained a pitiable and complicated one. For a few, the backward caste label became a passport to advancement. For the many, who were poverty stricken and landless, their social and economic conditions were unameliorated. In different parts of the country, scheduled castes or tribes were organized into vote banks to be drawn on by a ruling party in return for favors, such as extending the reservations. Sometimes, as in Gujarat, caste Hindus and opposition parties violently resisted such courting of votes.

In some areas, as Mathur shows in the case of Bihar, when backward castes asserted their legal and economic rights they were subjected to systematic brutality with the complicity of the police. Throughout the country, as Jurgensmeyer (1982:20) documents with reference to the Punjab, backward castes and tribes "are uncertain whether ultimately they should regard themselves as separate from, or part of, Hindu society." Their religious identity has been somewhat fluid, as they involved themselves in various religious movements within the Hindu framework but with a strong reformist element, such as those led by Guru Nanak in Kerala or Mangoo Room in the Punjab, or explicitly converted to Islam, Sikhism, or Christianity. Over recent decades, significant numbers converted to Buddhism, emulating their national leader Dr. B. R. Ambedkar. In 1981, Harijan leaders in Tamilnadu declared that they were tired of continued discrimination, threatening "that all 21 crores (210 million) Harijans of India would convert to Islam once the concessions were withdrawn." (*Far Eastern Economic Review*, 17 July 1981). The vociferously antagonistic reaction in the Indian press to the conversion to Islam of a few hundred scheduled caste families in the Tamilnadu village of Meenakshipuram at the time was an indication that their act of protest would not pass unnoticed.

In the 1950s, the Indian Parliament legislated reforms in Hindu personal law which affected marriage, inheritance, and the status of women, but Parliament did not initiate reforms in Muslim personal law. As Lateef (1983:358) explains, a disparate Muslim community in India, in its search for group cohesion in the 20th century, emphasized traditional unity symbols including unreformed personal law. Though private religious beliefs and social customs among Muslims of different classes responded to changes in the social environment, the community maintained a public profile of an orthodox religion with the support of men and women alike.

In post-partition India, individual Muslims found prominence through their participation in Congress governments, but the leadership of the Muslim masses was largely in the hands of traditionalist bodies such as the *Jamaat-e-Islami* which focused on non-economic sectarian interests. Their failure to pay attention to economic advancement in the modern world, or to build coalitions with economically powerful groups of non-Muslims, left the great majority of Muslims economically non-competitive. When

Muslims prospered, as in towns where artisans and merchants felt the stimulation of international trade, they became prone to chronic communal violence, as in Moradabad, Ahmedabad, and Bhiwandi. The Muslim leadership had traded electoral support to Congress in return for resting undisturbed, and safe, but in the 1970s and early 1980s neither Congress nor non-Congress governments were guaranteeing security of life, property, or honor of any group which became victim to criminal assault by un-named and frequently unpunished mobs. At the same time, Muslims were numerically strong enough in certain electoral districts to swing results. Their vote was courted by political parties other than Congress. The Muslim vote went to the Janata in the 1977 general elections, back to the Congress(I) in 1980, and was an unpredictable factor in 1985. Akbar (1985:313) takes encouragement from this fact as well as from the coming of age of a new, post-partition generation. He predicts greater commitment to democracy—and by implication, secularism—and a more constructive participation in national politics on the part of India's largest minority group.

The dominant influence on Indian politics has, no doubt, been that of Congress. Under Nehru's leadership, Congress was broad-based, inclusive, socialistic, and protective of minorities. During the 1960s, Congress' dominance and stability were weakened. Under Indira Gandhi's leadership it lost the institutional resilience which had provided strong but flexible links between grassroots workers —often dealing in terms of caste and community- –and a national secular leadership. With the increasing personalization and centralization of Congress in the 1970s, party leaders at all levels become dependent on New Delhi and thus more vulnerable to their opponents, and more prone to abandon pluralistic principles for electoral advantage.

The main opponents of Congress, as Nehru was acutely aware, were the parties and groups on the right which appealed to caste Hindus. The most coherent and best organized among them was the Rashtriya Swayamsevak Sangh (RSS), which is sympathetically portrayed by Malkani (1980) as having a clear cut philosophy of a Hindu Rashtra. The late RSS chief M. S. Golwalkar's attitude towards minorities is quoted by Prabha Dixit (1974:173): they must "adopt Hindu culture and language, must learn to respect and hold in reverence Hindu religion, must entertain no ideas but those of glorification of the Hindu race and culture... (they) must cease to be foreigner and claim nothing... far less preferential treatment." As Rudolph shows (1983), the Hindu Right waged its struggle within India's constitutional structure but attempted to push government cultural and educational policies in the directions it preferred. Installation of the Janata government in 1977 provided new opportunities for doing so. The question of which history books were to be used in schools became contentious; secular scientific and professional historians were ranged against "Hindu nationalistic" ones. The Arunachal Freedom of Religion Act passed in 1978 was perceived by Christians and Muslims as directed specifically against them, as it ruled against conversion but not against "reconversion" (to Hinduism). An ominous feature of the times was the absence of public opposition to such an erosion of tolerance. On the contrary, there was a rising tide of Hindu identification, first manifesting itself as insecurity and assertiveness. Dr. Karan Singh, Member of Parliament, former member of Congress and President of a newly formed Hindu Virat Samaj, expressed himself thus: "The day has gone when Hinduism was like some kind of helpless whale being constantly bitten into by aggressive sharks. We must be prepared to look after all our interests, and it is our responsibility to look after the interests of other religions" (Singh 1984:6). A new and notable feature of the late 1970s and early 1980s was the opening of doors by Hindu organizations to non-Hindus, including Muslims, and the cooperation in some states of Janata with parties labelled "communal" such as the Akali Dal or the Muslim League.

Though Mrs. Gandhi warned against "rabid communal forces" undermining India in the early 1980s, and though she counted on minority support at center and state, it was evident that she too looked to garner the "Hindu vote" in the 1985 elections—as she had done in the 1983 state elections in Kashmir (Hardgrave 1984:41). This fact, together with her intolerance for state governments which she did not control, led her to make a series of disasterous decisions in the Punjab and Kashmir. Sikhs and Muslims respectively formed majorities in those two border states, but had steadfastly demonstrated their preference in successive elections for moderate political leadership over secessionist demogogues. Without tracing the tortuous details of the Punjab problem, or like Brass (1974) comparing Nehru's handling of similar problems in the 1950s and early 1960s with that of his daughter, some comment must be made. By refusing to respond to legitimate grievances reasonably expressed, by failing to halt a deteriorating law and order situation in the Punjab or apprehend miscreants, by undermining the leadership of the moderate Akalis, by appearing to connive at the activities of Bhindranwale, and by using the army to assault the Golden Temple in Amritsar in June 1984 and then maintain security in the Punjab, Mrs. Gandhi's government alienated Sikhs. She was assassinated by two Sikh guards on 31 October 1984.

Independent witnesses to the atrocities committed against Sikhs resident outside the Punjab, especially in Delhi—and traditional supporters of Congress—have testified that the violence was not a spontaneous expression of mass hysteria, but a delayed and organized pogrom to "teach Sikhs a lesson" led by certain members of the Congress(I) (Mukhoty and Kothari 1984). When the subsequent election campaign of the Congress(I) capitalized on portraying Sikhs as threats to national unity, the gulf between two formerly close-knit communities widened perceptibly. A few individuals, such as the journalist Arun Shourie (1985), questioned seriously if Indians could survive united by teaching one another lessons. Too many others remained silently acquiescent. The debates of the 1930s on minority rights were not repeated in this totally different political system but did cast shadows of their own. There was a division of opinion between those who believed that a majority ruled while others depended on its concessions, and those who believed that all citizens of all communities could live together because each had rights and duties independently and equally derived from law and the constitution.

To conclude, contemporary South Asia shows no firm line of demarcation between the private religious beliefs of individuals and the public political behavior of social groups defined by religious adherence. As in the past, therefore, religious identity continues to be used for a variety of political purposes. The heads of weak state structures invoke religious nationalism to strengthen governmental control, as in Pakistan and Bangladesh, though it is evident that the commonality of Islam alone is not sufficient to bring about national consensus. Other instruments must be forged. Likewise some politicians in India and Sri Lanka have attempted to generate nationalistic fervor among Hindus and Buddhists, neither previously renowned for *machismo*. Social conservatives all over South Asia—as in other parts of the world— resist the egalitarian changes brought about by modernization, especially as changes affect the rights and behavior of women and other oppressed groups, in the name of religious or doctrinal purity.

Political aspirants so frequently mobilize followings among their co-religionists that it has become common electoral practice for Indian political parties to field candidates belonging to the majority community or caste in any given constituency. Group demands for governmental attention or special treatment in India appear to be bolstered rather than diluted when phrased in terms of protection for religious minorities. Thus, Muslim personal law remains unreformed; the neglected grievances of the state of Punjab gained the (not necessarily favorable) attention of New Delhi only when presented as Sikh demands; and groups most profoundly dissatisfied with their status have registered protest by public conversion to another religion. In short, the sacred in South Asia is frequently made to serve the temporal.

Our glance at South Asian history leads to five broad propositions. First, in every country and in every era, religious identity has been one of several factors molding individual careers, group politics, and governmental behavior. The importance of this factor has varied with prevailing standards of legitimacy, with the economic and political institutions of the time, and, above all, with the expediency of the moment.

Secondly, no religious elite in South Asia has been immune to the temptation of seeking political influence through indirect or direct involvement in matters of state. The conventional dichotomy drawn between contemplative, non-ecclesiastical religions (such as Hinduism) and congregational, clerical religions (such as Islam) is an overgeneralization in the field of public affairs. The South Asian experience demonstrates the ability of every faith to treat others either with a benign smile of tolerance or a malignant frown of intolerance—for political reasons!

Thirdly, while all political systems in South Asia have permitted the intertwining of religion and politics to some extent, it can be seen that the more narrowly based and autocratic a regime, the more likely it is to seek legitimization and reinforcement from religious leaders who can influence the masses.

Fourthly, democratic politics in which numbers of votes cast are vitally important, and in which interests are disaggregated, tend to underline religious identity as a short-run tactic of mass mobilization. In the long run, however, broad-based and participatory politics encourage the building of cross-community coalitions around shared interests.

Finally, the politics of different periods in South Asian history show that though the "secular state" is a new and evolving concept, it best encapsulates the ineffable spirit of that civilization. The torch-bearers of civilization there have known, as Derrett (1968:43) puts it, that "were it not tolerant of disunity and discrepancy it would have no survival of its own."

Consolidated List of References

Ahlstrom, Sydney E. 1972. *A Religious History of the American People.* New Haven: Yale University Press. Pages 263–329.

Ahmad, Abdul Monsur. 1964. "Secularism Versus Religion in Pakistan." *The Concepts of Pakistan* (No. 4): 21–29.

Ahmad, Aziz. 1964. *Studies in Islamic Culture in the Indian Environment.* Oxford: Oxford University Press.

Ahmad, Imtiaz. 1980. "India: Surprising Isolation." *World Focus* 1 (5): 23–26.

Ahmad, Khurshid and Zafar Ishaq Ansari. 1979. *Islamic Perspectives.* Leicester: The Islamic Foundation.

Ahmad, Mumtaz. 1981. "Islamic Revival in Pakistan." In C.A. Pullapilly, editor. *Islam in the Contemporary World.* Notre Dame: Crossroads Press. Pages 261–73.

_____. 1985. "Parliament, Parties, Polls, and Islam: Issues in the Current Debate on Religion and Politics in Pakistan." *American Journal of Islamic Social Sciences* 2(1): 15–28.

Ahmed, Qadeeruddin. 1983. "The Form of Government People Desire." *The Universal Message* (Karachi): 4: 12–13

Akbar, M.J. 1985. *India: The Siege Within: Challenges to a Nation's Unity.* Harmondsworth, England: Penguin Books.

Ali, Salamat. 1986. "India: A Minority Syndrome: Muslims Have Begun to Assert Their Rights." *Far Eastern Economic Review* (20 March): 32–33.

Anand, J.C. 1975. "The Punjab-Akalis in the Coalition." In K.P. Karunkarun, editor. *Coalition Governments in India.* Simla: Indian Institute of Advanced Study. Pages 237–250.

Arasaratnam, S. 1958. "Oratorians and Predikants: The Catholic Church in Ceylon under Dutch Rule." *The Ceylon Journal of Historical and Social Studies* 1(2):216–222.

Austin, Granville. 1966. *The Indian Constitution.* New York: Oxford University Press.

Babb, Lawrence A. 1986. "The Puzzle of Religious Modernity." In J.R. Roach, editor. *India 2000: The Next Fifteen Years.*

Riverdale, Maryland: The Riverdale Company. Pages 56–79.

Banerjee, Nitya Narayan. 1987. "Stop the Fissiparous Trend." *The Hindu* (17 February): 17.

Baxi, Upendra. 1985. "Reflections on Reservation Crisis in Gujarat." *Mainstream* (8 June): 15–22.

Baxter, Craig. 1969. *The Jana Sangh: A Biography of an Indian Political Party.* Philadelphia: University of Pennsylvania Press.

Bechert, H. 1972. "Buddhism in the Modern States of South East Asia." In B. Grossman. editor. *South East Asia and the Modern World.* Wiesbaden: Otto Harrassowitz. Pages 129–139.

Bihari Lal, Pandit. 1873. *Tajawiz Kameli Dharm Sabha.* Lahore: Koh-i-Nur Press.

Binder, Leonard. 1961. *Religion and Politics in Pakistan.* Berkeley: University of California Press.

Björkman, James Warner. 1984. "Indian Liberalism: Precursor to Indian Socialism and Democracy." In A.P. Padhi and K.V. Rao, editors. *Socialism, Secularism and Democracy in India.* Delhi: New Literature. Pages 44–78.

——————. 1986. Editor. *The Changing Division of Labor in South Asia: Women and Men in Society, Economy, and Politics.* Riverdale, Maryland: The Riverdale Company; and Delhi: Manohar Publications.

——————. 1988. "On Lions, Tigers and Peacocks: Indo-Lankan Ethno-Political Relations." In K.E. Corey, editor. *Sri Lanka: Recent Accomplishments and Future Prospects.* Riverdale, Maryland: The Riverdale Company.

Bolitho, Hector. 1954. *Jinnah: Creator of Pakistan.* New York: Macmillan Company.

Borthwick, Meredith. 1984. *The Changing Role of Women in Bengal, 1849–1905.* Princeton, New Jersey: Princeton University Press.

Boudens, Robrecht. 1979. *Catholic Missionaries in a British Colony: Successes and Failures in Ceylon, 1976–1893.* Immensee, Switzerland: Nouvelle revue de science missionaire.

Boxer, C.R. 1958. "Christians and Spices: Portuguese Missionary Methods in Ceylon, 1518–1658." *History Today* 8:346–354.

——————. 1960. "A Note on Portuguese Missionary Methods in the East: 16th–18th Centuries." *Ceylon Historical Journal* 10: 77–90.

Brass, Paul R. 1974. *Language, Religion and Politics in North India.* London: Cambridge University Press.

——————. 1985. "Separatism in India (with Special Reference to Punjab.)" Paper presented at the Conference on India's Democracy, 14–16 March.

Caplan, Lionel. 1980. "Class and Christianity in South India: Indigenous Responses to Western Denominationalism." *Modern Asian Studies* 14(4):645–671.

——————. 1985. "The Popular Culture of Evil in Urban South India," *The Anthropology of Evil.* Oxford: Basil Blackwell. Pages 110–127.

Chawdhery, G.W. 1974. *The Last Days of United Pakistan.* London: C. Hurst and Company.

Coupland, Reginald. 1944. *The Indian Problem: Report on the Constitutional Problem in India.* Oxford: Oxford University Press.

Das, A.N. 1983. *Agrarian Unrest and Socio-economic Change in Bihar, 1900–1980.* New Delhi: Manohar Publications.

Das, P.S. 1978. "Growth and Instability in Crop Output in Eastern India." *Economic and Political Weekly* 13: 1741–1748.

De, Krishna Prasad. 1976. *Religious Freedom Under the Indian Constitution.* Columbia, Missouri: South Asia Books.

Derrett, J. Duncan M. 1968. *Religion, Law and the State in India.* London: Faber and Faber.

de Silva, K.M. 1965. *Social Policy and Missionary Organizations in Ceylon, 1840–55.* London: Longmans, Green and Company, for the Royal Commonwealth Society.

——————. 1973. Editor. *History of Ceylon.* Colombo: University of Ceylon Press Board.

——————. 1975. "Christian Missions in Sri Lanka and Their Response to Nationalism, 1910–1948." In P.L. Prematileke, K. Indrapala, and J.E. van Lohuizen-de Leeuw, editors. *Senarat Paranavitana Commemoration Volume: Studies in South Asian Culture.* V. Leiden: Institute of South Asian Archaeology, University of Amsterdam. Pages 221–233.

——————. 1981. *A History of Sri Lanka.* Delhi: Oxford University Press.

——————. 1986a. *Managing Ethnic Tensions in Multi-Ethnic Societies: Sri Lanka 1880–1985.* Lanham, Maryland: University Press of America.

_____. 1986b. *Religion, Nationalism and the State in Modern Sri Lanka*. Tampa, Florida: University of South Florida (Monographs in Religion and Public Policy No. 1).

Dessuki, Ali E. Hillal. 1981. "The Resurgence of Islamic Organizations in Egypt: An Interpretation." In A.S. Cudsi and A.E.H. Dessouki, editors. *Islam and Power*. Baltimore: The Johns Hopkins University Press. Pages 107–118.

Dhar, H. and Kalyan Mukherjee. 1978. "Growing Peasant Revolt." *Economic and Political Weekly* 13:51.

Dil, Shaheen F. 1980. "The Myth of Islamic Resurgence in South Asia." *Current History* 78: 165–168, 185–186.

Dilgeer, Harjinder Singh. 1984. *Glory of the Akal Takht*. Jullundur: Punjabi Book Company.

Dixit, Prabha. 1974. *Communalism: A Struggle for Power*. New Delhi: Orient Longman.

Dube, S.C. and V.N. Basilov. 1983. Editors. *Secularization in Multi-Religious Societies: Indo-Soviet Perspectives*. New Delhi: Concept Publishing Company.

Dumont, Louis. 1970a. *Religion, Politics and History in India*. Paris: Mouton.

_____. 1970b. *Homo Hierarchicus: Implications of Caste*. London: Weidenfeld and Nicholson.

Engineer, Asghar Ali. 1984. Editor. *Communal Riots in Post-Independence India*. Hyderabad: Sangham.

Eschmann, Anncharlott *et aliter*. 1978. Editors. *The Cult of Jagannath and The Regional Tradition of Orissa*. New Delhi: Manohar.

Esposito, John L. 1984. *Islam and Politics*. Syracuse, New York: Syracuse University Press.

Forrester, Duncan B. 1980. *Caste and Christianity: Attitudes and Policies on Caste of Anglo-Saxon Protestant Missions in India*. London: Curzon Press.

Fox, Richard G. 1985. *Lions of the Punjab: Culture in the Making*. Berkeley: University of California Press.

Freud, Sigmund. 1928. *The Future of an Illusion* (translated by W.D. Robson-Scott, The International Psycho-Analytic Library, No. 15). London: The Hogarth Press.

Frykenberg, Robert Eric. 1977. "The Silent Settlement in South India, 1793–1863." In *Land Tenure and Peasant in South Asia*, edited by R.E. Frykenberg. Madison: University of Wisconsin Press. Pages 37–53.

_____. 1979. "Conversion and Crises of Conscience Under Company Raj in South India." In *Asie du Sud: Traditions et Changements,* edited by M. Gaborieau and A. Thorner. Paris: Colloques Internationaux du Centre National de la Recherche Scientifique. Pages 311–321.

_____. 1980. "On the Study of Conversion Movements: A Review Article and a Theoretical Note." *Indian Economic and Social History Review* 17(1): 121–138.

_____. 1985a. "Caste, Morality, and Western Religion under the Raj." *Modern Asian Studies* 19(2): 321–352.

_____. 1985b. "State, Empire, and Nation in South India: Demythologizing as a Scholar's Enterprise." In *Region and Nation in India,* edited by P. Wallace. New Delhi: Oxford Publishing Company. Pages 60–84.

_____. 1985c. "Religion and Company Raj in South India." *Fides et Historia* 12(2): 3–37.

_____. 1986. "The Concept of 'Majority' and Its Mischief in Modern India: An Historiographic and Theoretical Comment." *Journal of Commonwealth History.*

Ghose, Jogendra Chunder. 1885. *The English Works of Raja Ram Mohun Roy.* Calcutta: Bhowanipore Oriental Press.

Gill, S.S. 1987. "Religion and Politics in India." *Indian Express* (3 February): 8.

Glazer, Nathan and Daniel P. Moynihan. 1975. *Ethnicity: Theory and Experience.* Cambridge, Massachusetts: Harvard University Press.

Glock, Charles Y. 1962. "On the Study of Religious Commitment." *Religious Education* 42: 98–110.

Glock, Charles Y. and Rodney Stark. 1965. *Religion and Society in Tension.* Chicago: Rand MacNally.

Government of Bihar (GOB). 1982. *Plan Statistics.* Patna: Planning Department.

Government of India (GOI). 1923. *1921 Census of India.* Volume XV. *Punjab and Delhi.* Part I. Lahore: Superintendent, Government Printing.

_____. 1984. *White Paper on the Punjab Agitation.* New Delhi: 10 July.

Government of Punjab (GOP). 1945. *Pamphlet Showing the Systems Adopted by Departments of the Punjab Government to Ensure Equitable Recruitment of All Communities into Government Services.* Lahore: Superintendent, Government Printing.

_____. 1984. *Statistical Abstract of Punjab 1983*. Chandigarh: Economic Adviser to Government.

Gupta, Rakesh. 1983. *Bihar Peasantry and the Kisan Sabha*. New Delhi: People's Publishing House.

Haddad, Yvonne. 1980. "The Arab-Israeli Wars, Nasserism, and the Affirmation of Islamic Identity." In J.L. Esposito, editor. *Islam and Development*. Syracuse, New York: Syracuse University Press. Pages 107–121.

Hardgrave, Robert L. 1984. *India Under Stress: Prospects for Political Stability*. Boulder, Colorado: Westview Press.

Hardy, Peter. 1972. *The Muslims of British India*. Cambridge: Cambridge University Press.

Harrison, Selig S. 1960. *India: The Most Dangerous Decades*. Princeton: Princeton University Press.

_____. 1967. "Hindu Society and the State: The Indian Union." In K.H. Silvert, editor. *Expectant Peoples: Nationalism and Development*. New York: Vintage Books, 1967. Pages 267–299.

Hayami, Y. 1981. "Agrarian Problems in India: An East and South East Asian Perspective." *Economic and Political Weekly* 16: 707–712.

Heimsath, Charles H. 1964. *Indian Nationalism and Hindu Social Reform*. Princeton, New Jersey: Princeton University Press.

Hodgson, Marshall G.S. 1974. *The Venture of Islam*. Chicago: The University of Chicago Press.

Horowitz, D.R. 1980. *Coup Theories and Officers' Motives: Sri Lanka in Comparative Perspective*. Princeton, New Jersey: Princeton University Press.

Houghton, Graham. 1983. *The Impoverishment of Dependency: The History of the Church in Madras*. Madras: CLS.

Hudson, Michael C. 1980. "Islam and Political Development." In J.L. Esposito, editor. *Islam and Development*. Syracuse, New York: Syracuse University Press. Pages 1–24.

Ihtesham, Kazi, 1981. "Nationalism: Its Basis and Implications for Pakistan and Bangladesh" (mimeograph).

Ikram, S.M. 1965. *Modern Muslim India and the Birth of Pakistan. 1858–1951*. Lahore: Sh. Muhammad Ashraf.

Jahan, Rounaq. 1972. *Pakistan: Failure in National Integration*. New York: Columbia University Press.

Jain, Girilal. 1986. "Hindu Revival?" *The Illustrated Weekly of India* (7 December): 13.

Jalal, Ayesha. 1985. *The Sole Spokesman: Jinnah, The Muslim League and the Demand for Pakistan.* Cambridge, England: Cambridge University Press.

Jambunathan, M.R. 1961. Editor. *Swami Shraddhanand.* Bombay: Bharatiya Vidya Bhavan.

Janda, Kenneth. 1980. *Political Parties: A Cross National Survey.* New York: Free Press.

Jansen, G.H. 1979. *Militant Islam.* New York: Harper and Row, Publishers.

Jones, Kenneth W. 1973. "Ham Hindu Nahin: Arya Sikh Relations, 1877–1905." *The Journal of Asian Studies* 32: 3: 457–475.

_____. 1976. *Arya Dharm: Hindu Consciousness in 19th Century Punjab.* Berkeley: University of California Press.

_____. 1979. "Social Changes and Religious Movements in Punjab." In M.S.A. Rao, editor. *Social Movements in India.* Volume 2. New Delhi: Manohar Publications. Pages 1–16.

Joshi, Chand. 1984. *Bhindranwale: Myth and Reality.* New Delhi: Vikas Publishing House Pvt. Ltd.

Juergensmeyer, Mark. 1982. *Religion as Social Vision: The Movement Against Untouchability in 20th Century Punjab.* Berkeley: University of California Press.

R.G.K. 1986. "Are We a Soft People?" *Times of India Sunday Review* (17 August): IV.

Kagal, Ayesha. 1982. "Armed Coup in Golden Temple." *The Times of India, Sunday Review* (19 December): I, VI.

Kanya Mahavidyalaya, Jullundur. 1981. *Digest of the Annual Report for 1891.* Translated from the Urdu by Miss Selma Ajmeri. [Ditto 1896 and 1897 annual reports]

Kapur, Rajiv A. 1986. *Sikh Separatism: The Politics of Faith.* London: Allen and Unwin.

Katzenstein, Mary F. 1979. *Ethnicity and Equality.* Ithaca, New York; Cornell University Press.

Kaufmann, Susan Bayly. 1981. "A Christian Caste in Hindu Society: Religious Leadership and Social Conflict among the Paravas of Southern Tamil Nadu." *Modern Asian Studies* 15(2): 203–234. Also see her Ph.D. dissertation, "Popular Christianity, Caste, and Hindu Society in South India, 1800–1915: A Study of Travancore and Tirunelveli." University of Cambridge.

Kaye, John William. 1859. *Christianity in India: An Historical Narrative.* London: Smith, Elder and Company.

Kemper, Steven. 1984. "The Buddhist Monkhood, the Law and the State in Colonial Sri Lanka." *Comparative Studies in Society and History* 26(3): 401–427.

Kearney, R.N. 1967. *Communalism and Language in the Politics of Ceylon.* Durham, North Carolina: Duke University Press.

Khan, Liaquat Ali. 1951. *Pakistan, The Heart of Asia.* Cambridge, Massachusetts: Harvard University Press.

Khan, Mohammad Ayub. 1967. *Friends, Not Masters.* Karachi: Oxford University Press.

Khayal, G.N. 1985. "Valley of Unrest." *The Illustrated Weekly of India* (20 October): 5.

Khergamvala, F.J. 1987. "Rising Fundamentalism: A Blessing or a Curse?" *The Hindu* (21 January): 8.

King, Christopher R. 1974. "The Nagari Pracharini Sabha . . . of Bengal, 1893–1950." Ph.D. dissertation. Madison: University of Wisconsin.

Kopf, David. 1969. *British Orientalism and the Bengal Renaissance.* Berkeley: University of California Press.

———. 1979. *The Brahmo Samaj and the Shaping of the Indian Mind.* Princeton, New Jersey: Princeton University Press.

Kothari, Rajni. 1970. *Caste in Indian Politics.* New Delhi: Orient Longman Ltd.

———. 1986. "'Fundamentalism' is Not the Essence of Hinduism." *The Illustrated Weekly of India* (7 December): 16.

Lateef, Shahida. 1983. "The Status and Role of Women in a Minority Community: The Case of Muslims in India." D.Phil. dissertation. Brighton, England: University of Sussex.

Low, D.A. 1973. *Lion Rampant: Essays in the Study of British Imperialism.* London: Frank Cass and Company.

McLoughlin, William G. 1959. *Modern Revivalism: Charles Gradison Finney to Billy Graham.* New York: Ronald Press.

———. 1978. *Revivals, Awakenings, and Reform.* Chicago: University of Chicago Press.

Madan, T.N. 1983. "The Historical Significance of Secularism in India." In Dube and Basilov: 11–20.

———. 1986. "Secularisation and the Sikh Religious Tradition." *Social Compass: International Journal of the Sociology of Religion* 33: 257–273.

Malalgoda, K. 1973. "The Buddhist-Christian Confrontation in Ceylon, 1800–1880." *Social Compass* 20:171–200.

———. 1976. *Buddhism in Sinhalese Society, 1750–1900.*

Berkeley: University of California Press.

Malik, Hafeez. 1980. *Moslem Nationalism in India and Pakistan,* second edition. Lahore: People's Publishing House.

Malik, Lynda. 1982. "Measuring Consensus in Pakistan."*Journal of South Asian and Middle Eastern Studies* VI:33–47.

Malkani, K.R. 1980. *The RSS Story.* New Delhi: Impex.

Marsden, George M. 1980. *Fundamentalism and American Culture: The Shaping of Twentieth-Century Evangelicalism, 1870–1925.* Oxford: Oxford University Press.

————. 1984. Editor. *Evangelicalism and Modern America.* Grand Rapids, Michigan: Eerdmans.

Marshall, P.J. 1970. Editor. *The British Discovery of Hinduism in the Eighteenth Century.* Cambridge: Cambridge University Press.

Mathew, George. 1982. "Politicization of Religion: Conversion to Islam in Tamil Nadu." *Economic and Political Weekly* 17 (19 and 26 June).

Mehrottra, N.C. 1980. *Political Crises and Polls in India.* New Delhi: Deep and Deep Publications.

Memon, Muhammad Umar. 1983. "Pakistani Urdu Creative Writing on National Disintegration: The Case of Bangladesh." *The Journal of Asian Studies* 42: 105–127.

Merrian, Allen Hayes. 1980. *Gandhi vs. Jinnah: The Debate over the Partition of India.* Calcutta: Minerva.

Metcalf, Barbara Daly. 1982. *Islamic Revival in British India: Deoband, 1860–1900.* Princeton: Princeton University Press.

Minault, Gail. 1982a. *The Khilafat Movement: Religious Symbolism and Political Mobilization in India.* New York: Columbia Univerity Press.

————. 1982b. "Purdah's Progress: The Beginnings of Education for Indian Muslim Women." In J.P. Sharma, editor. *Individualist Ideas in Modern India.* Calcutta: Firma K.L. Mukhyopadyaya.

Mitra, H.N. and N.N. 1925. "The Sikh Movement" [based on the papers of Sardar Gurbachan Singh]. *The Indian Quarterly Register* I: 90.

Morris-Jones, W.H. 1962. "India's Political Idioms." In C.H. Philips, editor. *Politics and Society in India.* London: Allen and Unwin. Pages 133–154.

Mujahid, Sharif al. 1962. "Basis of Pakistani Nationalism."

Pakistani Nationhood. Dacca: Bureau of National Reconstruction. Pages 79–95.

_____. 1974 "Bangladesh: Was It a Failure of Ideology?" *Impact International* (London) 4(13–14): 9.

_____. 1976. *Ideological Orientation of Pakistan*. Islamabad: National Committee for the Birth Centenary Celebration of Quaid-i-Azam Mohammad Ali Jinnah.

Mukherjee, K. 1979. "Peasant Revolt in Bhojpur." *Economic and Political Weekly* 14: 1536–1538.

Mukherjee K. and Rajendra Yadav. 1982. "For Reasons of State: Oppression and Resistance: A Study of Bhojpur Peasantry." In A.N. Das, editor. *Agrarian Movements in India: Studies in 20th Century Bihar*. London: Frank Cass. Pages 119–147.

Mukherjee, S.A. 1968. *Sir William Jones: A Study of Eighteenth-Century British Attitudes to India*. Cambridge: Cambridge University Press.

Mukhia, Harbans. 1987. "The Connotations of Indian Secularism." *Express Magazine* (4 January): 2.

Mukhoty, Govinda and Rajni Kothari. 1984. *Who Are the Guilty? Report of a Joint Inquiry into the Causes and Impact of the Riots in Delhi from 31 October to 10 November*. Delhi: People's Union for Democratic Rights, and People's Union for Civil Liberties.

Mullick, R.P. 1980. "Not a Communal Riot." *Economic and Political Weekly* (6 September): 1507.

Naidu, Ratna. 1982. "The Communal Edge to Plural Societies: India and Malaysia." *ICSSR Newsletter* (October 1981–March 1982): 1–16.

Naim, C.M. 1979. Editor. *Iqbal and Jinnah and Pakistan: The Vision and the Reality*. Syracuse, New York: Maxwell School of Citizenship and Public Affairs, Syracuse University.

Naipaul, V.S. 1984. "Among the Republicans." *The New York Review of Books* 32:16 (October): 5–17.

Nandy, Ashis. 1983. *The Intimate Enemy: Loss and Recovery of Self under Colonialism*. Delhi: Oxford University Press.

_____. 1985. "An Anti-Secularist Manifesto." *Seminar* 314 (October): 1–11.

_____. 1986. "The Fate of Secularism—II." *The Forum Gazette* (16–31 July): 14.

Narang, Surjit Singh. 1980. "Role of the Chief Khalsa Diwan in Punjab Politics." M.Phil. Thesis. Amritsar: Department of

Political Science, Guru Nanak Dev University.

——————. 1981. "Chief Khalsa Diwan: An Analytical Study of Its Perceptions." In P. Wallace and S. Chopra, editors. *Political Dynamics of Punjab*. Amritsar: Guru Nanak Dev University Press. Pages 67–81.

Nayar, Baldev Raj. 1966. *Minority Politics in the Punjab*. Princeton, New Jersey: Princeton University Press.

Nayar, Kuldip and Khushwant Singh. 1984. *Tragedy of Punjab: Operation Bluestar & After*. New Delhi: Vision Books.

Nayyar, Rohini. 1977. "Poverty and Inequality in Rural Bihar." In *Poverty and Rural Landlessness in Rural Asia*. Geneva: International Labour Organisation. Pages 101–112.

Neill, Stephen. 1964. *A History of Christian Missions*. Harmondsworth: Pelican Books.

——————. 1984. *A History of Christianity in India: The Beginnings to AD 1707*. Cambridge: Cambridge University Press. Reviewed by P.J. Marshall in *The Times Literary Supplement* (4 May 1984): 501.

Niebuhr, H. Richard. 1937. *The Kingdom of God in America*. New York: Harper and Brothers.

Oddie, Geoffrey. 1977. *Religion in South Asia: Religious Conversion and Revival Movements in South Asia in Medieval and Modern Times*. Delhi: Manohar.

——————. 1978. *Social Protest in India: British Protestant Missionaries and Social Reforms, 1850–1900*. Columbia, Missouri: South Asia Books.

Omvedt, Gail. 1981. "Capitalist Agriculture and Rural Classes in India." *Economic and Political Weekly* 16:A140–A159.

Paige, Jeffrey M. 1975. *Agrarian Revolution, Social Movements and Export Agriculture in the Underdeveloped World*. New York: The Free Press.

Pakistan Institute of Public Opinion [PIPO]. 1980. "Religious Beliefs and Behaviour in Pakistan: An Empirical Study." Islamabad: Pakistan Institute of Public Opinion (mimeograph).

Prasad, Pradhan H. 1979. "Caste and Class in Bihar." *Economic and Political Weekly* 14 (Annual Number): 481–484.

Quddus, Muhammad A. 1982. *Pakistan: A Case Study of a Plural Society*. Columbia, Missouri: South Asia Books.

Quershi, Ishtiaq Husain. 1977. *Struggle for Pakistan*, second edition.

Karachi: Ma'arif Ltd.

Rahman, Fazlur. 1979. *Islam*. Chicago: University of Chicago Press.

Rahman, Mushtaqur. 1986. "Indian Muslims: A Perplexed Minority" (mimeograph).

Rahula, Walpola. 1959. *What the Buddha Taught*. London: Gordon Fraser.

_____. 1974. *The Heritage of the Bhikkhu*. New York: Grove Press.

Rao, M.S.A. 1979. *Social Movements and Social Transformation: A Study of Two Backward Class Movements in India*. Delhi: Macmillan Company.

Raychaudhuri, Tapan and Irfan Habib. 1982. *The Cambridge Economic History of India*, Volume I. London: Cambridge University Press.

Riggs, Fred W. and Ingetraut Dahlberg. 1982. Editors. *Conceptual and Terminological Analysis in the Social Sciences*. Frankfurt: INDEKS Verlag.

Roberts, M.W. 1982. *Caste Conflict and Elite Formation: The Rise of a Karava Elite in Sri Lanka, 1500–1931*. Cambridge: Cambridge University Press.

Rocher, Rosanne. 1983. *Orientalism, Poetry, and the Millennium: The Checkered Life of Nathaniel Brassey Halhed, 1751–1830*. New Delhi: Motilal Banarsidass and Columbia, Missouri: South Asia Books.

Rodinson, Maxime. 1980. *Marxism and the Muslim World*. Delhi: Orient Longman.

Rodrigues, Mario. 1986. "Maharashtra: Bhiwandi: Will the Peace Hold?" *Economic and Political Weekly* 21 (14 June): 1049–1050.

Rothermund, Dietmar. 1965. *Die Politische Willensbildung in Indien, 1900–1960*. Wiesbaden: Harrassowitz; Beitrage zur Sudasien-Forschung, Sudasien Institut, Universitat Heidelberg.

Rudolph, Lloyd I. 1983. "Establishing a Niche for Cultural Policy: An Introduction." *Pacific Affairs* 56 (1): 5–14.

_____. 1984. Editor. *Cultural Policy in India*. Delhi: Chanakya.

Rudolph, Lloyd I. and Susanne Hoeber Rudolph. 1967. *The Modernity of Tradition: Political Development in India*. Chicago: The University of Chicago Press.

_____. 1984. "Rethinking Secularism: Genesis and Implications of the Text Book Controversy, 1977–79." In L.I. Rudolph, editor. *Cultural Policy in India*. Delhi: Chanakya.

——————. 1987. *In Pursuit of Lakshmi: The Political Economy of the Indian State*. Chicago: The University of Chicago Press.

Rummel, R.J. 1970. *Applied Factor Analysis*. Chicago: Northwestern University Press.

Samuel, Valiyaveetil Thomas. 1973. "One Caste, One Religion and One God for Man: A Study of Sri Naryana Guru (1854–1928) of Kerala, India." A Thesis submitted to the Hartford Seminary Foundation.

Sandeen, Ernest R. 1970. *The Roots of Fundamentalism: British and American Millenarianism, 1800–1930*. Chicago: University of Chicago Press.

Saraswati, S. 1974. *Minorities in Madras State: Group Interests in Modern Politics*. Delhi: Impex India.

Sarkisyanz, E. 1965. *Buddhist Backgrounds of the Burmese Revolution*. The Hague: M. Nijhoff.

——————. 1978. "Buddhist Backgrounds of Burmese Socialism." In Bardwell L. Smith, editor. *Religion and Legitimation of Power in Thailand, Laos, and Burma*. Chambersburg, Pennsylvania: Anima Books. Pages 87–99.

Sayeed, Khalid Bin. 1968. *Pakistan; The Formative Phase, 1857–1948*, second edition. Karachi: Oxford University Press.

——————. 1967. *The Political System of Pakistan*. Boston: Houghton, Mifflin Company.

Sender, Henriette M. 1981. "Kashmiri Brahmans, Up to 1930." Ph.D. dissertation. Madison: University of Wisconsin.

Sharma, Hari P. 1973. "The Green Revolution in India: Prelude to a Red One." In K. Gough and Hari Sharma, editors. *Imperialism and Revolution in South Asia*. New York: Monthly Review Press.

Sharma, R.P. 1987. "Psychological Factor in Linguistic Agitations." *The Hindu* (13 January): 19.

Shastri, Sivanathas. 1911. *History of the Brahmo Samaj*, Volume I. Calcutta: R. Chatterjee.

Sheth, D.L. 1984. "Wooing the Hindu Voter." *Indian Express Magazine* (9 December): 1,6.

Shourie, Arun. 1985. "Can We Survive By Teaching Each Other Lessons?" *Illustrated Weekly of India* (13 January): 6–13.

Siddiqqi, A.R. 1980. "Need for a New Civil-Military Equation."

Dawn [Karachi] (6 September): 4.

Singh, Karan. 1984. "Keynote Address to Tenth World Hindu Conference." New York.

Singh, Khushwant. 1952. *The Sikhs*. London: George Allen and Unwin, Ltd.

_____. 1963. *A History of the Sikhs*. Princeton, New Jersey: Princeton University Press.

Singh, Mohinder. 1978. *The Akali Movement*. Delhi: The Macmillan Company of India, Ltd.

Singh, R.B., B.K. Dey and N.D. Roy. 1981. "Demand Supply of Foodgrains in Bihar 1982–83 and 1988–89." In M.N. Karna, editor. *Studies in Bihar Economy and Society*. New Delhi: Concept Publishing Company. Pages 29–44.

Singh, Rahul. 1986. "Punjab: The Politics of Terrorism." *Express Magazine* (21 December): 1,3.

Singh, Teja. 1922. *The Gurdwara Reform Movement and the Sikh Awakening*. Jullundur: The Desh Sewak Book Agency.

_____. 1944. *Essays in Sikhism*. Lahore: Sikh University Press.

Sinha, Arun. 1977a. "The Belchi Killings." *Economic and Political Weekly* 12:974.

_____. 1977b. "Landlords on the Rampage in Champaran." *Economic and Political Weekly* 12:1671.

Sinha, S. *et aliter* [Samata Era Editorial Team]. 1984. *Army Action in Punjab*. New Delhi: Samata Era.

Smith, Donald E. 1963. *India as a Secular State*. Princeton, New Jersey: Princeton University Press.

_____. 1965. *Religion and Politics in Burma*. Princeton, New Jersey: Princeton University Press.

_____. 1966. Editor. *South Asian Politics and Religion*. Princeton, New Jersey: Princeton University Press.

Spear, Percival. 1961. *India: A Modern History*. Ann Arbor: The University of Michigan Press.

Spellman, J.W. 1964. *Political Theory of Ancient India*. Oxford: Clarendon Press.

Sprinzak, Ehud. 1986. *Gush Enunim: The Politics of Zionist Fundamentalism in Israel*. New York: The American Jewish Committee, Institute of Human Relations.

Stark, Rodney and Charles Y. Glock 1974. *American Piety: The*

Nature of Religious Commitment. Berkeley: University of California Press.

Stein, Burton. 1980. *Peasant, State, and Society in Medieval South India*. New Delhi: Oxford University Press.

Stoeffler, F. Ernest. 1965. *The Rise of Evangelical Pietism*. Leiden: Brill.

——————. 1973. *German Pietism During the Eighteenth Century*. Leiden: Brill.

Suksamran, S. 1977. *Political Buddhism in South East Asia: The Role of the Sangha in the Modernization of Thailand*. London: Christopher Hurst and Company.

——————. 1982. *Buddhism and Politics in Thailand*. Singapore: Institute of South East Asian Studies.

Sumathipala, K.H.M. 1968a. *Bodu Samula Puranaya [Sinhalese: A History of the All Ceylon Buddhist Congress, 1919–1968]*. Colombo: The All Ceylon Buddhist Congress.

——————. 1968b. "History of Education in Ceylon, 1796–1965." *Ceylon Historical Journal* 13:i–xxii, 1–416. Colombo: Tisara Prakasakhayo.

Suri, Donna. 1981. "Portrait in Black: Notes from a University Hostel in Punjab." In P. Wallace and S. Chopra, editors. *Political Dynamics of Punjab*. Amritsar: Guru Nanak Dev University Press. Pages 257–263.

Swarup, Ram. 1986a. "Sikh Separatism: I—Its Genesis and Development; and II—The Development of Sikh Separatism." *The Times of India* (20–21 August).

——————. 1986b. "From Sikhs into Singhs: I—Alchemy of the Change; II—Transformation of Sikh Society; III—Arya Samaj and Singh Sabha." *The Times of India* (20–22 October).

Sweet, William W. 1944. *Revivalism in America: Its Origins, Growth and Decline*. New York.

Syed, Anwar H. 1979. "Iqbal and Jinnah on Issues of Nationhood and Nationalism." In C.M. Naim, editor. *Iqbal and Jinnah and Pakistan: The Vision and the Reality*. Syracuse, New York: Maxwell School of Citizenship and Public Affairs, Syracuse University. Pages 77–106.

Tambiah, S.J. 1976. *World Conqueror and World Renouncer: A Study of Buddhism and Polity in Thailand Against a Historical Background*. Cambridge: Cambridge University Press.

Tandon, Prakash. 1963. *Punjabi Century*. New York: Harcourt, Brace and World, Inc.

Taylor, David and Malcolm Yapp. 1979. *Political Identity in South Asia*. London: Curzon Press.

Tayyeb, A. 1966. *Pakistan: A Political Geography*. London: Oxford University Press.

Thapar, Romesh. 1986. "The Hindus: A Call to Arms." *The Illustrated Weekly of India* (7 December): 8–17.

Thapar, Romila. 1963. *Asoka and the Decline of the Mauryas*. London: Oxford University Press.

Timberg, Thomas A. 1982. "Bihar Backwardness: Does Feudalism Frustrate?" *Asian Survey* 22: 470–480.

Tully, Mark and Satish Jacob. 1985. *Amritsar: Mrs Gandhi's Last Battle*. London: Jonathan Cape.

Vijayavardhana, D.C. 1953. *Dharma-Vijaya (Triumph of Righteousness) or the Revolt in the Temple*. Colombo: Sinha Publications.

Voll, John O. 1982. *Islam: Continuity and Change in the Modern World*. Boulder, Colorado: Westview Press.

Wallace, Paul. 1980. "Plebiscitary Politics in India's 1980 Parliamentary Elections: Punjab and Haryana." *Asian Survey* 20:6:617–633.

_____. 1981. "Religious and Secular Politics in Punjab: The Sikh Dilemma in Competing Political Systems." In P. Wallace and S. Chopra, editors. *Political Dynamics of Punjab*. Amritsar: Guru Nanak Dev University Press. Pages 1–32.

_____. 1986. "The Sikhs as a 'Minority' in a Sikh Majority State in India." *Asian Survey* 26(3): 363–377.

Waterbury, John. 1981. "Egypt: Islam and Social Change." In P.H. Stoddard *et aliter*, editors. *Change and the Muslim World*. Syracuse, New York: Syracuse University Press. Pages 49–58.

Watt, W. Montgomery. 1966. *Islam and the Integration of Society*. London: Routledge and Kegan.

Weaver, Mary Ann. 1984. "Visit to Sikhdom's Damaged Symbol." *Christian Science Monitor* (20 June): 7.

Webster, John C.B. 1976. *The Christian Community and Change in Nineteenth Century North India*. Delhi: Macmillan.

Weeramantry, L.G. 1960. *Assassination of a Prime Minister*. Geneva: H. Studer, S.A., Printers.

_____. 1965. *Report on the Assassination of Prime Minister S.W.R.D. Bandaranaike, Sessional Paper*, III. Colombo: The Government Press.

Wickremeratne, L.A. 1985. *The Genesis of an Orientalist: Thomas Rhys Davids in Sri Lanka*. Delhi: Motilal Banarsidass; and Columbia, Missouri: South Asia Books.

Williams, Raymond Bradly. 1984. *A New Face of Hinduism: The Swami Narayan Religion*. London: Cambridge University Press.

Wilson, A.J. 1980. *The Gaullist System in Asia: The Constitution of Sri Lanka (1978)*. London: Macmillan and Company.

Wolpert, Stanley. 1984. *Jinnah of Pakistan: A Life*. New York: Oxford University Press.

Wriggins, W.H. 1960. *Ceylon: The Dilemmas of a New Nation*. Princeton, New Jersey: Princeton University Press.

Young, Richard Fox. 1981. *Resistant Hinduism: Sanskrit Sources on Anti-Christian Apologetics in Early Nineteenth-Century India*. Vienna: Gerold and Company, on behalf of Institut für Indologie der Universitat Wien, Sammlung De Nobili [De Nobili Research Foundation].

Zia-ul-Haq, Mohammad. n.d. *Interviews to Foreign Media*. Islamabad: Ministry of Information and Broadcasting, Volume I.

Author unspecified. 1949. *History of the Khalsa College Amritsar*. Amritsar: Khalsa College.

Index